T0199245

Cyber-Physical Systems

Chapman & Hall/CRC Cyber-Physical Systems

SERIES EDITORS:

Jyotir Moy Chatterjee
Lord Buddha Education Foundation, Kathmandu, Nepal

Vishal Jain
Sharda University, Greater Noida, India

Cyber-Physical Systems: A Comprehensive Guide
By: Nonita Sharma, L K Awasthi, Monika Mangla, K P Sharma, and Rohit Kumar

Introduction to the Cyber Ranges
By: Bishwajeet Pandey and Shabeer Ahmad

Security Analytics: A Data Centric Approach to Information Security
By: Mehak Khurana & Shilpa Mahajan

For more information on this series please visit: https://www.routledge.com/Chapman–HallCRC-Cyber-Physical-Systems/book-series/CHCPS?pd=published,forthcoming&pg=1&pp=12&so=pub&view=list?pd=published,forthcoming&pg=1&pp=12&so=pub&view=list

Cyber-Physical Systems

A Comprehensive Guide

Edited by
Nonita Sharma, L K Awasthi, Monika Mangla,
K P Sharma, and Rohit Kumar

CRC Press
Taylor & Francis Group
Boca Raton London New York

CRC Press is an imprint of the
Taylor & Francis Group, an **informa** business

A CHAPMAN & HALL BOOK

First edition published 2022
by CRC Press
6000 Broken Sound Parkway NW, Suite 300, Boca Raton, FL 33487-2742

and by CRC Press
4 Park Square, Milton Park, Abingdon, Oxon, OX14 4RN

CRC Press is an imprint of Taylor & Francis Group, LLC

Library of Congress Cataloging-in-Publication Data
Names: Sharma, Nonita, editor. | Awasthi, Lalit Kumar, editor. | Mangla, Monika, editor. | Sharma, K. P., (Krishna Pal), editor. | Kumar, Rohit (Computer scientist), editor.
Title: Cyber-physical systems. a comprehensive guide / edited by Nonita Sharma, L K Awasthi, Monika Mangla, K P Sharma, Rohit Kumar.
Description: First edition. | Boca Raton : Chapman & Hall/CRC Press, 2022. |
Series: Chapman & Hall/CRC cyber physical systems | Includes bibliographical references and index. |
Summary: "Cyber-Physical Systems: A Comprehensive Guide explores the complete system perspective, underlying theories, modelling, and the applications of Cyber Physical Systems (CPS). It aims to cover all topics ranging from discussion of rudiments of the system and efficient management to recent research challenges and issues. Editors aim to present the book in a self-sufficient manner and in order to achieve this, the book has been edited to include all the aspects of CPS. The book focuses on the concept map of CPS including latest technological interventions; issues, challenges, and the integration of CPS with IoT & Big Data Analytics. This aims to bring together unique contributions on cyber-physical systems research and education with applications in Industrial, Agriculture, and medical domains. The main aim of the book is to provide a roadmap to the latest advancements to provide optimal solutions in the field of CPS. The featured book aims to present the emergence of Cyber Physical Systems in response to revolutionary advancements in IoT. While discussing the associated challenges, the book also targets to devise efficient models which are competent to address these challenges. The book aims to cater to researchers and academicians working in the related field of CPS"-- Provided by publisher.
Identifiers: LCCN 2021052534 (print) | LCCN 2021052535 (ebook) | ISBN 9781032065489 (pbk) | ISBN 9781032065465 (hbk) | ISBN 9781003202752 (ebk)
Subjects: LCSH: Cooperating objects (Computer systems)
Classification: LCC TJ213 .C8848 2022 (print) | LCC TJ213 (ebook) | DDC 006.2/2--dc23/eng/20211227
LC record available at https://lccn.loc.gov/2021052534
LC ebook record available at https://lccn.loc.gov/2021052535

ISBN: 978-1-032-06546-5 (hbk)
ISBN: 978-1-032-06548-9 (pbk)
ISBN: 978-1-003-20275-2 (ebk)

DOI: 10.1201/9781003202752

Typeset in Palatino
by MPS Limited, Dehradun

Contents

Preface

The technological development during the past few decades has revamped the life of mankind. This revolutionary change in lifestyle is primarily due to the advancement in the Internet of Things (IoT) that has significantly influenced the human life from multiple perspectives. IoT has completely revolutionized the facet of health care, agriculture, education, and other industrial fields. Advancement of IoT has also led to another avenue of research, the cyber-physical system (CPS), where physical systems are monitored and controlled by a computing core. The CPS also transformed the manner in which mankind interacts with the world. Hence, the CPS has grabbed the attention of researchers, academicians, and industrialists.

The prime focus of the proposed book, Cyber-Physical Systems: A Comprehensive Guide, *is to explore the CPS by including the CPS framework, various issues, challenges, and research directions. This book delves into the complete system perspective, underlying theories, modelling, and the applications of the CPS. It aims to cover all topics ranging from discussion of rudiments of the system, efficient management to recent research challenges, issues, and future directions. The table of contents is designed in a manner so as to provide the reader with a broad list of its applications. Thus, the book plans to discuss the recent research trends and advanced topics in the field of cyber-physical systems, which will be of interest to industry experts, academicians, and researchers working in related areas. Considering the interest of researchers and academicians, the editors aim to present this book in a multidimensional perspective that will cover the CPS in breadth.*

Editors

Dr. Nonita Sharma is working as an assistant professor at the National Institute of Technology, Jalandhar. She has more than 10 years of teaching experience. Her major area of interest includes data mining, bioinformatics, time series forecasting, and wireless sensor networks She has published several papers in international/national journals/conferences and book chapters. She received a best paper award for her research paper in the Mid-Term Symposium organized by CSIR, Chandigarh. She has authored a book titled *XGBoost: The Extreme Gradient Boosting for Mining Applications*.

Prof. Lalit Kumar Awasthi is currently heading the Dr. B. R. Ambedkar National Institute of Technology Jalandhar as the director. An academician par excellence, he has more than 30 years of teaching experience. His areas of research are mobile distributed systems, cloud computing, network security, and wireless sensor network. He has published several research papers in peer-reviewed journals. He is senior member of the IEEE and has received the best Faculty Award in view of recognition of contributions, achievements, and excellence in computer science and engineering at the NIT Hamirpur. He is the reviewer of many peer-reviewed journals and contributed to academic research in terms of projects, papers, and patents.

Dr. Monika Mangla received her Ph.D. from the Thapar Institute of Engineering and Technology, Patiala, Punjab, in 2019. Currently, she is working as an Associate Professor in the Department of Information Technology at Dwarkadas J. Sanghvi College of Engineering, Mumbai. Her interest areas include IoT, cloud computing, algorithms and optimization, location modelling, and machine learning. She has guided many projects at the UG and PG level. She has published several research papers and book chapters (SCI and Scopus Indexed) with reputed publishers and she is also the editor of a book on the topic of Internet of Things to be published by Apple Academic Press, CRC Press, Apple Academic Press. She has also been associated with several SCI indexed journals like TUBITAK, IMDS, etc. as a reviewer. She has been associated with several reputed conference as a session chair. She has also qualified the UGC-NET for computer science in July 2018. She has two patents applied to her credit is a life member of CSI and IETE.

Dr. Krishna Pal Sharma is an assistant professor at the Dr B R Ambedkar National Institute of Technology, Jalandhar Punjab India. He received his B.Tech degree in computer science and engineering from the Uttar Pradesh Technical University, Lucknow in 2005, M.Tech in computer science and engineering from the Graphic Era University, Dehradun (UK), India in 2010 and Ph.D. from the National Institute of Technology Hamirpur HP India 2016, respectively. His research interests include computer networks, wireless sensor ad hoc networks, and the Internet of Things. He has published many papers in international journals and conferences.

Dr. Rohit Kumar is currently a postdoctoral researcher at the University of Southern California, Los Angeles, USA. Prior to this, he completed his Ph.D. from the National Institute of Technology Delhi, India. He was also the visiting researcher at the National Chiao Tong University, Taiwan, Indian Institute of Technology Bombay, Indraprastha Institute of Information Technology Delhi. He has published several articles in reputed journals that include *IEEE Transactions on Mobile Computing, IEEE Systems Journal, IEEE Communication Letter, IEEE Wireless Communication Letter*, etc. He is also an active reviewer of *IEEE Systems Journal* and *IEEE IoT Journal*. He has been awarded Best Graduate Forum Presenter Award in 11th International Conference on Communication Systems and Networks (COMSNETS 2019), Bangalore, India and Best Lightening Talk Award in 20th International Conference on Distributed Computing and Networking (ICDCN 2019) as Doctoral Symposium paper, IISC Bangalore, India. His research interests include dynamic spectrum access, reinforcement learning for cognitive radio and IoT networks, distributed computing, and blockchain.

Contributors

Ashutosh Deshwal
Dept. of Computer Sci. and Engg.
Thapar Institute of Engineering and
　　Technology
Punjab, India

Amritpal Singh
Assistant Professor, Dept. of Computer Sci.
　　& Engg. Dr B.R. Ambedkar National
　　Institute of Technology
Jalandhar, India

Azra Nazir
Computer Science & Engineering
　　Department National Institute of
　　Technology Srinagar Hazratbal
Jammu & Kashmir, India

Dr. Abhijit V. Chitre
EnTC Engineering Department,
　　Vishwakarma Institute of Information
　　Technology
Pune, India

Dr. Gurjinder Kaur
Department of Computer Science &
　　Engineering, Sant Longowal Institute of
　　Engineering & Technology Longowal
Punjab, India

Dr. Kirti Wanjale
Computer Engineering Department,
　　Vishwakarma Institute of Information
　　Technology
Pune, India

Dr. Monika Mangla
Department of Information Technology,
　　Dwarkadas J. Sanghvi College of
　　Engineering
Mumbai, India

Faisal Rasheed Lone
Baba Ghulam Shah Badshah University
Rajouri
Jammu & Kashmir, India

Harsh K Verma
Dr. B.R. Ambedkar National Institute of
　　Technology Jalandhar
Punjab, India

Nonita Sharma
Department of Computer Sci. and Engg.
Dr. B.R. Ambedkar National Institute of
　　Technology Jalandhar
Punjab, India

Pranjali Singh
Research Scholar, Dept. of Computer
　　Science & Engineering
Dr B.R. Ambedkar National Institute of
　　Technology
Jalandhar, India

Ravi Sharma
Dr. B.R. Ambedkar National Institute of
　　Technology Jalandhar
Punjab, India

Roohie Naaz Mir
Computer Science & Engineering
　　Department National Institute of
　　Technology Srinagar Hazratbal
Jammu & Kashmir, India

S. Miglani
Assistant Professor, Dept. of CSE
Thapar Institute of Engineering and
　　Technology
Punjab, India

Shaima Qureshi
Computer Science & Engineering
　　Department, National Institute of
　　Technology Srinagar, Hazratbal
Jammu & Kashmir, India

Surbhi Khullar
Department of Computer Science &
　　Engineering, Thapar Institute of
　　Engineering & Technology Patiala
Punjab, India

Tanya Garg
Department of Computer Science &
  Engineering, Thapar Institute
  of Engineering & Technology
  Patiala
Punjab, India

Tawseef Ayoub Shaikh
Department of Computer Science &
  Engineering
Baba Ghulam Shah Badshah University
  Rajouri
Jammu & Kashmir, India

Younis Ahmed Malla
Department of Computer
  Engineering
Aligarh Muslim University
Uttar Pradesh, India

Vibha Nehra
Department of Computer Sci. and Engg.
Amity University
Uttar Pradesh, India

Najeeb-ud-Din Hakim
National Institute of Technology
  Srinagar
Jammu & Kashmir, India

Mohd Rafi Lone
Baba Ghulam Shah Badshah University
  Rajouri
J&K, India

Radha Krishna Rambola
Computer Engineering, SVKM's NMIMS
  MPSTME Shirpur
Mumbai

Amrit Raj
Department of Computer Sci. and Engg.
National Institute of Technology
Meghalaya Shillong, India

Arun Kumar Verma
Department of Computer Sci. and Engg.
National Institute of Technology
Meghalaya Shillong, India

Kamal Mehta
SVKM's NMIMS MPSTME Shirpur
Mumbai

Vikramjit Singh
Dr. B.R. Ambedkar National Institute of
  Technology Jalandhar
Punjab, India

Pradeep Tomar
Department of Computer Sci. and Engg.
Gautam Buddha University, Greater Noida
Uttar Pradesh, India

Amitesh Garg
Associate Intern, Sabre Travel
  Technologies Pvt. Ltd.
India

Sourabh Yadav
Department of Computer Sci. and Engg.
Gautam Buddha University, Greater Noida
Uttar Pradesh, India

Sameer Farooq
Lovely Professional University
Jalandhar, Punjab, India

Soumen Moulik
Department of Computer Sci. and Engg.
National Institute of Technology
Meghalaya Shillong, India

Priyanka Chawla
Lovely Professional University Jalandhar,
  Punjab, India

Shubham Joshi
Department of Computer Engineering,
  SVKM's NMIMS MPSTME
Shirpur, Mumbai

Krishna Pal Sharma
Dr. B.R. Ambedkar National Institute of
  Technology Jalandhar
Punjab, India

Tabasum Rasool
Research Associate, Interdisciplinary
  Centre for Water Research (ICWaR)
Indian Institute of Science
Bangalore

Shabir Sofi
Department of Information Technology,
  National Institute of Technology,
  Srinagar
Jammu & Kashmir, India

1

Applications of Artificial Intelligence in Cyber-Physical Systems

R. Sharma and N. Sharma

Dr. B.R. Ambedkar National Institute of Technology Jalandhar, Punjab, India

1.1 Introduction

Helen Gill of the National Science Foundation coined the term "Cyber Physical System (CPS)" in 2006 [1]. "CPS contains communicating digital, analog, physical, and human elements designed for operation by integrated physics and logic," according to Griffor [2]. One may infer from the above description that CPS is an intersection of the physical and cyber worlds, where physical refers to a real-world object, and cyber refers to the network connections that link all physical entities and enable them to interact. These technologies will support our critical infrastructure, act as the foundation for future intelligent networks, and enhance our quality of life in several ways. For example, traffic flow control, health services, and emergency response will all benefit from CPS. It is a novel digital system that integrates the physical and cyber worlds [3]. It is a combination of communication, control, computation, and the physical world. CPS has two main functional components: CPS system has high-speed connectivity for data gathering from the real world and cyberspace to provide the result by analyzing the data [4]. In addition, CPS aims to improve the system's functionality, reliability, usability, and safety.

The industry is now witnessing the fourth Industrial Revolution in CPS [5]. These are industrial automation systems that allow a wide range of innovative functionalities through networking and virtual world access, significantly altering our everyday lives [6]. Different new and advanced technologies such as smart homes, driverless cars, smart cities, Internet of Things (IoT), renewable energy, and 3D printing now exist [7,8]. The devices can be adapted to automate traffic management, precision robotic surgery, smart manufacturing, perform in hazardous or impossible conditions, autonomous search and rescue systems, large-scale distributed coordination (e.g., supporting technologies), and ubiquitous monitoring and deployment in health care [9]. Other than advancement in technology in CPS, these devices work without human intervention and can communicate with each other and produce huge amounts of data. This data is analysed and different services are provided to the user.

DOI: 10.1201/9781003202752-1

CPS is also called an industrial application of IoT that can control physical objects with the help of cyberspace [10]. The concept of industrial IoT has emerged with CPS that provides machine-to-machine communication without human intervention. With this automation, a machine can work with its full potential and also offer optimized services. Different sensors and actuators are used in these systems to make them autonomous.

As CPS systems become more commonly utilised, the number and quality of attacks is increasing. Protecting these systems from different attacks is challenging in a human-free environment [11,12]. If proper security measures are not taken into consideration, it is easy to attack the system. So, it is a concern of prime importance to secure the design and provide a good service simultaneously.

This chapter demonstrates the application of artificial intelligence (AI) in CPS. The following section introduces the concept of CPS to readers, followed by the introduction of AI, and the application of AI in CPS.

1.2 Cyber-Physical System

CPS is an interconnection of a physical entity with communication and computation infrastructure [6,13]. CPS focuses on networking several embedded devices so that they can work together. There are different embedded systems such as smartphones, cars, and other devices; without these devices, we cannot imagine our modern life. All of these devices cannot be accessed remotely. With the help of CPS, these devices can be integrated and communicate with each other and can be accessed remotely. Connected car technology is an example of CPS; these days, most cars come with this technology and it helps us remotely turn on and off the car engine, check the location of the vehicle, and turn on the air conditioning before we reach the car. It'd be perfect if one could switch on the home air conditioning on the way back from work, bringing the indoor room temperature back to normal. Or an electric kettle could start making tea while the person is still in bed in the morning. System monitoring may also benefit from remote access to process data. The details obtained from remote diagnostics assists service members in bringing the appropriate instrument and replacement component. The device will order replacement parts on its own, using the corresponding network infrastructure. Also, now, there are many areas of use for CPS, such as surgical devices, driving machines, etc.

Figure 1.1 represents a structure of a CPS, which is mainly composed of the physical world, access layer, and cyber world [14]. Wireless or wired communication may connect CPS to cyber-level systems such as control centers to physical components. The computing and control portion, which also sends control commands and receives sensed data, contains the intelligence. Sensors that track physical components and actuators that control them connect CPS to the real world [15]. A CPS is made up of a control panel, which usually consists of microcontroller(s) that control the actuators and sensors required to communicate with the other entity and process the data received [16]. These systems need a networking interface to share data with other embedded systems or the cloud. The most critical aspect of a CPS is data exchange, which allows data to be exchanged. The Internet-enabled CPS is often referred to as the IoT. In other words, a CPS is a network-capable integrated device that can send and receive data [6].

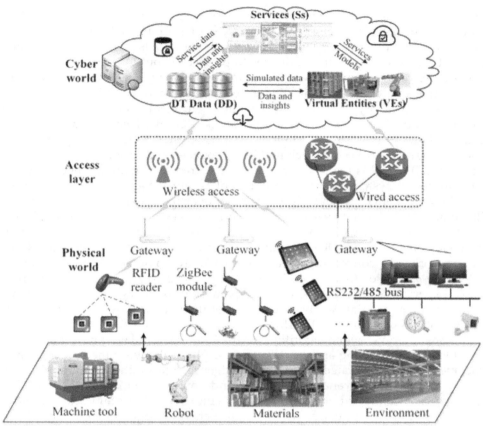

FIGURE 1.1
Cyber-Physical System Structure [14].

1.3 Artificial Intelligence

According to John McCarthy [17], the father of AI, "artificial intelligence is the science and engineering of creating intelligent machines, brilliant computer programs." AI is a field of computer science that deals with creating programs that exhibit "intelligence." There are two forms of AI: narrow and universal AI. Many of the features of human intelligence would be present in ubiquitous AI, such as the ability to comprehend words, distinguish between objects and sounds, erudition, and problem solving. On the other hand, narrow AI shows certain aspects of human intelligence and can perform certain functions exceptionally well but lacks in other fields. A software that can recognize photographs but not anything else is an example of narrow AI.

To achieve the idea of AI, different algorithms and models are used. These learning algorithms and models are called machine learning (ML). ML is a learning process that is used to make a machine intelligent. Different learning methods are used to make machines intelligent, and they are broadly classified into three categories: unsupervised,

supervised, and reinforcement learning. Supervised learning is learning where a device is provided with the label data means the machine knows for a specific input and its output during the training phase. In the testing phase, the machine is given data where the label is provided only on input data and it tries to predict the output label.

On the other hand, in unsupervised learning, there is no label on output data during any phase, machine try to find out hidden features in the data. Reinforcement learning works on the concept of agent and environment where agents learn from the surrounding environment and try to improve their performance. On the basis of learning, there are different techniques that are not limited to: decision tree, K-nearest neighbour (KNN), random forest, support vector machine (SVM), logistics regression, and artificial neural network (ANN). ANN is the technique that is inspired by the human neural system. In the human neural system, there are millions of neurons that work together to tmke a decision in same manner when we use a number of artificial neural networks to make an intelligent machine is called deep neural network and a new term to come into the picture is known as deep learning (DL). DL is an extension of ML that has the same task to make a machine intelligent, but in DL, the number of artificial neurons are very large. Recurrent neural network and convolution neural network are some of the most popular DL models. Applications of AI are used in different domains to improve their performances and user experiences: web search engine, spam detector, image recognition, voice recognition, and sensory data analysis are some of the applications in which tremendous improvement has been done with AI.

A CPS uses computer-aided algorithms to track and manipulate physical elements that are capable of manipulating and reacting to their physical environment, using a mixture of machine sensors, integrated computer intelligence, and multiple communication mechanisms. With rapid advancements in AI and connectivity, demand for CPS is increasing, such as connected and autonomous vehicles that track and interact with their environments, and smart devices that maximise energy usage depending on the atmosphere and the occupant's conduct.

A CPS is becoming data-rich, allowing new and higher degrees of automation and autonomy. For making this automation possible, AI plays a very important role. AI provides the result with great accuracy and precision. AI not only is used to make the system automated and fast but it is also used to secure the system and provide privacy.

1.4 Applications of Cyber-Physical Systems

A CPS is focused on information-processing computer systems installed in goods such as vehicles, aeroplanes, and other equipment. A computer machine is used to execute a complex operation. The brakes of a car, for example, are controlled by an integrated ABS system (anti-lock braking system). Since a CPS contains both cyber and physical elements, it is referred to as a cyber-physical device. To put it another way, a CPS is a system that combines digital and physical controls. The components of cyber-physical systems, such as networked control systems (NCS) and feedback systems, are distributed and interconnected through communication networks. Cyber-based manufacturing, smart grids, water, and wastewater networks are examples of NCS. Data moving between various areas of an NCS may be vulnerable to a variety of attacks.

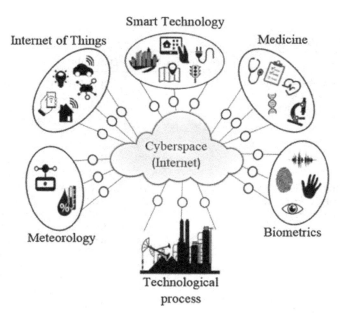

FIGURE 1.2
Applications of CPS [18].

CPSs have intelligent features such as increased and streamlined physical device stability, quality, protection, wellness, performance, running costs, longevity, and maintainability. CPSs are integrated software and hardware components that are attached to humans and embedded in the real environment. Sensor-assisted, communicable autonomous systems are the most popular CPS implementations. Many wireless sensor networks, for example, track various facets of the atmosphere and send the processed data to a central node. Smart grids, autonomous vehicle systems, medical tracking and process control systems, distributed robots, automatic control, and avionics are some of the examples of CPS. The following are the major characteristics of a CPS: To incorporate calculations into physical processes, it is integrated in physical structures and networked via wireless sensor networks. Manufacturing, water treatment networks, logistics, health care, and smart cities are all examples of information-intensive technology industries where CPS applications have the ability to make major improvements. Figure 1.2 shows different domains that use CPS applications [18]. The next few sections provide details of different domains that use CPS applications.

1.4.1 Biomedical and Healthcare Systems

CPS research in healthcare and biomedical sciences shows a number of opportunities and benefits. Some of the aspects that have benefited from the recent growth in image-guided surgery and other technology include the development of operating rooms and clinics that are technologically advanced, clinically and industrially more effective, medical fluid circulation systems, and other neural implants, among many others. Health care relies on networked medical devices and services that meet patients' needs and emergencies. As a result, medical devices and services can be reconfigured, distributed, and communicated

TABLE 1.1

AI in Medical Cyber Physical System

Reference	Objective	Technology Used	Description
[20]	Cognitive Cybersecurity for CPS-IoT Enabled Healthcare Ecosystems	AI	Authors provide a cognitive cybersecurity model for predicting and responding to current and evolving privacy threats and cybersecurity to critical infrastructure and CPS-IoT systems. It involves the design and definition of a layered architecture that incorporates AI, cognitive processes, and novel security mechanisms.
[21]	Verification of Wireless Medical Cyber-Physical System (MCPS)	Decision Support System (DSS)	For wireless MCPS, they suggested a lightweight real-time data-based runtime verification methodology. The first step is to create a user-friendly domain specific language (DRTV) for defining real-time details and dynamic temporal properties of medical care practices. A runtime verification approach is suggested and formalised based on the DRTV model to improve the medical decision support system. It integrates structured information engineering approaches with medical practise protocols to automatically check runtime temporal properties, and it can be applied and plugged into emerging cellular MCPS to improve health care.

to patients and caregivers in different environments and needs. Numerous operating rooms use ventilators and oxygen delivery systems for respiratory assistance, infusion pumps for sedation, as well as a variety of sensors to track patient conditions. To meet specific patient or procedural specifications, these instruments are often reassembled into a new device configuration. The objective is to build and operate systems that are certifiable, secure, reliable, and accurate. In [19], authors proposed a smart ontology-based IoT framework for remote patient monitoring.

A CPS study can be used in neuroscience, which is concerned with discovering the basic concepts of human intelligence processes and applying this knowledge in engineered environments. Examples include brain-computer interfaces, medicinal robots, orthotics and exoskeletons, and prosthetics. These dynamically interconnected systems are made up of multifunctional modules, computation and feedback loops running at varying intervals and length scales, signals, parallel processing, and redundant fault-tolerant architectures, rather than simple modularity concepts. Table 1.1 provides details of research that uses CPS and AI in healthcare systems. Two studies are discussed here on the technology used in studies and their brief description.

1.4.2 Next-Generation Air Transportation Systems and Smart Cars

Building and managing complex networks can be challenging. Many devices work together to accomplish a shared purpose in certain situations, such as at an airport or in a smart car. A cyber-physical structure can be so dynamic that it necessitates the use of several CPSs.

Relevant areas of research include: New functionality aimed at increasing capability, protection, and performance, as well as the interactions, advanced flight deck implementations, ranging from pilot screens and models to potential (semi)autonomous systems; vehicle health monitoring and management; and aircraft control system safety testing [13]. One of the major technological difficulties is the verification and validation of complex flight-critical technologies, with an emphasis on supporting efficient, stable, and safe operations. If device sophistication grows, costs associated with verification and certification, as well as safety assurance, would almost certainly raise the cost of developing and constructing next-generation vehicles. Verification and evaluation methodologies and principles have been described as a key research field by the wider aeronautics community.

Smart cars are environmentally friendly, fuel-efficient, and safe vehicles that also offer enhanced entertainment and convenience features. These advances are made possible by the use of electronic control systems, which are a group of many electronic control units (ECUs) that are networked together. Engine pollution control, brake control, entertainment (radio and video players), and convenience features (cruise control and windows opening and closing) are all monitored and regulated by ECUs. Each ECU is assigned to the required subnetwork based on the essence of the tasks it is supposed to perform. Gateways enable ECUs from various subnetworks to connect with one another. Table 1.2 provides details of research that uses CPS and AI in smart transportation systems. Two studies are discussed here and their objective, technology used in study, and brief description.

TABLE 1.2

Use of AI in Smart Transportation System

Reference	Objective	Technology Used	Description
[22]	Obstacle Recognition with ML for Cyber-Physical System	ML	This paper provides a set of artificial intelligence–based obstacle detection approaches. A multi-layer perceptron neural network, a self-organizing map, and a support vector machine comprise the library. Within a given scenario, the whole device is tested in a specific use case constructed from two types of sensory data (LiDAR on-chip and GPS sensors). The comparative analysis demonstrates that the suggested methods to obstacle detection are good at detecting pedestrians
[23]	ML for Next-Generation Intelligent Transportation Systems (ITS)	ML	The authors of this survey look at how ML, which has recently gained a lot of attention, can be used to allow ITS. They provide a concise overview of how ML technology has been applied to a wide variety of ITS technologies and facilities, such as cooperative driving and road hazard notification, as well as potential guidance on how ITS will use and benefit from ML

1.4.3 Renewable Energy and Smart Grid

The research and implementation of smart grid and renewable energy technologies have risen to the forefront of the public's focus list, rendering them a top priority for policy-makers. The objective is to improve energy quality by modernising the energy system. The following are the strategic factors behind renewable energy and smart grids: By 2030, energy demand is expected to increase by more than 75%; electricity generation contributes more than 40% of greenhouse gas emissions; and the expense of generating 1 kW-h is four times that of saving 1 kW-h [13]. According to [24] report, California passed a bill mandating a renewable-energy standard that would require zero-carbon electricity to be generated in its grid by 2045. The generation of renewable energies from wind and solar energy is highly variable and depends on resources such as sunshine duration, wind, and generation time. Variable-power generation brings new challenges for grid design and base load supply. Additional technologies are needed to meet the new challenges of operating the California electricity grid. About 4.5 million smart metres will be deployed in personal and commercial buildings throughout the United States to develop and demonstrate demand control, distribution automation, substation technology, distributed generation, and communication system innovations. The aim is to demonstrate an increase in energy consumption by demand control and distributed automation by significantly reducing peak load.

Advances in modular transmission devices such as phasor measurement units (PMUs) open up new opportunities for smart grids and wider area control. The North American Synchro-Phasor Initiative, funded by the U.S. Department of Energy, has made significant investments in PMU hardware. Future initiatives will focus on data fusion and processing, dynamic real-time tracking, and system operation simulation. A greater emphasis will be placed on the wide range of communication and control to optimise system operation and the close coupling of cyber systems with physical system components needed for smart grids. Advances in systems science, hybrid digital/analogue systems, dynamic emerging systems, sophisticated software systems, and widely time-varying scattered systems will present critical gaps and common challenges. Improving the performance of smart grids in terms of security, efficiency, reliability, and cost-effectiveness will require progress in optimizing stochastic dynamic systems and distributed control. The academic group has identified these concerns in many seminars concerned with information infrastructure and smart grids.

The smart grid is made up of two main parts: the electricity application and the required infrastructure [25]. The power application is where the smart grid's core functions are, such as energy generation, transmission, and distribution. The supporting infrastructure, on the other hand, is the intelligent aspect that is primarily concerned with coordinating and tracking the smart grid's core operations through the use of software, hardware, and communication networks. Table 1.3 provide details of research that uses CPS and AI in smart grids. Two studies are discussed here with their objective, technology used in the study, and their brief description.

1.4.4 Cyber Manufacturing System

This definition describes an automated industrial environment associated with technologies such as the IoT, cloud computing, sensors, networks, and AI. Some academic groups have expressed this concern in many seminars on information infrastructure and smart networks. CMS stands for cyber manufacturing system and is a vision for the future of the manufacturing infrastructure [28].

TABLE 1.3

AI in Smart Grid

Reference	Objective	Technology Used	Description
[26]	AI Techniques in Renewable Energy and Smart Grid Systems	AI	In this article, the author will look at some new AI implementation examples in energy fields. These applications include automatic design of current wind generation systems and health monitoring in use, fault pattern recognition of a smart grid subsystem, and real-time simulator-based smart grid power. These application example definitions can be used to create a variety of other programmes. The basic features of AI that are applicable to these applications were briefly evaluated
[27]	ML Methods for Attack Detection in the Smart Grid	ML	In this study, the smart grid attack identification problems are presented as mathematical learning problems for various attack situations, with measurements taken in batch or online environments. ML algorithms are used in this approach to identify measurements as stable or invaded. In the suggested solution, an attack detection architecture is given to leverage some previous information about the method and overcome restrictions resulting from the problem's sparse nature. In the proposed attack detection paradigm, experiment results show that ML algorithms outperform attack detection algorithms that use state vector estimation methods

Compared to traditional experience-based management systems, cyber manufacturing provides an evidence-based environment that informs devices and consumers about the status of connected assets and converts raw data into actionable intelligence. The design of cyber-physical networks is a convergence of technical experience in computer science and information technology driven by technology. A growth in sectors such as retail, consumer goods, and health care, is due to the widespread availability of Internet-based services, is linked to an increase in demand in these industries, and is the phenomenon of cyber manufacturing. The manufacture of mobile devices is an example of particular importance for industry and science. Cyber manufacturing is a term that originates in virtual physical systems and refers to a digital manufacturing infrastructure that provides information and a transparent ecosystem that enables inventory management, provides reconfigurability, and maintains competitiveness.

System integration, data acquisition, machine condition forecasting, fleet-based asset management, and manufacturing reconfigurability are some of the expected functions of a cyber manufacturing system. The current production companies make their decisions according to an approach based on the overall efficiency of the equipment and the allocation of production requirements, without taking into account the condition of the machinery. This can lead to instability in plant management due to a lack of linkage between plants, potential spare parts overstock, and unintentional computer failures. Production properties, on the other hand, are more networked and available in real time

TABLE 1.4

AI in Cyber Manufacturing System

Reference	Objective	Technology Used	Description
[29]	CPS for Smart Factories Project	DL	Industry 4.0 plants are highly complicated, increasing maintenance costs. Reduced costs by controllers using cyber physical (CP) will ensure the smart plant project results in commercialization of CPS. In the following fields, multi-adaptive CP controllers are implemented: industrial robot arms, automotive manufacture, processing of steel, and general assembly lines
[28]	Detecting Attacks in Cyber Manufacturing Systems with ML Methods	ML	The use of ML on physical data to detect cyber-physical threats is being investigated. Two examples were created using modelling and experiments: a malicious 3D printing attack and a malicious computer numerical control (CNC) milling machine attack. The anomaly detection algorithm achieved 96.1% accuracy in detecting cyber-physical attacks in the 3D printing process by applying ML methods in physical data; the random forest algorithm achieved 91.1% accuracy in detecting cyber-physical attacks in the CNC milling process by implementing ML methods in physical data

compared to other Internet-enabled industries. These conditions require computer network–based analysis, in addition to the requirements for computer networks, to convert raw data into information to facilitate consumer decision making.

The development of cyber-manufacturing solutions involves a number of technologies. A brief overview of these developments and their applications in cyber manufacturing follows: The cornerstone of cyber manufacturing is the cyber-physical structure. A CPS's tools and techniques make it possible to achieve cyber-manufacturing targets. The other important technology in the design and production of cyber-manufacturing processes is big data analytics. Cyber manufacturing is no exception. Connected computers in every sector pose the question of adequate data management and processing. Cyber manufacturing will benefit from customised advances in cloud computing, AI, and predictive analytics. Table 1.4 provide details of research that uses CPS and AI in a cyber manufacturing system. Two studies are discussed here with objective, technology used in the study and their brief description.

1.4.5 CPS Security

A CPS tracks physical elements with computer-based algorithms linked to the Internet, using a mixture of computers, sensors, integrated computer intelligence, and different connectivity mechanisms. This implies that a CPS can operate independently of its physical surroundings. CPSs control vital and dynamic operating services for most of the nation's strategic infrastructure. The frequency and sophistication of cyber-attacks have risen due to the proliferation of physical cybersecurity processes and the increasing alignment of these systems with enterprise and Internet-based applications.

The greatest problem in industrial protocols is tight radio efficiency, high reliability, availability, and protection as key requirements for wireless networks in plants. Expert devices use wireless sensors (pressure, temperature, sounds, cameras, and so on) to figure out what's going on, forecast potential issues, and avoid errors. A main concern is secure connectivity between physical machines and the cloud. Automated data collection, storage, and analysis in the cloud are needed for related processes. Machines can optimise their efficiency and communicate with the environment as computing methods and AI in sensor and actuator-level communication increase.

A successful attack on CPS can result in significant damage to the environment. Each layer can be individually addressed, or the entire system can be challenged. In addition to traditional IT systems, CPS is more vulnerable to attacks, including attacks not just on the CPS but also on network, including the Internet. Attacks may be active or passive. Active attacks are those in which the attacker attempts to exploit the system's functionality and facilities. These attacks include, but are not limited to, Sybil, man-in-the-middle, and denial of service attacks. Passive attacks, on the other hand, occur when an attacker gains access to a user's information without their consent. Passive attacks include traffic monitoring and eavesdropping. Passive attacks result in privacy leakage. Details of most common attacks on CPS are given below.

Denial of Service (DoS): Affects behaviour by blocking traffic and rendering the network and service inaccessible; for example, by filling a resource with fake requests and exploiting a protocol flaw. Furthermore, DDoS is a typical attack that simultaneously attacks various tools, such as end devices and networks, blocking access to information and services.

Man-in-the-Middle: Sends a forged message to a targeted resource, and then performs unintended behaviour, such as manipulating a primary feature, based on the received message, which could result in an unwanted occurrence. This form of attack can also affect the network layer, which can lead to eavesdropping in certain situations.

Eavesdropping: The device intercepts any data that is being transmitted. For example, transferring control information from sensor networks to applications in the CPS for monitoring purposes may be vulnerable to eavesdropping. Furthermore, since the device is being tracked, user privacy could be compromised.

Spoofing: Pretends to be a genuine member of the system and therefore engages in system operations. After successfully gaining entry, the intruder will have access to information and will be able to alter, delete, or inject data.

Wormhole: Creates network knowledge gaps by announcing fake paths from which all packets are routed.

Jamming: Introduces noise or a signal of the same frequency into the wireless channel between sensor nodes and the remote base station. By causing deliberate network interruption, this attack may result in a DoS.

Table 1.5 provides details of research that uses AI in CPS security. Three studies are discussed here with their objective, technology used in the study, and their brief description.

Cyber-physical systems security [33] is a project that tackles CPSs and IoT device security issues. These involve intelligent, wired devices with embedded sensors, processors, and actuators that capture and communicate with the physical environment in real time to ensure essential application efficiency and protection. These IoT devices are crucial in vital infrastructure, governance, and everyday life.

TABLE 1.5

AI in CPS Security

Reference	Objective	Study Type	Technology used	Description
[30]	DL for CPS Security	Survey	DL	The authors of this paper aim to provide a succinct overview of regularisation methods for DL algorithms used in security-related applications in CPSs
[31]	ML for Security in Connected Medical Devices	Experimental	ML	Developed a feature set for medical device to check that device is working normally or not and to detect different security attacks. ML techniques were used to check the performance
[32]	Effective ML in Smart City	Experimental	ML	Analyse the performance of five ML algorithms to detect cyber-attacks in IoT system with a BoT-IoT data set

1.5 Conclusion

CPS and AI have changed our life and the way we are doing our work. Applications of these technologies can be seen in every domain from the home to industry and from a small car to a big aeroplane. This chapter provides a brief introduction of a CPS and AI and different domains that use these technologies. This chapter also includes studies on the various domains of a CPS. Security plays a very important role in everyone's life. There are different types of attacks that can alter the security of a CPS. ML and DL models are used to prevent a CPS from attacks. This chapter covers the security part of a CPS and elaborates on the most common attacks on the system and gives a description of recent studies that use AI to secure CPSs.

References

[1] Lee, E.A., (Feb. 2015). "The past, present and future of cyber-physical systems: A focus on models,". *Sensors (Switzerland)*, *15*, 3, 4837–4869, doi: 10.3390/s150304837.

[2] Griffor E.R., Greer C., Wollman D.A. and Burns M.J., (Jun. 2017). "Framework for Cyber-physical Systems: Volume 1, Overview," Gaithersburg, MD, doi: 10.6028/NIST.SP.1500-201.

[3] Chen, H., (Sep. 2017). "Applications of cyber-physical system: A literature review,". *J. Ind. Integr. Manag.*, *0203*, 1750012, doi: 10.1142/s2424862217500129.

[4] Lee, J., Bagheri, B. and Kao, H.A., (Jan. 2015). "A cyber-physical systems architecture for Industry 4.0-based manufacturing systems,". *Manuf. Lett.*, *3*, 18–23, doi: 10.1016/j.mfglet.2014.12.001.

[5] Aydos, M., Vural, Y. and Tekerek, A., (Jun. 2019). "Assessing risks and threats with layered approach to Internet of Things security,". *Meas. Control*, *52*, 5–6, 338–353, doi: 10.1177/0020294019837991.

[6] Jazdi, N., (2014). "Cyber physical systems in the context of Industry 4.0,", doi: 10.1109/ AQTR.2014.6857843.

[7] Nur Altun, S., Dorterler, M. and Alper Dogru, I., (Oct. 2018). "Fuzzy Logic Based Lighting System Supported with IoT for Renewable Energy Resources," in *2018 Innovations in Intelligent Systems and Applications Conference (ASYU)*, 1–4, doi: 10.1109/ASYU.2018.8554 026.

[8] Almada-Lobo, F., (2015). "The Industry 4.0 revolution and the future of Manufacturing Execution Systems (MES),". *J. Innov. Manag.*, 3, 4, 16–21, doi: 10.24840/2183-0606_003.004_ 0003.

[9] "cyber-physical systems (CPS) (nsf10515)," (2010). https://www.nsf.gov/pubs/2010/ nsf10515/nsf10515.htm., (accessed April 25, 2021).

[10] Wang, L., Törngren, M. and Onori, M., (2015). "Current status and advancement of cyber-physical systems in manufacturing,". *J. Manuf. Syst.*, 37, 517–527, doi: 10.1016/j.jmsy.2015. 04.008.

[11] Sicari, S., Rizzardi, A., Grieco, L.A. and Coen-Porisini, A., (2015). "Security, privacy and trust in Internet of things: The road ahead,". *Comput. Networks*, 76, 146–164, doi: 10.1016/ j.comnet.2014.11.008.

[12] Jing, Q., Vasilakos, A.V., Wan, J., Lu, J. and Qiu, D., (Oct. 2014). "Security of the Internet of Things: Perspectives and challenges,". *Wirel. Networks*, 20, 8, 2481–2501, doi: 10.1007/s112 76-014-0761-7.

[13] Baheti, R. and Gill, H., (2011). "Cyber-physical systems,". *Impact Control Technol.*, 12, 1, 161–166. [Online]. Available: www.ieeecss.org, (accessed April 23, 2021).

[14] Tao F., Zhang M. and Nee A.Y.C., (2019). "Digital twin, Cyber–Physical System, and Internet of Things,". *Digital Twin Driven Smart Manufacturing*, United Kingdom: Elsevier Science, 243–256.

[15] Humayed, A., Lin, J., Li, F. and Luo, B., (Dec. 2017). "cyber-physical systems security - A survey,". *IEEE Internet Things J.*, 4, 6, 1802–1831, doi: 10.1109/JIOT.2017.2703172.

[16] Bocciarelli, P., D'Ambrogio, A., Giglio, A. and Paglia, E., (Aug. 2017). "A BPMN extension for modeling Cyber-Physical-Production-Systems in the context of Industry 4.0,". In *Proceedings of the 2017 IEEE 14th International Conference on Networking, Sensing and Control, ICNSC 2017*, 599–604, doi: 10.1109/ICNSC.2017.8000159.

[17] McCarthy, J., (2017). "What is AI? / basic questions,". *John McCarthy's Original Website*, http://jmc.stanford.edu/artificial-intelligence/what-is-ai/index.html, (accessed May 06, 2021).

[18] Alguliyev, R., Imamverdiyev, Y. and Sukhostat, L., (Sep. 2018). "Cyber-physical systems and their security issues," *Comput. Ind.*, 100, 212–223, doi: 10.1016/j.compind.2018.04.017.

[19] Sharma, N., *et al.*, (Jul. 2021). "A smart ontology-based IoT framework for remote patient monitoring," *Biomed. Signal Process. Control*, 68, 102717, doi: 10.1016/j.bspc.2021.102717.

[20] Abie, H., (May 2019). "Cognitive cybersecurity for CPS-IoT enabled healthcare ecosystems,". In *International Symposium on Medical Information and Communication Technology, ISMICT*, vol. 2019-May, doi: 10.1109/ISMICT.2019.8743670.

[21] Jiang, Y., Song, H., Wang, R., Gu, M., Sun, J. and Sha, L., (Aug. 2016). "Data-centered runtime verification of wireless medical cyber-physical system,". *IEEE Trans. Ind. Informatics*, 13, 4, 1900–1909, doi: 10.1109/TII.2016.2573762.

[22] Castaño, F., Beruvides, G., Haber, R.E. and Artuñedo, A., (Sep. 2017). "Obstacle recognition based on machine learning for on-chip lidar sensors in a cyber-physical system," *Sensors (Switzerland)*, 17, 9, 2109, doi: 10.3390/s17092109.

[23] Yuan, T. *et al.*, (Nov. 2020). "Machine learning for next-generation intelligent transportation systems: A survey,". [Online]. Available: https://hal.inria.fr/hal-02284820v2, (accessed May 05, 2021).

[24] Speer, B.*et al.*, (2015). "The role of smart grids in integrating renewable energy,"[Online]. Available:www.nrel.gov/publications, (accessed May 08, 2021).

[25] Sridhar, S., Hahn, A. and Govindarasu, M., (2011). "Cyber-physical system security for the electric power grid," *Proc. IEEE, 100*, 1, 210–224, doi: 10.1109/JPROC.2011.2165269.

[26] Bose, B.K., (Nov. 2017). "artificial intelligence Techniques in smart grid and renewable energy systems - Some example applications,". *Proc. IEEE, 105*, 11, 2262–2273, doi: 10.1109/JPROC.2017.2756596.

[27] Ozay, M., Esnaola, I., Yarman Vural, F.T., Kulkarni, S.R. and Poor, H.V., (Aug. 2016). "machine learning methods for attack detection in the smart grid,". *IEEE Trans. Neural Networks Learn. Syst., 27*, 8, 1773–1786, doi: 10.1109/TNNLS.2015.2404803.

[28] Wu, M., Song, Z. and Moon, Y.B., (Mar. 2019). "Detecting cyber-physical attacks in cyber manufacturing systems with machine learning methods,". *J. Intell. Manuf., 30*, 3, 1111–1123, doi: 10.1007/s10845-017-1315-5.

[29] Sonntag D., Zillner S., van der Smagt P. and Lörincz A., (2017). "Overview of the CPS for Smart Factories Project: deep learning, Knowledge Acquisition, Anomaly Detection and Intelligent User Interfaces," Springer, Cham, 487–504.

[30] Wickramasinghe, C.S., Marino, D.L., Amarasinghe, K. and Manic, M., (Dec. 2018). "Generalization of deep learning for cyber-physical system security: A survey,". In *Proceedings: IECON 2018 - 44th Annual Conference of the IEEE Industrial Electronics Society.* 745–751, doi: 10.1109/IECON.2018.8591773.

[31] Gao, S. and Thamilarasu, G., (Sep. 2017). "Machine-learning classifiers for security in connected medical devices,", doi: 10.1109/ICCCN.2017.8038507.

[32] Shafiq, M., Tian, Z., Sun, Y., Du, X. and Guizani, M., (Jun. 2020). "Selection of effective machine learning algorithm and Bot-IoT attacks traffic identification for internet of things in smart city,". *Futur. Gener. Comput. Syst., 107*, 433–442, doi: 10.1016/j.future.2020.02.017.

[33] "CPSSEC | Homeland Security.", (2021). https://www.dhs.gov/science-and-technology/cpssec, (accessed May 06).

2

Enhancement of the Healthcare Sector and the Medical Cyber-Physical System with the Help of Blockchain Technology

A. Deshwal and S. Miglani

Department. of CSE, Thapar Institute of Engineering and Technology, Punjab, India

2.1 Introduction

Blockchain is a new technology that has changed the world scenario. Suddenly, a parallel universe has been established by blockchain. The popularity gain of blockchain is so high that big companies and banks have started adopting this technology. The integrity, transparency, user-friendliness, peer-to-peer connection, and safety against hackers make blockchain an ideal model to use in the future. The most famous use of blockchain is in cryptocurrency; whenever someone says blockchain, Bitcoin strikes our mind. The reason is the amount of work or research done on Bitcoin and ethereum. It does not mean there are no other areas where blockchain cannot be used. The central pillar of blockchain is a smart contract. In this paper, we have used the same vision of a smart contract to use in fields other than Bitcoin. The idea of smart contracts in blockchain to work with hospital management systems has been proposed in this paper. Our main aim is to achieve the results based on smart contracts in blockchain without the involvement of any third party. Blockchain is an unexplored area to work on, and it is a small step towards a more fantastic future to improve or secure the healthcare system from corruption or corrupted persons.

Nowadays, one of the most crucial sectors for every individual is health care. Health care is the one which people trust a lot because it is only one sector that can give a new life to an individual. However, in this revolutionary era where this sector is growing in multiple fields like research, infrastructure, testing, and many more on the other side, some people are using it to earn more money using corruption and playing with people's lives. A coronavirus pandemic (COVID-19) has affected the lives of ordinary people and shook most of the countries of the world. This pandemic also continues to have extensive global economic and environmental consequences. In developing countries, economies, and regions, the pandemic's disruption in the healthcare sector has made it difficult for poor, lower-middle-class, and middle-class people to get their treatments. People faced this problem during the COVID-19 pandemic where some of the private hospitals charged huge amounts of money to patients for treatment and medicines.

DOI: 10.1201/9781003202752-2

This problem is not of a single country. Many people throughout the world reported how this COVID-19 pandemic is affecting health care and its services. Many healthcare workers reported how this pandemic is making a person sick [1]. The report states that there is also corruption in personal protective equipment (PPE). The government contracts also have been riddled corruption, described in the same article [2]. This pandemic shut down everything, which affected imports and exports a lot. This resulted in a higher cost of raw materials used to produce medicines. This also increased the corruption when medicine prices increased. According to an article [3], the National Pharmaceutical Pricing Authority (NPPA) has allowed a one-time 50% hike on the price of a heparin injection on its ceiling price. In an article [4], it was mentioned that in around 80 countries of the world, the cost for ten of the common widely used medicines for treating coronavirus patients increased 4% just between February and June 2020. The most significant hike increased the price of Remdesivir when it was approved for the treatment of COVID-19 patients. In India, lots of corruption took place on this medicine due to its higher price. In different parts of India, many people were found selling Remdesivir at higher prices and on the black market [5,6]. This black market is not for Remdesivir, but this also happened for tocilizumab, where patients and their families were forced to pay 1.4 lacs for 400 mg of the drug mentioned in the article [7,8,9,10].

However, before the coronavirus pandemic, India's healthcare sector already hit international headlines of corruption [11]. Many ways enhance the corruption in the healthcare sector. These factors are in front of everyone, and an ordinary person can also observe these factors. The present scenario of the healthcare system or hospitals is just a business to earn lots of money from people. Everyone understands how the hospital charges a massive amount of money in fees like consultation fees, testing fees, etc. One can also observe the enormous difference between the charges of two labs, doctor's private clinics, or even hospitals, especially if one of them belongs to the government and the second to a private company. Most of the time, the government gives lots of funds to improve these sectors, but some people are corrupted and do not like to improve the services of this sector. To solve this problem, the Internet is also used to maintain records, but it also did not work well because they use a centralized server and authorities have the permission who can view, alter, etc., these data. No ordinary person has access to see the database of an organization. Also, if someone wants to see the records in the database, they can alter them quickly, and no authority or government can track them.

Nevertheless, most of the time, there are also chances that hackers can hack the system and can retrieve confidential information like healthcare departments, employees' account numbers, patient banking details, government information, etc. One can also alter the amount of booked goods like ventilators, machines, etc. So, this problem is common for the public and private healthcare systems.

Now here, a question arises that in this digitalization world, is there any method or technology use that can stop or reduce this problem to an extent or not? Yes, we have technology called blockchain, which can reduce system insecuries to a great extent.

The main reason for choosing blockchain is that, as we know, it is easy to hack the distributed system for a hacker; once a server is hacked, all the data present becomes vulnerable. We are unable to detect if a hacker is sitting between us and keeps fetching our data. Because a third person does not need to hack our database, most of the time, a person in the network shares confidential information with others or does some changes in funds. Due to these activities done by few people, the entire staff and authorities must feel shame, which is not a good thing; it is terrifying. Several challenges concern the management of medical records. Among the solutions that promise to solve many problems concerning this critical point is the blockchain, through its decentralized form and security mechanisms. So, we need something transparent and secure and cannot be hacked easily. Here, blockchain comes into action.

However, technology may promise to improve conditions for poor people even in crises such as the COVID-19 period. This article discusses a smart contract of a healthcare system using blockchain technology and a ganache blockchain. We discuss how using blockchain technology in the healthcare system can reduce the corruption and high fees of treatment, medicines, and testing. This will help lower-class families get their treatment in any hospital at cheap and fixed prices mentioned by the government during this pandemic period. It will also help the government and ordinary people easily track the healthcare's database and charges as it will provide immutable privacy, transparency, and a shared ledger. This smart contract will also develop a secure framework between all the entities of the healthcare sector that promise to follow a secure transaction among all. This smart contract helps all the entities to get their amount of money timely, securely, and transparently without alteration.

The rest of the chapter is organized as follows: Section 4.2 describes the work in the related area of the healthcare sector. Section 3 describes how the coronavirus affected the world using visualization and analysis. Section 4 presents the proposed system; section 5 provides the materials used in which required software and environment setup is discussed. Section 6 describes the design flow architecture; section 7 presents the implementation and work of the proposed smart contract. Finally, section 8 offers a conclusion with a summary and section 9 presents future work.

2.2 Literature Review

In the healthcare system, we can find many challenges upon which some researchers also tried to cover such challenges in their work, but there were few loopholes in their study. In this section, we will discuss those works and their limitations in work.

Nowadays, many services that the health sector provides to us face many challenges like health problems, medical, insufficient health services, and many more incremental healthcare difficulties. Along with the same, it also results in the need for a better and safe healthcare system. Wan et al. (2013) [11] discussed the information technology (IT) trend in medical facilities such as e-medical records, good health of people, patients' database, and more can be easily explained with the help of IT. Healthcare sector has substantially improved owing to availability of records [12] as mentioned by Kim, Trimi, and Chung (2014).

Sharing the records may be the best application in the healthcare sector as it will help the patient get treatment at a new place. They can get their data from their old doctor or hospital and use all their data for better treatment if they are at a new location. Dubovitskaya et al. (2017) [13] tried to implement such a system by sharing the cancer patient data, which was EMR data. A similar framework was used by Xia et al. (2017) in their work [14] used the cloud to share the patient's medical records or data. They proposed a system with the name of MeDShare, which uses cloud service providers to share data. Azaria et al. (2016) [15] proposed a system with the name of MedRec, which provides three services to the users: authentication, confidentiality, and accountability in sharing the data. This study provides much more security to people, but something was missing that can make the system more secure and beneficial. Interoperability was something left out in their study, and they also mentioned it in their future reference section. As the institutions used different data formats, it acts as one of the main barriers to the data sharing process.

In their paper, Magyar (2017) [16] stated that solving the problems related to record lifelong patient health data can be solved easily with the help of the health information ecosystem, powered by blockchain technology. The Gabor Magyar uses the open extendable network, decentralized network, and cryptography techniques to simplify data accessibility without affecting personal information and privacy. The paper focused on the privacy issues and research available for the EHR data.

Prisco (2016) discussed a network based on the ethereum named Gem Health network [17] that was launched. The information in the infrastructure can be shared efficiently among multiple parties. It uses a transparent channel used to avail the latest data of treatments. This helps prevent the use of old data, but it also allows one to check out the previous interaction between the doctors and patients.

In health care, along with medicines, many also use counterfeit drugs. Tasatanattakool and Techapanupreeda (2018) created a hyperledger-based project named Counterfeit Medicines [18], where the produced drugs acted as timestamps and further added to the public network, i.e., blockchain. The motive to add the drugs as timestamps was to avoid alteration [19]. Doing so helps prevent fraud, and from this, the ownership can be easily detected. Another research in this field was Estonia's digital health infrastructure, which was created to help insurance companies check all the patient's medical treatments.

Dey et al. (2017) [20] propose a model for managing the transaction systematically, which is carried out by the sensors used in medical care and some devices. This blockchain acted as a base for this proposed Internet of Things (IoT) model. Mainly biosensors were connected to the Internet of Things (IoT) platform as the primary agents. The MQTT protocol utilization was proposed in the architecture. InterPlanetary File System (IPFS) consisted of the architecture used to case out the changes or state entries in the blocks whenever hardly any of the transactions are added to the blocks to lessen the stored transactions duplication.

Budida and Mangrulkar (2017) [21] presented an interactive environment concerning healthcare management operated by the Internet of Things (IoT). The proposed framework reposes on the core of generative statistics ingestion from intelligent wearable gadgets and biosensors. It follows up with feedbacks and with some solutions that are beneficial for the patients.

Sivagami, Revathy, and Nithyabharathi (2016) [22] presented a smart hospital system that unifies the effectiveness of sensors and encourages people's response for a time, and quickly counsels the patients. The approach promotes the use of smart wearables, WSN, and RFID, which set off with each other to bring off determined tasks. The tasks are sensing the patient's environment, allocating patients to the ward as per the requirement of a doctor, monitoring and analyzing data based on patient movement by the system, and finally posting the data collected with the help of sensors over a single platform.

Theodouli et al. (2018) [23] facilitated a data sharing system for health care that surpasses the current system by unshackling the sobriquet of privatizing the credentials of customers whose information is being utilized and shared by the team of medical research centers. This work also demonstrated the notion of "proof of interoperability," a consensus algorithm that would let the institutes organize a system with efficient and smoother transactions entirely reliant on the interoperability of the multiple nodes on a blockchain network. The authors also suggest a three-level architecture on the various stages.

Wang et al. (2018) [24] promote a parallel healthcare system based on a blockchain network around the ACP approach. The framework determines the use of the system based on the experience and knowledge of both the patients and doctors, including artificial intelligence. The other chunk of the ACP approach amalgamates doctors' clinical consequences and experience to determine the non-proprietary clinical and experimental approaches that must be accomplished on patients. The final chunk of the ACP approach allows the actual health care and artificial health care to execute simultaneously, which regulates the way for doctors and virtual doctors. The entire healthcare system is consolidated with a blockchain network. This network has a group of patients, hospitals, doctors, medical researchers, and healthcare bureaus. They all have the right to share and review the data.

Alhadhrami et al. (2017) [25] discussed the basis and architectures of various available blockchain networks in the current scenario. The authors also discussed how a blockchain network could be utilized in maintaining, storing, and validating data in the healthcare sector. The proposed system uses the consortium blockchain for storing healthcare data. These networks are permissible, which means the miner and node owner get exclusive access control. Moreover, this blockchain network is based on consensus theory, where most nodes or stakeholders are associated with the network.

Liu et al. (2017) [26] proposed a framework describing e-healthcare systems using blockchain architecture. The critical coverage of the work concentrated more on the growth of interoperable and versatile networking solutions for productive and actual transferring of the healthcare statistics within multiple stakeholders. The framework follows the methodology of crucial inspection by the stakeholders such as the hospitals, insurance companies, and doctors, considering the credibility and authenticity of documentation that must be shared over the platform.

Ahram et al. (2017) [27] evolved a blockchain network for the healthcare sector where HIPAA eases all the privacy rules. These rules were addressed using data that consisted of geographic and race-related particulars of the patients . Work also demonstrated a generative framework of a blockchain network consisting of the three kinds of networks. These networks have been named urgent care, referral, and primary care physician network.

Raj, Jain, and Arif (2017) [28] created a novel and unique methodology for monitoring and observing health status. This methodology also supports telemedicine technology in rural areas where robust and better connectivity always remains a vital concern. The authors developed a mobile system for measuring the health status of patients in remote locations. This mobile system contains many health sensors for measuring the health status of people like ECG, pulse oximeter, and many more. The system is also capable of working in both modes: online mode and offline mode. Another exciting thing about the system is that people's health status can be stored in a database that can further be used during the patient's treatment. This mobile system also supports a multichannel framework. This multichannel framework is designed for doctors, and it will help the doctors to take over the patient cases from any of the remote centers.

Liang et al. (2017) [29–32] created a blockchain network for the transferring of statistics and data. The proposed system usually pursued a group with the interoperability of entities. The entities include doctors, patients, hospitals, insurance companies, and private clinics. All the entities have access to collaborating and sharing the data. The devices attached to the patients are directly linked with the cloud storage or database. All the health data of the patients are stored in this cloud storage. For better processing of this massive data, it is stored in batches, and for smooth processing of data, the actual data is stored in a Merkle tree. The patient also has the right to share their record with any insurance companies and avail of their insurance. This right makes this system user-centric, which means the patient has total control over their data or records. In simple terms, patients can share their data wherever they want. Such types of systems may be fruitful to research organizations. Where security and privacy of data are a vital concern, such a system can also be used effectively and efficiently.

The comparison of the above works can be seen in Table 2.1.

TABLE 2.1

Tabular Analysis of Related Work and the Proposed Work

References	Work Done/Proposed	Technology Used	Methodology to Secure Transactions	Methodology to Reduce Cyber Attacks	Methodology to Reduce Corruption
[12, 13]	Storing patient data digitally	Information Technology	no	no	no
[14, 15, 16]	Sharing of data	Cloud	no	no	no
[17, 28]	Privacy issues, used cryptography to secure patient data	Blockchain	no	yes	no
[18, 22, 23, 29]	Used blockchain and sensors to share latest data of patients with doctors and past communication between patient and doctor. Person's data from rural areas can be shared with the help of sensors, which is available online as well as offline so that doctors can easily monitor the health status	Blockchain and IoT	no	no	no
[19, 20]	Motive was to reduce frauds in health care and to detect ownership	Blockchain Hyperledger	no	yes	no
[21]	Securing the duplication of the transactions using sensors and storing transactions in blocks	Blockchain – IoT	yes	no	no
[24, 25, 30]	Organising the shared data on multiples nodes of blockchain efficiently. Parallel healthcare system based on blockchain consisting of all members of healthcare sector and establishing an artificial network between patients and doctors where virtual doctors also assist the patients in absence of doctors	Blockchain – Proof of interoper-ability consensus algorithmArt-ificial Intelligence	no	no	no
[26]	Utilization of blockchain network in maintaining, storing, and validating data of a healthcare sector	Consortium Blockchain	no	yes	no
[27]	Sharing of documents between various stakeholder of healthcare sector after authenticating and validating the data	Blockchain	no	yes	no
Proposed work	Visualizing COVID-19 cases and describing a methodology to reduce corruption in the healthcare sector by securing the transactions, which also reduces the chance of cyber-attacks	Blockchain – Smart Contract	yes	yes	yes

After studying the above papers and after analyzing the work done by researchers, we can conclude that blockchain will be the best implementation in improving the healthcare sector. In the above papers, we studied various applications of a blockchain network in the healthcare sector. Besides so many applications, a loophole was found in the above studies, and there is a requirement to work around this loophole. The loophole is related to maintaining and securing the transactions. The transactions are the ones where there are many chances of corruption. In this proposed work, we worked on blockchain technology and the healthcare sector to maintain and secure these transactions with the help of smart contracts and a ganache blockchain. Once the transactions are secure, immutable, and transparent, corruption in the healthcare sector will automatically reduce.

2.3 Data Analysis

We are aware of how coronavirus cases are increasing a lot in India. With the help of machine learning approaches, we can easily visualize the data.

Before visualizing the data, we need to import the set of libraries and the data set, as shown in Figure 2.1.

```
In [1]:  # ------- Start of the project -------#
         # ------- Visualizing the spread of CoronaVirus in six countries using python
         --------#

         # Author:- Ashutosh Deshwal

         #Step 1 :- Import useful libraries for the project

         %matplotlib notebook
         import pandas as pd
         import matplotlib.pyplot as plt
         import matplotlib.animation as animation
         from time import sleep
```

```
In [2]:  # Step 2:- Download the data Set
         URL_DATASET = r'https://raw.githubusercontent.com/datasets/covid-19/master/dat
         a/countries-aggregated.csv'
         df = pd.read_csv(URL_DATASET, usecols = ['Date', 'Country', 'Confirmed'])

         # to see the information about data set, run following command
         print(df.info())

         <class 'pandas.core.frame.DataFrame'>
         RangeIndex: 51030 entries, 0 to 51029
         Data columns (total 3 columns):
         Date        51030 non-null object
         Country     51030 non-null object
         Confirmed   51030 non-null int64
         dtypes: int64(1), object(2)
         memory usage: 1.2+ MR
```

FIGURE 2.1
Libraries and Data Set Used for Visualizing COVID-19 Cases.

The data on which we are working should be up to date to easily visualize the recent data. So before going ahead, we will first check out the latest date of which data is available in our data set, as shown in Figure 2.2.

The lists of dates available in the database are up to date. Now we can easily visualize the data of all the current cases of COVID-19 throughout the world, as shown in Figure 2.3.

Now there are lots of countries in the world and we cannot visualize them all. Here we will pick up some countries where coronavirus cases are increasing more rapidly, as shown in Figure 2.4.

Visualizing with the help of animation is easier and more straightforward compared to graphs and figures. The following code is used to generate the visualization in the form of a video file, and the mp4 format of the visualization will also get saved automatically, as shown in Figure 2.5.

```
In [3]:   # Step 3 :- Create a list containing of all the dates
          list_of_dates = df['Date'].unique()

          # To see the dates, run the following commands
          print(list_of_dates)
```

FIGURE 2.2
Code to Find Out Dates Available in Data Set.

```
          2020-09-23   2020-09-24   2020-09-25   2020-09-26   2020-09-27
          '2020-09-28' '2020-09-29' '2020-09-30' '2020-10-01' '2020-10-02'
          '2020-10-03' '2020-10-04' '2020-10-05' '2020-10-06' '2020-10-07'
          '2020-10-08' '2020-10-09' '2020-10-10' '2020-10-11' '2020-10-12'
          '2020-10-13' '2020-10-14' '2020-10-15' '2020-10-16' '2020-10-17']
```

FIGURE 2.3
Set of Dates Available in Data Set.

```
In [4]:   # Step 4 :- Pick some countries about which you want to focus.
          # Also create an ax object

          fig, ax = plt.subplots(figsize=(15, 8))

          # Where the virus is spreading a lot, we will animate only for those six count
          ries.

          list_of_countries = ['India', 'US', 'Brazil', 'Russia', 'South Africa', 'Mexic
          o']

          # List of colors for the 6 horizontal bars are as follows

          list_of_colors = ['red', 'orange', 'black', 'blue', 'yellow', 'green']
```

FIGURE 2.4
Choosing the Countries for Visualization.

```
In [6]:   # Step 6 :- Now create a FuncAnimation object
          covid_animation = animation.FuncAnimation(fig = fig, func = plot_bar_graph,
                          frames= list_of_dates, blit=True,
                          interval=20)
```

```
In [7]:   # Step 7 :- Finally save the animation to a video file of mp4 format

          # Set the path where you want to save the video file.

          my_path = r'C:\Users\lenovo\Desktop\covid_visualization.mp4'

          covid_animation.save(filename = my_path, writer = 'ffmpeg', fps=30,
                          extra_args= ['-vcodec', 'libx264', '-pix_fmt', 'yuv420p'
          ])
          plt.show()
```

FIGURE 2.5
Creating Animation and Saving Animation in Video Format.

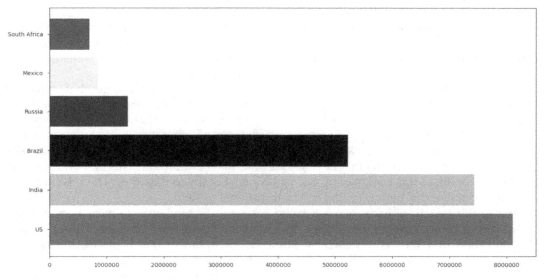

FIGURE 2.6
Countries with Number of COVID-19 Cases.

After the complete execution of the code, we can quickly check out how the coronavirus cases increase and decrease in different countries. The final output of recent cases of the coronavirus is as shown in Figure 2.6.

From Figure 2.6, we can see many coronavirus cases in the United States, followed by India. In the animated visualization, we saw how coronavirus cases in India were very few initially and then rapidly increased.

2.4 Proposed Model Theory

In this work, an intelligent contract is proposed for a transaction of a clinic or a hospital. The smart contract has all the leading entities: patients, doctors, pathologists, receptionists, and chemists. As the proposed model, we are using blockchain technology to reduce corruption in the healthcare system. The cryptocurrency that might be used in the smart contract may be equal to any country's standard currency. For example, if we talk about India, we use INR in the country. We could also set a cryptocurrency equal to INR so that a person who wants to use it does not have to pay more like other cryptocurrencies like Bitcoin and ethereum.

So, when a patient is in health care, he/she will be a part of the blockchain network, and they have to purchase cryptocurrency as they are required to pay for their treatment. To reduce corruption, say a central authority fixes the charges, including consultancy fees, testing fees, and medicines. In health care, these are three main factors where doctors charge a lot of money to people, which is not affordable. In this manner, this irregularity of doctor's consultancy fees and testing fees will be reduced slightly.

As the charges are fixed, the patient will pay the fee to different entities like the receptionist, chemist, and pathologist. The doctors also have their commission in receptionist fees and chemist bills; keeping this in mind, the intelligent contract is prepared in such manner so that all the entities will get their money once the patient pays the fee. There are chances of corruption when sometimes one entity does not give another entity their amount. The use of smart contracts makes this system properly clear and transparent. No entity must rely on others to get their amount.

Sometimes the patient pays a fee in advance, and later, they want to get their payment back. Most of the time, the management refunds the amount, but sometimes the management does not make the refund. Management also ignores that you did not pay it to us, but blockchain technology also resolves such issues. Each transaction has a transaction hash from where one can quickly get the details of any transaction, or the patient can also show the entire transactions that he/she did from his/her account. This system is evident and open for all; as it is transparent, one can connect easily to the other. There is no role of a central database in between, like in the traditional system.

This entire system is more helpful in the coronavirus pandemic as there is no vaccine available and no doctors are using the medicine prescribed by the World Health Organization and the central medical authority of India. In many places, the hospital charges a lot money to people for their treatment; some private pathologists are also charging more money than the price fixed by the central government. Similarly, many chemists are selling higher prices than the MRP by saying there is a shortage of medicine. This all leads to corruption, and they are affecting the healthcare system. As there are many entities between and all have their central servers and databases, tracking all those transactions is difficult for a central authority. However, with the help of this smart contract and blockchain technology, we can resolve this issue also. As the system is transparent, one can quickly check out all the transactions by entering the hash and one can easily trace in which transaction someone is doing transactions with higher prices. For example, the central set the testing price at Rs 4000 and say a country pathologist is charging Rs 5000; so from this, Rs 5000 can easily track out that something is happening. After reviewing the transaction, one can easily find out the hash address of both sender and receiver, and from that hash, one can easily reach to the person, and they can take appropriate action on them.

2.5 Required Software

In this proposed model, we want the following software to build and execute the smart contract:

Remix IDE: It uses an object-oriented programming language known as solidity to write and deploy smart contracts in various environments. Mainly it is used to implement smart contracts on an ethereum blockchain platform.

Ganache Blockchain: It is used to set up a personal blockchain environment of ethereum. It is used to test the smart contracts written in solidity language.

Meta Mask: A cryptocurrency wallet is a web browser extension for accessing distributed applications (Dapps). It is widely used to send, store, and receive ethers. This extension allows the users to use any ethereum-enabled Dapps and make transactions through any regular website.

2.6 Design Flow and Architecture Design

For ordinary persons, it is not easy to understand the backend or coding part as all are not familiar with them. Following is an architecture that visualizes the workflow of the proposed solution (Figure 2.7).

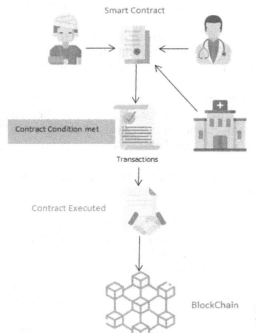

FIGURE 2.7
Design Flow and Architecture Design of Smart Contract.

2.7 Implementation and Working

In this section, we will see the implementation and the workings of the smart contract.

2.7.1 Deploying Smart Contract on JavaScript Virtual Machine (VM)

To run an application, we must check it on the virtual machine network to check whether it is running well or not. The same with the smart contract; in the smart contract, remix's IDE provides us a JavaScript virtual machine where we can deploy the smart contract and check out its functionalities.

To deploy the smart contract on the JavaScript VM, we have to choose JavaScript VM in the environment, and after that, we can deploy it as shown in Figure 2.8.

Once the contract gets deployed, we can check out the initial balance of all the entities of a smart contract, as shown in Figure 2.9.

Now the smart contract is fully ready for operation. When patients visit the hospital or a clinic for their treatment, they have to pay the consultancy fee to the receptionist. In this fee, the doctor also has a commission fee. Similarly, doctors also commission the chemist for the medicine that doctors prescribe to the patients. So, in this smart contract, we already set the doctor commission to 25% of the consultancy fees and the total bill of medicine.

To better understand the workings of the smart contract, we initially set the fees and bills that patients must pay in the clinic. The receptionist fee is Rs 500, and to the chemist, they must pay Rs 300, and to the pathologist, they must pay Rs 200.

Now let us see whether the smart contract can handle all of these things or not. The patient will have their unique hash address, which will be used to transfer all the fees, and this hash value will be public in the network. This transparency makes the system more secure and transparent.

When a patient visits the hospital, they have to pay the consultancy fees to the receptionist. The patient will pay the fee to the receptionist's account by entering the amount. Once they make the payment, the required amount gets transferred to the receptionist's and doctor's account, as shown in Figure 2.10A.

After consulting with the doctor, the patient will get the medicine, and they will pay the amount to the chemist. As the patient made the payment successfully, both the chemist and doctor will receive the payment in their account, as shown in Figure 2.10B. This will help all the entities as the transactions will automatically credit to receiver accounts, as shown in Figure 2.10.

As the pathologist does not contact the doctors or other entities, when a patient pays a fee to the pathologist, the total amount will be credited into the pathologist's account, as shown in Figure 2.11.

Once payment is made by the patient, immediately a new transaction gets recorded in the list. Now we will see the beauty of using this smart contract and how it is helpful to ordinary people. The transactions that we made can be done with the help of any wallet or payment gateway. These transactions will be a central server of the gateway authority to which ordinary people do not have access to see their database. If a hacker hacks the account, hackers can also steal confidential information like account number, password, contact number, and others.

However, this smart contract with blockchain technologies provides us many benefits. It uses cryptography in its base, due to which we can say it is secure. The reason for

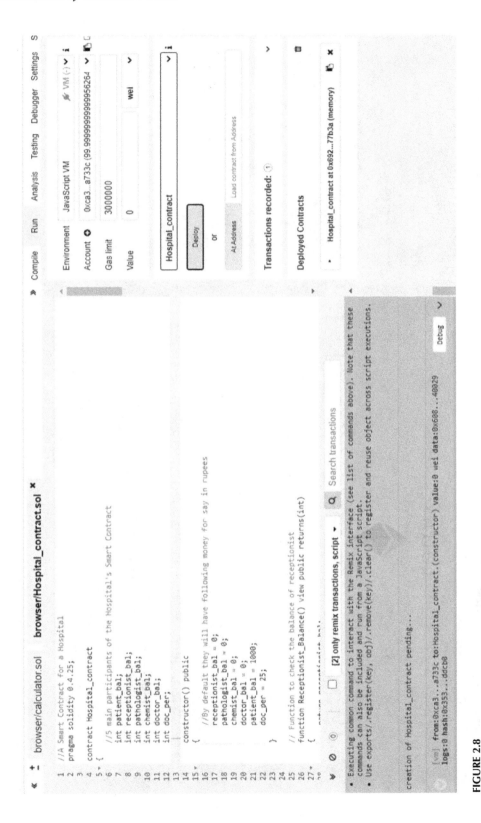

FIGURE 2.8

Deploying Smart Contract on JavaScript VM.

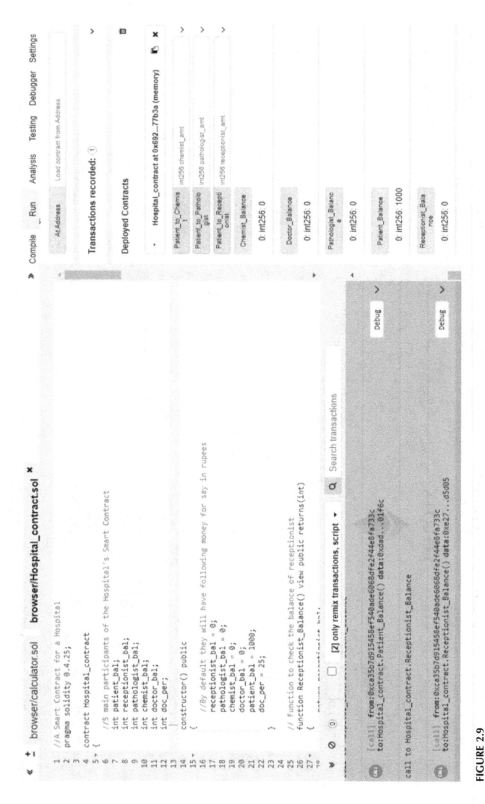

FIGURE 2.9

Initial Balance of all Entities in Smart Contract.

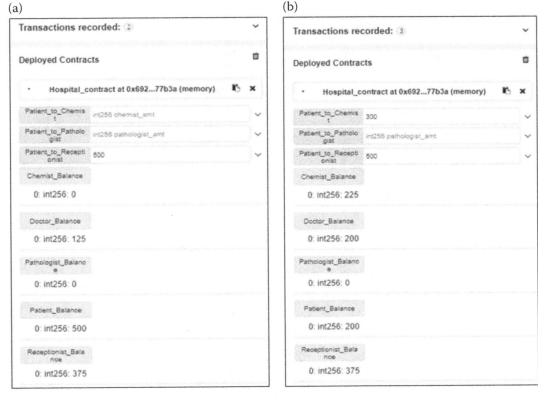

FIGURE 2.10
Distribution of Transactions.

saying it is secure is it uses hash despite a value. In this network, every account of each entity is in the form of a hash value. It also provides non-repudiation, which means if one person did a transaction and it becomes successful, another person cannot say they did not receive the payment. As it is transparent and open for all network entities, they can check out the transactions and prove them. It provides us many details, as shown in Figure 2.12.

From the figure, we can see that everything is clear and transparent, and one can easily see the transactions taking place between two or more entities.

However, what if we are doing a transaction amount that is more significant than our current account's balance. The smart contract much capable of handling such types of situations also. The smart contract will pop up with one error message if such a situation occurs, as shown in Figure 2.13.

2.7.2 Deploying a Smart Contract on a Rinkeby Environment

Deploying the smart contract on the virtual machine is just to check out the functionalities of the smart contract. However, it is not how Bitcoin and ethereum run. To better understand the workings of smart contract applications on a blockchain network, we require to deploy it on a Rinkeby Environment.

Transactions recorded: ④   ⌄

Deployed Contracts   🗑

| Hospital_contract at 0x692...77b3a (memory) | 🗐 ✖ |

Patient_to_Chemist	300	⌄
Patient_to_Pathologist	200	⌄
Patient_to_Receptionist	500	⌄

Chemist_Balance

0: int256: 225

Doctor_Balance

0: int256: 200

Pathologist_Balance

0: int256: 200

Patient_Balance

0: int256: 0

Receptionist_Balance

0: int256: 375

FIGURE 2.11
Transaction between Patient and Pathologist.

Rinkeby's environment of solidity provides us almost the same network and interface as Bitcoin and ethereum use. On the Rinkeby network, metamask will come into action. Because of JavaScript VM, when a patient was making any transaction, it was complete. However, in the Rinkeby environment, metamask will pop up always, whenever a transaction initiates.

On the blockchain network, we have to pay some fees in the form of gas fees. These gas fees help us to complete our transaction faster from a miner. So, in the Rinkeby environment, we will initiate some transactions. Metamask asks us for a gas fee like on a Bitcoin and ethereum environment.

When we deploy our smart contract initially, we have to pay slightly more gas fees for creating a new contract on the blockchain, as shown in Figure 2.14.

Once we pay the gas fee for any operation, either deploying or for a transaction, we will get a link to find details about some of the critical terms of blockchain.

FIGURE 2.12
Details of a Transaction in Smart Contract.

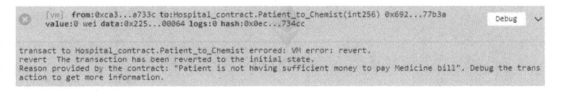

FIGURE 2.13
Error Message.

These terms are transaction hash, status, block, timestamp, sender address, receiver address, transaction fees, gas fees, nonce, and many more. After clicking on the link, we will be redirected to a page to find all these details, as shown in Figure 2.15 (Figures 2.16 and 2.17)

The solidity uses virtual ether; that is why all these details we can found on the ether scan website as it uses ethereum, not Bitcoin. The Rinkeby network helps us to understand how a smart contract application runs on the blockchain network.

Whenever someone has to pay an amount, the metamask will generate a pop-up from where one can easily allow a transaction if he/she wants to make a transaction or not.

Whenever the patient makes any transaction, the patient has to confirm the transaction, as shown in Figure 2.18.

After making the transaction, if the patient wants to check out details about their transaction, they can quickly check it out. This will help in easily tracking the transaction at any time. Others can also check it out by visiting the ether scan website, or they can find out a transaction with the help of a block or transaction hash. After entering the details, one can easily find out all the details about the transactions, as shown in Figure 2.19.

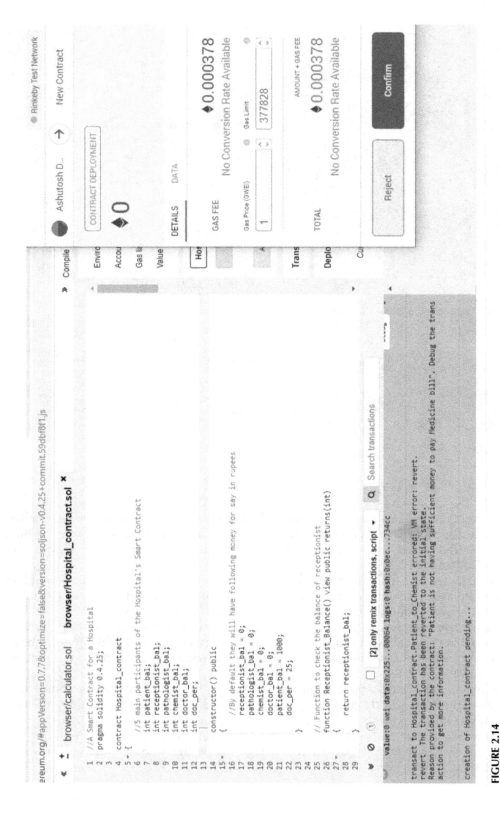

FIGURE 2.14
Metamask Pop-up for Validating Smart Contract.

FIGURE 2.15
Transaction Link.

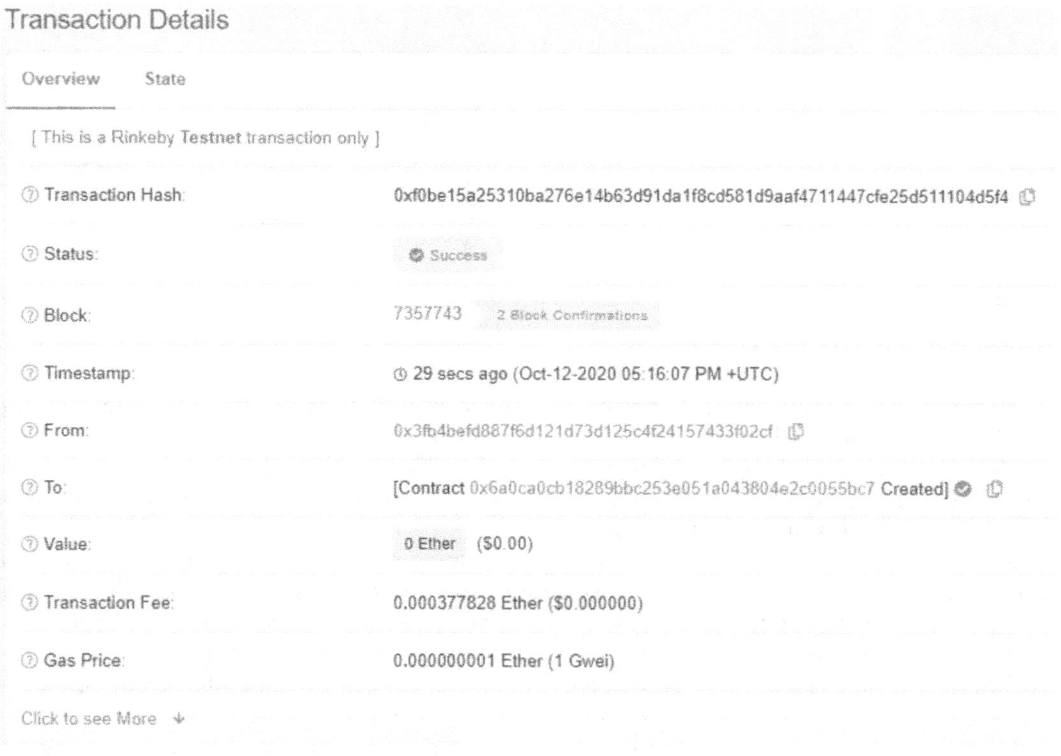

FIGURE 2.16
Fewer Transaction Details.

Once the transaction is complete, the entities will receive the amount in their account, as shown in Figure 2.20.

Whenever a patient wants to make a transaction value more than the current value, then a pop-up occurs, giving the warning message shown in Figure 2.21.

2.7.3 Deploying a Smart Contract on a Ganache Blockchain Using Web3 Provider

We discussed the deployment of the smart contract on the virtual machine and the Rinkeby network. However, the implementation should be on a blockchain to quickly understand the working of the smart contract on a blockchain network. Now we will

Overview   State

Timestamp: 29 secs ago (Oct-12-2020 05:16:07 PM +UTC)

From: 0x3fb4beld887f6d121d73d125c4f24157433f02cf

To: [Contract 0x6a0ca0cb18289bbc253e051a043804e2c0055bc7 Created]

Value: 0 Ether   ($0.00)

Transaction Fee: 0.000377828 Ether ($0.000000)

Gas Price: 0.000000001 Ether (1 Gwei)

Gas Limit: 377,828

Gas Used by Transaction: 377,828 (100%)

Nonce   Position   56   24

Input Data:

FIGURE 2.17
More Transaction Details.

deploy this smart contract on the ganache blockchain. To run the smart contract on the blockchain, we need to deploy the smart contract on the Web3 Provider.

After deploying the smart contract on the Web3 Environment, it provides us ten accounts with 100 ethers each, as shown in Figure 2.22. The user can choose any account for the implementation of the transaction.

Once the user chooses one account, the transaction count of the same account increases, and the balance of that account will also reduce from 100 ethers, as shown in Figure 2.23.

We are aware that we have blocks where the transactions get stored and mined by miners in the blockchain. Similarly, when the smart contract gets deployed on the ganache blockchain, block 0 will be created. A new block will be generated in the ganache blockchain whenever a new transaction occurs, as shown in Figure 2.24.

All the smart contract transactions will be reflected in the ganache blockchain, which is available to all. Anyone can see these transactions easily in the ganache blockchain, as shown in Figure 2.25.

The available transactions in the ganache blockchain will also be available in the solidity smart contract. One can also view all the transactions or the current balance on the solidity smart contract, as shown in Figure 2.26.

If we check out the blocks in the ganache blockchain, we can see in front of each block that we have the complete details about that respective block. The details like how much gas is used to mine and the block and how many transactions occur in particular blocks are all mentioned easily, as shown in Figure 2.27.

The benefit of using the ganache blockchain is that it provides us the complete log of all the procedures and steps. One can also save these logs if someone wants to look at them for any future requirement. These logs also contain the complete details about each operation, as shown in Figure 2.28. These logs are also easy to read by a person, and they are immutable, which means no one modifies these logs. This immutability feature helps a lot in reducing corruption.

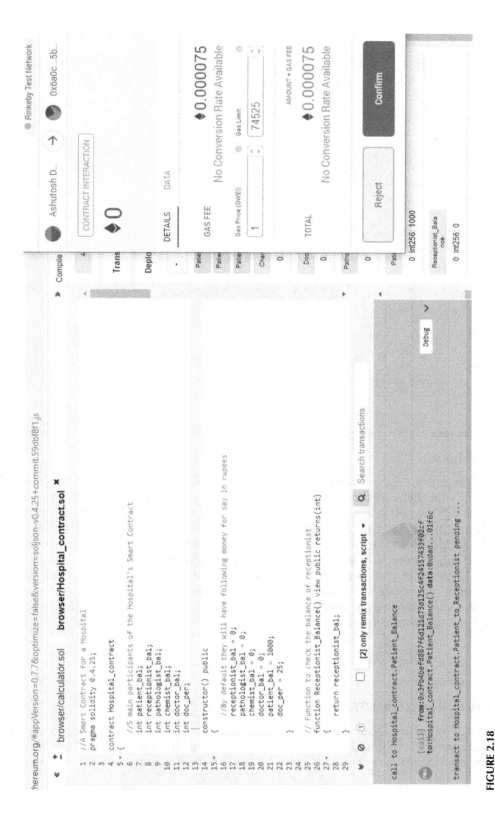

FIGURE 2.18
Confirmation of Transaction Using Metamask.

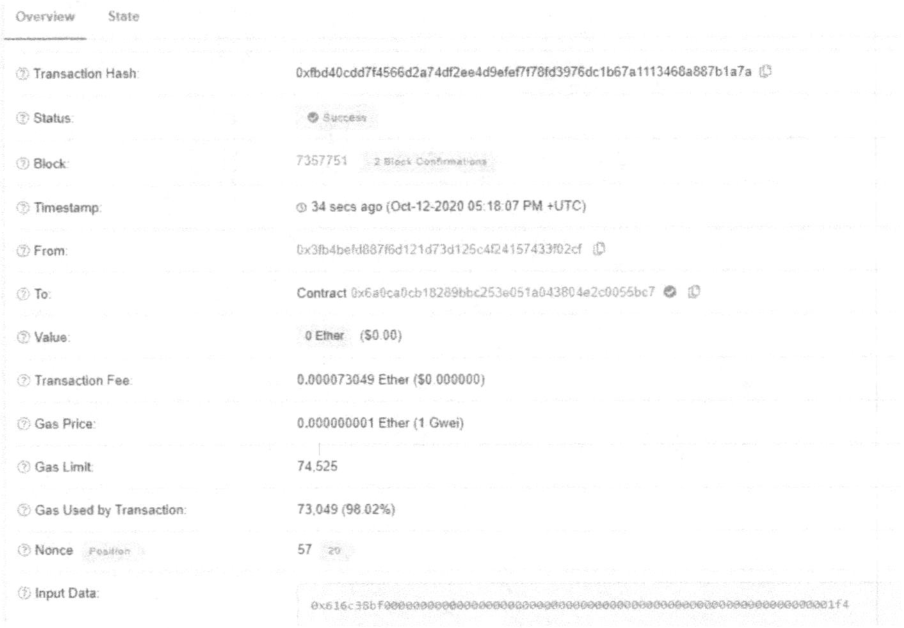

Overview   State

⑦ Transaction Hash:	0xfbd40cdd7f4566d2a74df2ee4d9efef7f78fd3976dc1b67a1113468a887b1a7a
⑦ Status:	✓ Success
⑦ Block:	7357751 2 Block Confirmations
⑦ Timestamp:	⏱ 34 secs ago (Oct-12-2020 05:18:07 PM +UTC)
⑦ From:	0x3fb4befd887f6d121d73d125c4f24157433f02cf
⑦ To:	Contract 0x6a9ca0cb18289bbc253e051a043804e2c0056bc7 ✓
⑦ Value:	0 Ether ($0.00)
⑦ Transaction Fee:	0.000073049 Ether ($0.000000)
⑦ Gas Price:	0.000000001 Ether (1 Gwei)
⑦ Gas Limit:	74,525
⑦ Gas Used by Transaction:	73,049 (98.02%)
⑦ Nonce Position	57 29
⑦ Input Data:	0x616c38bf0000000000000000000000000000000000000000000000000000000000001f4

FIGURE 2.19
Transaction Details from Transaction Hash.

2.8 Conclusion

Implementing the "Enhancement of Healthcare Sector and Medical Cyber-Physical System with the help of Blockchain Technology" is successfully achieved and fulfills the objectives. The software utilized in this introduced model performed its functioning precisely as per the need to obtain the desired result, which is required for the patients and ordinary people in the healthcare sector. The use of blockchain in health care makes it secure and transparent with less complexity. Using this module, the people who indulge in the healthcare sector will not rely on others to get their payment. They will also get rid of corruption and non-repudiation. The system is automatically monitored and controls the entire transaction taking place on time. This all will result in designing a secure medical cyber-physical system.

2.9 Future Research Directions

This concept in the future can gain ground by making the system more intelligent. A tract may be prepared that will utilize slightly less quantities of software and perform better. It should be made simpler or more advanced by using the following upcoming technologies

Transactions recorded: ③   ⌄

Deployed Contracts   🗑

⌄   Hospital_contract at 0x6a0...55bc7 (blockchain)   📋 ✕

Patient_to_Chemist	300	⌄
Patient_to_Pathologist	int256 pathologist_amt	⌄
Patient_to_Receptionist	500	⌄

Chemist_Balance

0: int256: 225

Doctor_Balance

0: int256: 200

Pathologist_Balance

0: int256: 0

Patient_Balance

0: int256: 200

Receptionist_Balance

0: int256: 375

FIGURE 2.20
Entities Balance after a Set of Transactions.

Gas estimation failed   ✕

Gas estimation errored with the following message (see below). The transaction execution will likely fail. Do you want to force sending?
gas required exceeds allowance (10000000) or always failing transaction

Send Transaction   Cancel Transaction

FIGURE 2.21
Warning Message.

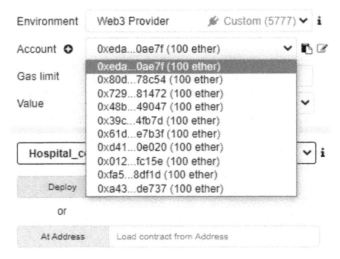

FIGURE 2.22
Group of Ten Accounts with 100 Ethers Each.

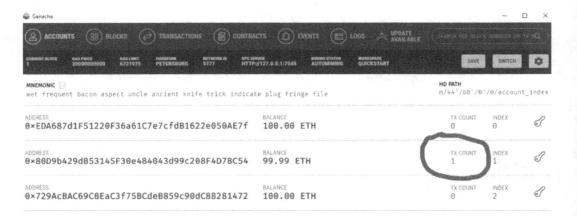

FIGURE 2.23
Increment in Transaction Count after Deploying.

FIGURE 2.24
New Block Creation.

FIGURE 2.25
List of Transactions in Ganache Blockchain.

FIGURE 2.26
Entities Balance in Remix IDE.

FIGURE 2.27
Block Details.

FIGURE 2.28
Logs of a Smart Contract in a Ganache Blockchain.

or sensors. Despite using a browser, an application can be developed to be executable from any mobile device and have some more features in a single application.

References

[1] How corruption is making people sick. 2020, September 14. Transparency.org. https://www.transparency.org/en/news/how-corruption-is-making-people-sick#.

[2] Corruption is rife in the COVID-19 era. Here's how to fight it. 2020, July 15. World Economic Forum. https://www.weforum.org/agenda/2020/07/corruption-covid-19-how-to-fight-back/.

[3] Dey, S. 2020, July 2. Coronavirus drug update: Supply constraints push up COVID-19 drug price by 50% | India business news – Times of India. The Times of India. https://timesofindia.indiatimes.com/business/india-business/supply-constraints-push-up-covid-19-drug-price-by-50/articleshow/76740210.cms.

[4] Prices of essential COVID-19 medicines have increased 4% globally since February. 2021, January 14. IHS Markit. https://ihsmarkit.com/research-analysis/prices-essential-covid19-medicines-increased-4-percent-globally.html.

[5] PTI. 2020, July 19. Seven held for selling Remdesivir injections at higher cost. The Hindu. https://www.thehindu.com/news/cities/mumbai/seven-held-for-selling-remdesivir-injections-at-higher-cost/article32130672.ece.

[6] Remdesivir sold at high prices in Mumbai black market; some doctors suggest cheaper alternatives. 2020, July 8. The Economic Times. https://economictimes.indiatimes.com/industry/healthcare/biotech/pharmaceuticals/remdesivir-sold-at-high-prices-in-mumbai-black-market-some-doctors-suggest-cheaper-alternatives/articleshow/76861773.cms?from=mdr.

[7] Bhuyan, A., & IndiaSpend.com. 2020, July 7. In India, Black markets for tocilizumab spring up as demand for the COVID-19 drug surges. Scroll.in. https://scroll.in/article/966644/in-india-black-markets-for-tocilizumab-spring-up-as-demand-for-the-covid-19-drug-surges.

[8] Bhuyan, A., & IndiaSpend.com. 2020, June 7. In the middle of a pandemic, Indian hospitals are inflating the cost of even non-coronavirus care. Scroll.in. https://scroll.in/article/963885/in-the-middle-of-a-pandemic-indian-hospitals-are-inflating-the-cost-of-even-non-coronavirus-care.

[9] PharmaNewsIntelligence. 2020, July 15. Pharmaceutical companies hike drug prices during COVID-19 pandemic. https://pharmanewsintel.com/news/pharmaceutical-companies-hike-drug-prices-during-covid-19-pandemic.

[10] Www.ETHealthworld.com. 2015, March 11. Healthcare corruption in India hits international headlines. ETHealthworld.com. https://health.economictimes.indiatimes.com/news/industry/healthcare-corruption-in-india-hits-international-headlines/46532567.

[11] Wan, J., Zou, C., Ullah, S., Lai, C.F., Zhou, M., & Wang, X. 2013. Cloud-enabled wireless body area networks for pervasive healthcare. *IEEE Network*, 27(5), 56–61.

[12] Kim, G.H., Trimi, S., & Chung, J.H. 2014. Big-data applications in the government sector. *Communications of the ACM*, 57(3), 78–85.

[13] Dubovitskaya, A., Xu, Z., Ryu, S., Schumacher, M., & Wang, F. 2017. Secure and trustable electronic medical records sharing using blockchain. In AMIA annual symposium proceedings (Vol. 2017, p. 650). American Medical Informatics Association.

[14] Xia, Q.I., Sifah, E.B., Asamoah, K.O., Gao, J., Du, X., & Guizani, M. 2017. MeDShare: Trustless medical data sharing among cloud service providers via blockchain. *IEEE Access*, 5, 14757–14767.

[15] Azaria, A., Ekblaw, A., Vieira, T., & Lippman, A. 2016, August. Medrec: Using blockchain for medical data access and permission management. In 2016 2nd International Conference on Open and Big Data (OBD) (25-30). IEEE.

[16] Magyar, G. 2017. November. Blockchain: Solving the privacy and research availability tradeoff for EHR data: A new disruptive technology in health data management. In 2017 IEEE 30th Neumann Colloquium (NC) (pp. 000135–000140). IEEE.

[17] Prisco, G. 2016.The blockchain for healthcare: GemGem launches gem health network with philips blockchain lab Bitcoin Magazine 26.

[18] Tasatanattakool, P., & Techapanupreeda, C. 2018, January. Blockchain: Challenges and applications. In 2018 International Conference on Information Networking (ICOIN) (pp. 473–475). IEEE.

[19] Williams-Grut, O. 2016. Estonia is using the technology behind bitcoin to secure 1 million health records. Bus Insid.

[20] Dey, T., Jaiswal, S., Sunderkrishnan, S., & Katre, N. 2017, December. HealthSense: A medical use case of Internet of Things and blockchain. In 2017 International conference on intelligent sustainable systems (ICISS) (pp. 486–491). IEEE.

[21] Budida, D.A.M., & Mangrulkar, R.S. 2017, March. Design and implementation of smart HealthCare system using IoT. In 2017 International Conference on Innovations in Information, Embedded and Communication Systems (ICIIECS) (pp. 1–7). IEEE.

[22] Sivagami, S., Revathy, D., & Nithyabharathi, L. 2016. Smart health care system implemented using IoT. *International Journal of Contemporary Research in Computer Science and Technology*, 2(3), 641–646.

[23] Theodouli, A., Arakliotis, S., Moschou, K., Votis, K., & Tzovaras, D. 2018, August. On the design of a blockchain-based system to facilitate healthcare data sharing. In 2018 17th IEEE International Conference On Trust, Security And Privacy In Computing And Communications/12th IEEE International Conference On Big Data Science And Engineering (TrustCom/BigDataSE) (pp. 1374–1379). IEEE.

[24] Wang, S., Wang, J., Wang, X., Qiu, T., Yuan, Y., Ouyang, L., Guo, Y., & Wang, F. 2018. Blockchain-powered parallel healthcare systems based on the ACP approach. *IEEE Transactions on Computational Social Systems*, 5(4), 942–950. 10.1109/tcss.2018.2865526.

[25] Alhadhrami, Z., Alghfeli, S., Alghfeli, M., Abedlla, J.A., & Shuaib, K. 2017, November. Introducing blockchains for healthcare. In 2017 international conference on electrical and computing technologies and applications (ICECTA) (pp. 1–4). IEEE.

[26] Liu, W., Zhu, S.S., Mundie, T., & Krieger, U. 2017, October. Advanced block-chain architecture for e-health systems. In 2017 IEEE 19th International Conference on e-Health Networking, Applications and Services (Healthcom) (pp. 1–6). IEEE.

[27] Ahram, T., Sargolzaei, A., Sargolzaei, S., Daniels, J., & Amaba, B. 2017, June. Blockchain technology innovations. In 2017 IEEE technology & engineering management conference (TEMSCON) (pp. 137–141). IEEE.

[28] Raj, C., Jain, C., & Arif, W. 2017, March. HEMAN: Health monitoring and nous: An IoT based e-health care system for remote telemedicine. In 2017 International Conference on Wireless Communications, Signal Processing and Networking (WiSPNET) (pp. 2115–2119). IEEE.

[29] Liang, X., Zhao, J., Shetty, S., Liu, J., & Li, D. 2017, October. Integrating blockchain for data sharing and collaboration in mobile healthcare applications. In 2017 IEEE 28th annual international symposium on personal, indoor, and mobile radio communications (PIMRC) (pp. 1–5). IEEE.

[30] Remix – Ethereum IDE. https://remix.ethereum.org/.

[31] Truffle Suite. https://www.trufflesuite.com/ganache.

[32] MetaMask. https://metamask.io/.

3

Applications of Cyber-Physical Systems for Industry 4.0: A Comprehensive Review

Dr. Kirti Wanjale
Computer Engineering Department, VIIT, Pune

Dr. Monika Mangla
Department of Information Technology, Dwarkadas J. Sanghvi College of Engineering, Mumbai

Dr. A.V. Chitre
EnTC Engineering Department,VIIT, Pune

3.1 Introduction: Industry 4.0 and the Cyber-Physical System

The fourth revolution in industry, which is referred to as Industry 4.0, is initiated by the massive integration of physical and computational worlds. Instead of having mass and semi-customized products, it has turned to mass and fully customized products, the meaning of Industry 4.0. It gives Internet-enabled and innovative services, Internet-based diagnostics, and maintenance in an efficient way [1]. It aids in the comprehension of novel business models, operating principles, and intelligent controls, while also focusing on the user and their unique demands. These are industrial automation systems that provide revolutionary functionality via the Internet, affecting lives every day.

The cyber-physical system (CPS) is an integration of cyberspace and physical space. In cyberspace, it has computation and networking, and in physical space, it consists of physical devices. It is an embedded system that is powered by the Internet. These systems are high in economic and societal potential from an industry perception. It is a more advanced and improved form of embedded systems, computers, and embedded software. Automobiles, toys, medical devices, and scientific tools all exhibit the CPS. Life in the modern era is plagued with cell phones, automobiles, and domestic appliances that have become an intrinsic and inseparable part of our lives [2]. It is no longer a distant fantasy but a possible reality if we could turn on the heating system on our way home and arrive at a warm house. Coffee machines start to brew the coffee recognizing the wake-up time of the user before he/she gets up, thus significantly reducing the waiting time. Remote access to process data may also be used for system maintenance. Further development of the CPS can be observed in the tasks of big data management and providing machine interconnectivity, aiming at the final goal of developing decision making and intelligent machines [3,4].

DOI: 10.1201/9781003202752-3

The CPS can be further improved to manage big data and to connect machines to achieve the objective of intelligent and self-adapting machines.

In this chapter, we are going to produce a detailed study of how current existing industrial practices in production, manufacturing, and logistics can be enhanced to the next level of Industry 4.0 by CPS integration [1].

3.2 Industry 4.0

It refers to the digitalization of industrial processes as well as production in the sector. The definition of Industry 4.0 is the intelligent way of networking of machines and various processes for industry using information and communication technology. Certain aims must be understood in order to fully appreciate Industry 4.0, and they are as follows:

- Automate the process of decision making
- Monitor various processes and assets in real time
- Assist stakeholders in establishing value-creation networks that are interdependent
- Implement IT and OT convergence.
  a. **Automate the decision-making processes**: Partially transferring autonomy and autonomous decision making is essential to Industry 4.0. The application and potential of cyber-physical systems and machines, as well as information systems, makes it possible to accomplish this goal.
  b. **Monitor various assets and processes in real time**: In Industry 4.0, it is important to monitor various assets of the industry and the different processes the industry is following.
  c. **Enable equally connected value creation networks by involving stakeholders**: Involvement of stakeholders is also equally important when it comes to Industry 4.0. We need to enable the value creation networks with the help of stakeholders. It is critical to comprehend the industry's entire value chain. It contains information about the sources of the materials. Additionally, components required for multiple types of smart manufacturing are critical for improved output. The end client, which serves to be the eventual destination, must be understood irrespective of the number of intermediary procedures and stakeholders.
  d. **Implement IT and OT convergence**: For better production, we need to implement vertical and horizontal integration among various processes. Information technology (IT) is converging with operational technology (OT). There is no industrial transformation without this. For example, cloud and server infrastructure, storage, and edge infrastructure are part of a converged IT, OT, and their backbones. When it comes to convergence between IT and operations, the main characteristics include data, procedures, and people or teams. In fact, we can say that Industry 4.0 surely gives increased productivity but along with that, it helps in increasing quality, flexibility, and efficiency, as shown in Figure 3.1.

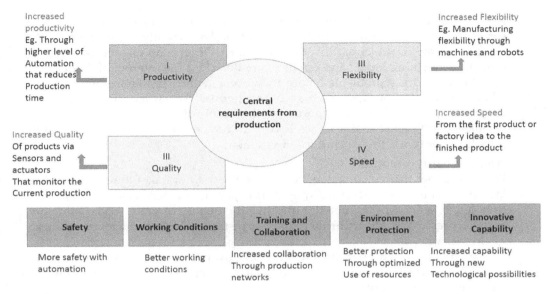

FIGURE 3.1
Advantages of Industry 4.0.

Let's have a quick look at the benefits of Industry 4.0.

3.2.1 Benefits of Industry 4.0

a. **Efficiency enhancements by optimization and automation**
The first advantage that anyone can see in Industry 4.0 is process and efficiency optimization. Essentially, it is one of the primary objectives of Industry 4.0 programs. Alternatively, it cuts costs, boosts profitability, and eliminates waste. Automation can help eliminate errors and delays, speed up output, and increase the overall value chain, among other benefits. Industry 4.0 provides several optimization opportunities, ranging from improved asset efficiency and simpler manufacturing processes to improved logistics and inventory management.

b. **Supply chain management in real time in a real-time work environment**
Additionally, Industry 4.0 places a premium on increased customer-centricity. It is concerned with the entirety of a product's and manufacturing's life cycle. When we understand the whole supply chain and environment, we see that process manufacturing involves a large number of stakeholders. They are all clients. And regardless of where they are in this whole cycle or supply chain, a consumer still needs increased efficiency. If the final customer desires high-quality goods quickly and has raised standards for customer engagement, quality, and service, this affects the entire supply chain, from procurement to manufacturing and beyond.

c. **Improved operational continuity as a result of enhanced maintenance and control capabilities**
Consider the case when a failure is detected in an industrial robot in a car manufacturing plant, in which case it is not just the robot that is broken. Output

is harmed, resulting in money being wasted and disgruntled consumers, and sometimes production is completely disrupted. Additionally, replacing or rectifying the error could jeopardize the credibility. Orders can also be canceled. If industrial assets are linked and can be e-monitored via the Internet of Things, it is possible to address problems before they occur, which has enormous benefits. Alarm or notification systems may be configured. When assets are managed proactively, real-time diagnosis and monitoring become attainable. Unsurprisingly, asset maintenance and management are becoming the second-largest sector of manufacturing IoT investment.

d. **Higher-quality products**

While it is true that customers want pace, this does not mean they will sacrifice quality. If your manufacturing system incorporates numerous sensors and IoT techniques, you will undoubtedly improve the quality of your goods. More automation results in fewer mistakes, which results in higher efficiency and also assures quality.

At the same time, indeed, robots will not take over all human jobs anytime soon. Numerous businesses have increased their reliance on robotics while also increasing their workforce.

e. **Better work environment**

Improving the working atmosphere in a plant or warehouse based on real-time physical parameters like temperature and humidity is a more vital component of Industry 4.0. Rapid identification and improved security in the event of any negative events or injuries can result in a safer working atmosphere for employees as well.

f. **Customization and personalization for the "new"market**

We are all aware that digital technologies have altered the way we work, shop, and live in the modern era. Consumption habits and tastes are altered. People have become more demanding; they expect prompt responses and information/ delivery. Additionally, customers prefer some level of personalization, depending on the context. They are more concerned with customization to meet their specific requirements. Consumers expect to engage directly with brands and their production capabilities. As previously stated, digital channels are used to configure goods, resulting in shorter lead times between development and distribution. These things already occur in a large number of industrial industries. Along with the customer world, businesses often benefit from customization in a business-to-business (B2B) sense.

g. **Adopting cutting-edge models to increase venue revenue**

Although it is possible to transform processes, basic roles, customer support, and interactions, true value comes from diversifying revenue streams and ecosystems. it is also challenging to manage new capabilities in order to provide specialized repair services to consumers.

3.3 Cyber-Physical System (CPS)

NIST, Engineering Lab had given a very clear definition of CPS: "Cyber-Physical systems or 'smart' systems are co-engineered interacting networks of physical and computational

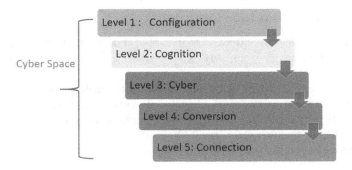

FIGURE 3.2
5C Architecture – Comprising Five Levels.

components. These systems will provide the foundation of our critical infrastructure, form the basis of emerging and future smart services, and improve our quality of life in many areas."

As per definition, the word *computational* is cyber and physical, meaning in which systems are operating. It is an interaction between the cyberworld and the physical world. These systems will serve as the cornerstone for vital infrastructure; this could include any public or private industry environment. Because of the CPS the quality of life will be improved as the smarter world. CPS will increase the smartness, which means smarter systems offering smarter services [5].

The CPS is a combination of embedded systems and the physical world. We need to understand what an embedded system is. It is software embedded in hardware like medical instruments, vehicles, defense systems, robotic equipment, process monitoring factory automation, and so on. Embedded systems have capabilities of computing, communication, and control.

In CPS there are various layers like physical layer, network layer, storage layer, and application layer, as shown in Figure 3.2. Interaction between these layers is called the CPS.

In physical space, we have objects like sensors, actuators, RFID tags, etc. Communication objects like cell phones, Wi-Fi, and General Packet Radio Service (GPRS) are in the network layer. The objects in the physical layer will sense data and send it to servers through network layers. The servers are from the storage layer known as cyberspace. Ultimately data will be sent to cyberspace. Data processing will be done in cyberspace and, based on the results, will be sent back to physical space, which will be used to actuating different devices placed in the application layer. The physical objects will be operated like starting the washing machine or starting AC in the room. Let's consider the simplest example of the CPS in real life. In the case of air conditioners, the sensors placed in AC will sense the real-time temperature which will be sent to servers. After data analysis is done in cyberspace, the decision will be sent back to physical space, which is the air conditioner, to adjust the temperature accordingly. So in all, we can say that cyberspace is actuating physical space [5].

The CPS is a term that refers to the integration of computational capability, underlying physical process, and more prominently networking ability. It is a set of many heterogeneous structures with the primary goal of controlling a physical process and adapting to changing circumstances in real time.

3.3.1 Cyber-Physical Systems in Industry 4.0

In Industry 4.0, the data is subsequently analyzed and secured with the help of the cyber-physical system (CPS). So we can say that Industry 4.0 is only possible because of the CPS.

As previously mentioned, cyber-physical systems are integrations of intelligent physical components and computing/storage systems. Networks bind the intelligent physical components and systems. Simply put, cyber-physical structures link the digital (cyber) and physical worlds in an industrial context.

The cyber-physical systems will help industries in the following areas:

1. Conceptualization, prototyping, and production of products;
2. Remote control, operation, and diagnosis; and
3. Monitoring, preventive, and predictive maintenance.
4. Tracking structural and system health;
5. Planning, creativity capacity, and agility, among other things.

The CPS's expanded capabilities contribute to the creation of the phenomena of "smart anything." Intelligent grids, intelligent infrastructure, and intelligent logistics are all examples of intelligent facilities [6]. Additionally, it includes intelligent buildings and intelligent plants. Additionally, it provides smart services for smart manufacturing, smart factories, and smart cities, as mentioned previously.

Industry 4.0 is a term that refers to the process of transforming an industry into a smart one. It takes advantage of technological advances in embedded and cyber-physical systems. Decentralized intelligence offers autonomous intelligent object networking and process management. Industry 4.0 is based on the current trend of industrial technology becoming more automated and data driven. This includes cyber-physical systems, the Internet of Things, and cloud computing. Industry 4.0 enables the creation of a "smart factory." So, if you want to understand the cyber-physical system, you'll need to understand the features of the CPS.

3.3.2 Features of the CPS

1. Reactive computation
   a. Interaction of the system with the environment in a continuous manner
   b. The sequence of inputs and outputs in the system that need to be deal with

2. Concurrency
   a. Concurrent execution of several processes
   b. Processes share data to achieve the desired outcome
   c. Synchronous or asynchronous activity modes

3. Control of the physical world through feedback
   a. Equipped with control systems that incorporate a feedback loop
   b. Sensors track the environment and actuators exert control over it
   c. Hybrid control structures for the performance of complex tasks

4. Computation in real time
   a. Time-sensitive operations such as resource distribution and coordination

5. Applications requiring extreme caution (safety critical)
   a. Prior to development, precise modeling, and validation

3.3.3 CPS Architecture for Industry 4.0

Figure 3.3 is showing the 5 C architecture – comprising five levels.

1. **Connection:** Smart connection to ensure that accurate data is obtained from IoT devices. Data acquisition for processes is done at this level. Two factors that need to be considering while acquiring the data is to obtain it seamless and tether-free data. And the other one is a selection of sensors with proper specifications.

2. **Conversion:** Conversion of machine data to meaningful information. It can be done using data analytics tools and various methodologies. So there is a need of developing different methodologies for prognostics and health monitoring of machine components and for multidimensional data collection and data correlation analysis.

3. **Cyber:** Analysis of data, which is gathered from information hubs, comprises of some high-end workstations, servers, cloud, etc. This data will be used further for data analysis, data mining, storing the data. Then some algorithms will be run on it to derive some results out of it.

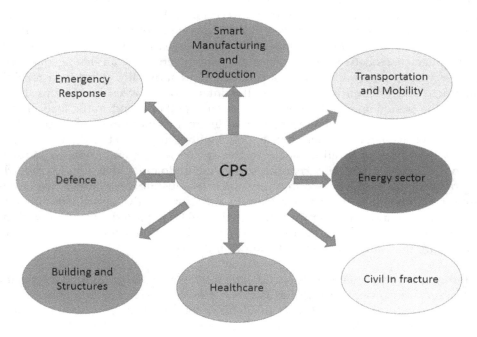

FIGURE 3.3
The Broad Categorization of Applications of the CPS.

4. **Cognition:** Proper presentation of information to users for generating knowledge of the system. Collaborative diagnostics, decision making for prioritization, optimization processes, etc.

5. **Configuration:** Supervisory control to determine actions to be taken by the machines, e.g., self-configuration for resilience, self-adjustment for variations, self-optimization for disturbances. The machine should become self-adaptive.

Industry 4.0 is mostly comprised of cyber-physical systems. It makes use of information technology–enabled control systems, embedded systems, and their interconnection. It enables new modes of production, value creation, and real-time optimization in this way. Through the use of IT infrastructure, industry items and methods of production are networked and communicate with one another. Cyber-physical systems are critical for the development of smart factories.

Additionally, Industry 4.0 must place a premium on security. The security of data, communication mediums, and networks is a critical component that must be handled. Additionally, the security of industrial control systems is critical. Industry 4.0 places a premium on the protection and security of people, industrial assets, essential infrastructure, and "physical security."

3.3.4 Need for the CPS in Industry 4.0

Similarly, the Internet has altered how people communicate with knowledge. Human interaction with engineered systems has shifted due to the advent of cyber-physical systems [7]. Humans will continue to play a key role in this scenario. In this scheme, the human being is the most adaptable and intelligent "entity." They function as a kind of supreme governing force, supervising the execution of largely automated processes.

A cyber-physical system is composed of a large number of heterogeneous components, necessitating the use of complex models to describe each subsystem and its conduct. Dynamic interactions between subsystems are then governed by an intelligent model that ensures each subsystem's deterministic conduct. The bandwidth, speed, and reliability of the Internet have a significant impact on this interaction between subsystems. For Wi-Fi networks, the positioning of devices, propagation conditions, and traffic load all have an impact on communication. This means that an Internet connection or communication network is often considered an intermediate model within the context of the CPS as a whole.

CPSs will be present in all business sectors in the future, assuming an Industry 4.0 scenario. CPSs will allow new manufacturing methodologies that will become the industry norm of the future. Self-configuring and self-adjusting development processes will be used. It will result in increased versatility and cost-effectiveness. As outlined below, any functional component of a production chain will be impacted, beginning with design and continuing through manufacturing, supply chains, and customer care and support. Following are the challenges for switching to Industry 4.0:

1. Information management: An actionable intelligence and connected information are very much necessary in Industry 4.0. Process excellence in a context of relevance, innovation, and timely availability for any desired business is equally important. All of the information either received or generated while following processes should be managed properly and this is one of the big challenges in Industry 4.0.

2. Cybersecurity or data privacy: Information or data security has also become a major challenge. The increase in the number of attacks on the industrial Internet became a big issue when the industry decided to go for certain advancements.

3.4 Applications of the CPS in Industry

Nowadays, the CPS has a plethora of applications. It is used in smart healthcare wearable devices, the smart grid, smart water networks, smart manufacturing, smart factories, monitoring and regulation of gas and oil pipelines, unmanned and autonomous underwater vehicles, hybrid electric vehicles, and greenhouse control. Figure 3.3 shows the broad categorization of applications of the CPS.

The CPS would create unprecedented opportunities for economic development. Additionally, it will generate skilled employment. The CPS will contribute to the nation's health, safety, and defense. Also, the CPS can spur creativity across a wide range of industries and can result in new products. Advanced and computer-controlled manufacturing processes, such as digital design software, will increasingly depend on CPS technologies. Additionally, it can inject vitality into the management of production lines, warehouses, and supply chains [8]. Refer to Figure 3.4(a–f) for applications of the CPS in industries.

1. Smart Manufacturing and Production
   - CPS in manufacturing systems used for logistics integrated with communication abilities. In manufacturing sectors, it will be used in sensors and actuators, ROBOT operated machines, Laid machines, and mining machine welding machines to improve the efficiency of production.
   - Agile manufacturing and supply chain connectivity
   - Intelligent controls, process, and assembly automation

Advantages:

- It helps to enhance global competitiveness.
- It has increased the efficiency, agility, and reliability.

3.5 CPS-Enabled Use Cases

Additionally, the new capabilities provided by cyber-physical systems, such as structural health monitoring, tracking, and tracing, are basically Internet of Things use cases; in other words, what the CPS allows you to do. Several of them are used in industries, not just in manufacturing.

The following are two examples of previously discussed CPS-enabled capabilities and how they are truly IoT use cases.

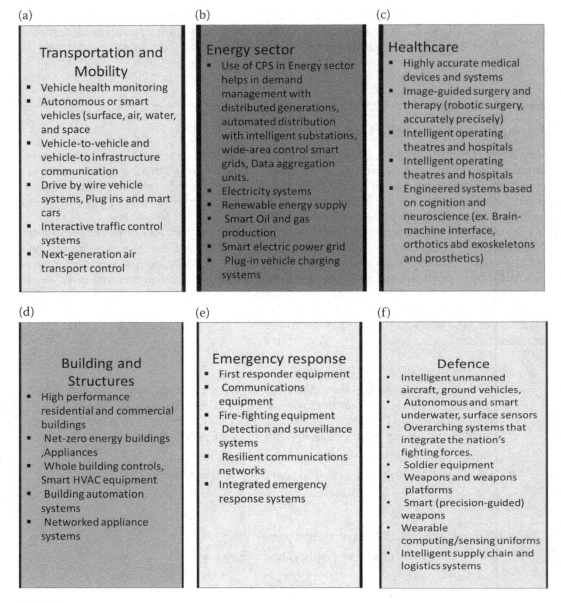

FIGURE 3.4
(a–f) Applications of CPS in Industries.

In practice, track and trace capabilities allow a variety of IoT use cases in a variety of industries, including health care, logistics, warehousing, shipping, mining, and even consumer-oriented Internet of Things use cases. There are various implementations for the latter, which incorporate a variety of solutions and technologies.[10] You can use IoT to track and trace your skateboard, your pets, or something else.

Additionally, structural health monitoring is ubiquitous, especially in industries such as architecture, building maintenance, and facility management. With the appropriate sensors and systems, you can track the structural health of a wide variety of items, ranging from bridges and objects inside buildings to manufacturing properties and cyber-physical assets in Industry 4.0.

3.6 CPS in Health Care: A Case Study

Active user input, such as smart feedback systems and digital patient records, combined with passive user input, such as biosensors or smart devices in healthcare facilities, would help collect data for efficient decision making in the context of CPS and help improve decision making [13]. Data gathering and decision making have not been thoroughly examined in healthcare applications; therefore, this is a high-priority area for further investigation. Healthcare CPS applications include the implementation of organized interoperation of autonomous and adaptive devices, novel concepts for managing and operating medical physical systems through computation and control, miniaturized implantable smart devices, body area networks, and programmable materials, as well as novel fabrication techniques.

Although numerous CPS architectures have been proposed in the literature, very few CPS architectures have been proposed for healthcare applications. Hu et al. suggested a medical CPS concept based on service-oriented architecture (SOA); however, they did not include a full architectural structure. Wang et al. [1] defined a stable CPS architecture for health care that is based on an integrated WSN-cloud platform. Banerjee et al. suggested medical CPS modeling and analysis. However, it falls short of resolving security and privacy concerns.

Figure 3.5. shows (1) data is collected from patients through various sensors and sent to the cloud through a gateway; (2) processed sensor data is sent to the cloud server; real-time queries are processed; (3) historical sensor data is processed in the event of a query response; (4) computation is performed; an alarm is produced and sent to the observation center if appropriate; (5) clinicians in observation centers access patient data from the cloud; (6) clinicians consult with other healthcare systems as needed; (7) clinicians and specialists communicate with other healthcare systems; (8) clinicians and specialists communicate with the actuation component; and (9) appropriate measures are performed on patients as shown in Figures 3.6 and 3.7.

3.6.1 Applications

The CPS has a variety of uses in health care that prominently include hospital, elderly care, and assisted living. The complex design of a system is highly application-dependent [11,12]. Architectural elements can require special organization depending on the application. In a controlled environment, like a hospital's intensive care unit, the architecture may employ controlled elements. On the contrary, in an assisted living facility, it might be necessary to incorporate a significant amount of automated elements into the design. CPS implementations in health care can be classified into two categories: (a) supported and (b) managed.

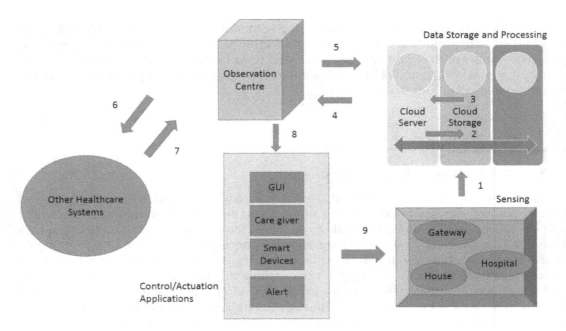

FIGURE 3.5
A Healthcare CPS Based on the Literature [6–8].

Assisted: These applications require monitoring of the health of the patient without impairing their ability to live normally. Individual patients can be counseled by real-time physiological data acquired via biosensors. With individual medical needs considered, it is quite possible to help and provide care for a growing number of elderly people in both assisted living facilities and private homes. Computing technologies, such as Angelah [9], may provide intriguing opportunities for in-house security and autonomy.

3.6.2 Controlled

In a supervised setting, this is applicable in hospitals and intensive care units where medical assistance is readily available. In a regulated area, there is a strong and intense degree of observation. In hospitals, information from a variety of sources is combined to guide therapies. These sources include bedside monitors, biosensors, and clinician observations. Closed-loop networked systems with people in the loop have the potential to augment patient safety and medical workflow. By combining these two distinct aspects of health care, the healthcare system will be transformed into a vast, complex, and mission-critical cyber-physical system with a plethora of benefits and drawbacks [7] (Figure 3.8).

3.6.3 Architecture

The CPS's quality and performance are vital to the healthcare architecture. To allow the CPS for healthcare use, you will need to design for the domain, user data, and system integration. A CPS consists of three important factors: Infrastructure, data, and composition.

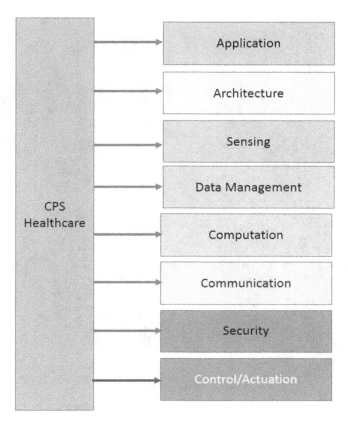

FIGURE 3.6
Taxonomy of CPS for Health Care (First Level).

3.6.3.1 Data Requirements

To handle CPS architecture, you will need to manage input data, historical data, and output data. The data size will depend on the kind of biosensor used [13]. Data such as temperature can be processed, but huge image data such as magnetic re-sonance (MRI) cannot be processed. There are differences in the data collection and transfer processes. Temperature and blood pressure are low data applications, whereas the electro-gram (EMG) has a high data rate. Additionally, you can go and get data from the folder. Thus, the architecture is divided into two categories: light and heavy.

3.6.3.2 Composition

Computation and collaboration tasks often go hand in hand in CPS health care. The framework should be able to determine the application's composition. They must be developed in accordance with the settings or preferences of the system. For instance, see Avrun et al. [10] who developed a quick and convenient guide for human participants to help and direct them when they do tasks. Computers and software can communicate

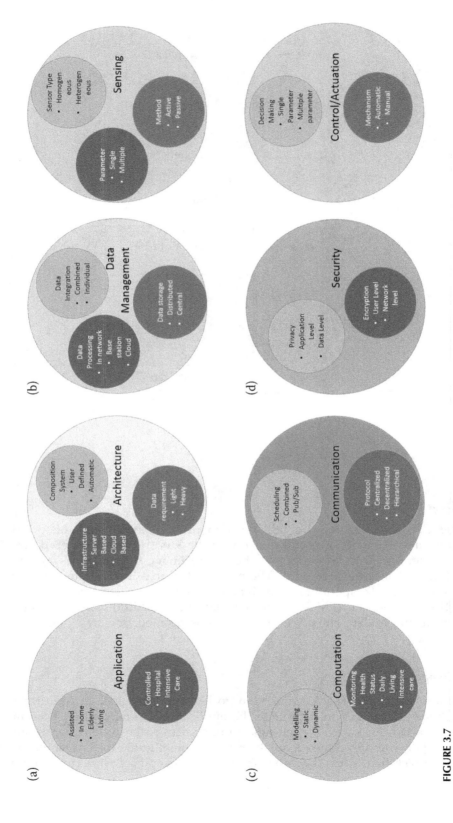

FIGURE 3.7

(a–d) Detailed Split of Taxonomical Blocks of CPS in Health Care.

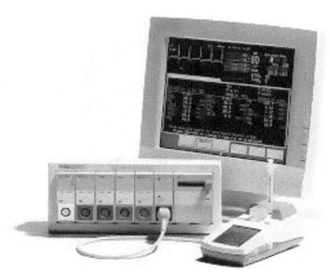

FIGURE 3.8
Monitoring Equipment.

with the system as well. Composition is based on dynamic computation and communication.

3.6.4 Sensing

The CPS is about the physicality of wellness. Biomedical sensors gather critical data, which are then processed by the computing and communication system. Sensing is a must for medical devices because parameters are input parameters. Diabetic blood testing includes pricking the finger and collecting a sample. A non-invasive BGL method is used that allows the use of radio sensors. On the sensing side, there are sensors, (a) electrodes, and (b) a mechanism.

The number and type of sensors used in healthcare applications differ. They may be identical or diverse. a single sensor can be used to monitor the health of a community, or multiple sensors can be used to monitor the health of one person primarily dependent on the sensing technique [11]. The number of sensors used in CPS collect a wide range of data. Sensors will often, on occasion, intercept important as well as questionable predictions [12]. To the efficiency of the method and decision making, information should be processed using a multidimensional analysis [13] (Figure 3.9).

3.6.4.1 Methods

The number and type of sensors used in healthcare applications differ [14]. They may be identical or diverse. A single sensor can be used to monitor the health of a community, or multiple sensors can be used to monitor the health of one person primarily dependent on the sensing technique [15]. The number of sensors used in the CPS collects a wide range of data. Sensors will often, on occasion, intercept important as well as questionable predictions. To the efficiency of the method and decision making, information should be processed using a multidimensional analysis [16].

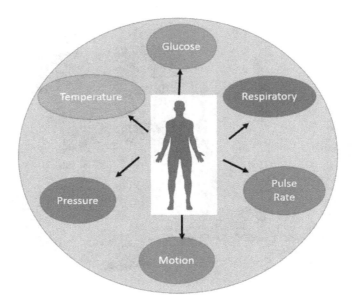

FIGURE 3.9
Wearable Sensors.

3.6.4.2 Parameters

Computation and communication are both improved when parameters are better defined. While a simple one-variable system is enough for personal use, a multi-parameter one will be needed. Wearable and wireless sensors monitor vital signs, such as heart rate, breathing, movement, muscle tone, and blood oxygen levels, transmit the data to a multiparameter [17]. The variety of measuring sensors and approaches makes monitoring the status of health difficult.

3.6.5 Data Management

Data management in health care means designing a strategy for data storage and management. Data from various sensors is required in the future. Gathering information is greatly facilitated by data processing "slow" data can't be provided due to excessive bandwidth and slow processing; several excepts apply.

Researchers Kang et al. [18] showed a novel and safe system for embedded databases that interacted with wireless sensors in real time to provide dynamic information. This database has raw data features. The nRTD features real-time data handling, reliable event handling, and efficient event detection. Three components make up the data management: (a) integration, (b) storage, and (c) processing.

3.6.5.1 Data Integration

Data integration gathers data from several sensors in order to provide information. This also limits the amount of data transmitted. Manual control is a must in most cases. The resolution to this ever-expanding gap between data extraction and processing is data fusing [19]. The data integration is done in two phases: (combined and person). The data obtained from multiple sensors can be integrated for further study. Combined data collection pulls and compiles data from sensors.

Wang used data to ascertain human behavior or human health. Sensors may be placed inside or applied to the body, such as a wall. Zhang et al. [20] developed a system to detect network interferences for localized body systems (WBAN). They used the equipment that could send and receive acoustic waves via cell phones. The acoustics are used with Bluetooth to measure the range between the mobile phones that serve as gateways.

3.6.5.2 Data Storage

The machine must be able to get the information from the real-time database regardless of the urgency of that information. In a sensor-oriented approach, sensors are viewed as databases. So, real-time data management research is being developed to include both local and distributed approaches.

3.6.5.3 Data Processing

To efficiently process and communicate data, data processing is needed. Data processing may be done either on premises or in the cloud, or off premises, making processing decisions that are commensurate with available resources and the application. Sensing and capture of sensed data in healthcare applications is crucial.

Additionally, health care has an urgent need for real-time data analysis. Kang recommended a systematic trade-off between transaction latency and freshness for data-intensive CPS applications. As a result, the proposed solution will be far more applicable to real-time database approaches than past designs.

3.6.6 Computation

For these two main tasks, computerized patient record systems are used: (a) to perform equations and (b) to keep track of outcomes. To determine the most suitable computational structure for healthcare applications, it is important to establish a computational model specification. If you're constantly monitoring the health of your patients, physicians and clinicians must be able to track and observe them from any place and at any time. It must be possible to always connect to the relevant patient's information. Electronic health records are easier to gather and track with cloud computing. It is critical to perform various processing techniques, such as data compression, data measuring, and the other techniques needed to achieve optimal data throughput. Because cloud computing allows us to easily provide computing services, it can be used for a lot of things. Additionally, cloud computing makes it possible for high-performance computing, facilitates mobile computing convergence, and the virtualization of existing and multiple operating systems.

3.6.6.1 Modeling

Due to the existence of massive networks and the surrounding environment, designing cyber-physical systems in health care requires a significant amount of computing. Often, the environment encompasses multiple domains, such as control, communication, input, and reaction. To validate the design, model-based computations are employed. These models might be static or dynamic. Static models are generated by specifying parameters or by utilizing a predetermined simulation environment. Dynamic models, on the other hand, require sophisticated computation and design since they incorporate estimation and a just-in-time approach. Model-based calculations begin with a concept-based idea. This helps the designer to form the design more precisely and effectively.

3.6.6.2 Monitoring

Computational architecture in health care is extensive due to vast networks and the physical environment that surrounds them. The environment is all four parts: power, contact, input, and response, depending on how you define them. Model-based design computations are used throughout the design and testing phase. They can be either the solution or the source of a complex process. You use predefined simulation parameters to construct static models. Complex models and on-the-the-the-fly architecture are needed since they use estimation and need to go out on the fly. The computations were model-based prior to implementation. This allows the designer to produce designs that are more focused and economical.

Due to the size of the network and the healthcare setting, complex cybernetic systems are seen frequently in health care. The environment also includes four distinct domains: power, communication, and input, as well as output. Model-based calculations are employed to find out if the concept is accurate. Static or dynamic models are possible. The user-defined or predefined parameters will generate a static model. Approaches that use computation and design are simpler in comparison, but incorporate estimation into their just-just-in-time design strategy are far more complex. This allows the designer to produce designs that are more focused and economical (Figure 3.10).

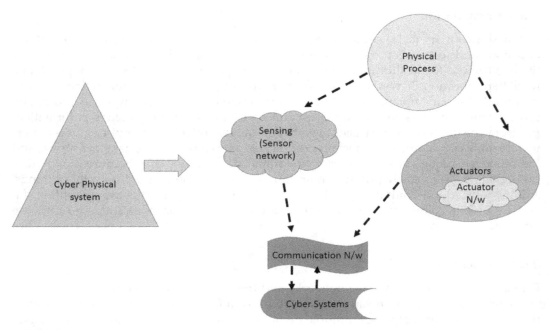

FIGURE 3.10
Computation and Communication in CPS.

3.6.7 Communication

Healthcare management applications use two types of communication methods in a CPS architecture: sensing data and connecting to the cloud. Smaller contacts may also happen within the system, such as contacts between healthcare providers and observation points. Recent advancements in wireless sensor networking (WSN) can allow the CPS to transmit energy-efficient extracted and compressed images. This helps to keep track of patients and collects various image-related information. To effectively communicate, a plan must be established and proper scheduling is essential.

S. Huang et al. [21] has put forward a data management and analysis strategy for large patient populations. A number of research studies have been done to assess the best approach to establishing a relationship with a healthcare provider. The general characteristics of a few CPSs proposed for various applications are summarised in Figure 3.11.

3.6.7.1 Scheduling

Scheduling is the method of determining the most effective contact time mapping to ensure that communication activities are completed satisfactorily. Project scheduling, concurrency monitoring, and data management can all be utilized to ensure the timeliness of real-time data transactions from biosensors. Scheduling is classified into two types: mixed and publish/subscribe. Combining scheduling and publish/subscribe scheduling is a synchronous method, while publish/subscribe scheduling is an asynchronous approach.

3.6.7.2 Protocols

The interaction of the sensors is facilitated by the employment of specialized communication protocols classified as centralized, decentralized, and hierarchical. Because the sensors exhibit heterogeneous behavior, it is vital to choose a suitable communication protocol to ensure efficient and effective communication. Limited data available from numerous sensors can complicate the protocol design [22].

The data exhibits substantial heterogeneity, which facilitates the need for additional research efforts to design a connectivity protocol for access confidential and restricted data of patients during a time of requesting medical service delivery.

Technology	System	Data Rate	Cell size	Frequency Range
IEEE 802.11g/WiFi	BAN / PAN	54 Mbps	50-60 m	2.4 GHz
IEEE 802.11n/WiFi	BAN / PAN	540 Mbps	50-60 m	2.4 GHz
IEEE 802.15.4	BAN / PAN	240 Mbps	10-30 m	2.4 GHz
IEEE 802.16r/Wi Max	WAN	30 Mbps	Upto 70-80 Km	2-6 GHz
IEEE 802.20	WAN	16 Mbps	>15 Km	3.5 GHz
IEEE 8802.22	WAN	18 Mbps	40 Km	54-862GHz
WiBro	WAN	1 Mbps	1 Km	2.3-2.4 GHz

FIGURE 3.11
General Characteristics of a Few CPSs Proposed for Various Applications.

3.6.8 Security

Security is critical in this case, as patient data is considered confidential by both legal and ethical standards. Thus, when developing a CPS architecture for healthcare applications, careful consideration must be given to data protection. There are two components to security: (a) privacy and (b) encryption.

3.6.8.1 Privacy

Professionals in health care are bound by patient-doctor confidentiality and patient data protection. Sensors, facilities, and confidential patient details are becoming increasingly accessible in health care. Managing both of these is cumbersome, considering that the device design is incapable of responding to unpredictable future events. As a result, protecting data protection is critical at both the application and data levels.

Healthcare applications include a large number of users and clinicians; as a result, their communications must be safe. Although cloud servers are protected by security protocols, encrypting data at the user level offers an additional layer of protection [17]. It is possible to deploy mechanisms that monitor for unauthorized data access and corruption [17]. A procedure for verifying the loss of confidentiality can be used in which the base station can detect the attack [1]. Data protection can be ensured at both the application and data levels. The selectivity of the data protection type varies according to the application type.

3.6.8.2 Encryption

Due to the enormous number of users and professionals involved in this healthcare application, the interactions between them must be secure. Encrypting data will assist in ensuring its security. Data encryption can occur at the user or network level, depending on the sophistication and security requirements of the application. While cloud servers are secured by security standards, encrypting data at the user level adds another degree of protection [17]. Attribute-based encryption (ABE) may be used to encrypt data. Any authorized staff member can decrypt the data using a security key. Protection is crucial, even more so when dealing with sensitive and personal patient data because the public cloud service provider is a third party. Any revelation of patient information may raise ethical and legal concerns. Additionally, methods can be employed to identify illegal data access and alteration [17].

3.6.9 Control/Actuation

Current healthcare networks are ineffective at detecting and alerting approved medical caregivers to emergency patient data. The majority of warning systems are currently programmed as threshold alarms. When a vital sign exceeds a preset value, a threshold warning is triggered. Control/actuation consists of two components: (a) decision making and (b) process.

3.6.9.1 Decision Making

Medical data provides vital insight into the behavior (treatments) necessary to save a patient's life. In this accordance, all the data should be immediately available and accessible to authorized medical personnel at all times and from any location. Additionally, healthcare applications require a high level of computational capacity to make intelligent judgments based on massive volumes of patient data [24].

Currently deployed healthcare networks are inadequate at recognizing and notifying authorized medical caregivers of emergency patient data [23]. At the moment, the overwhelming majority of warning systems are configured as threshold alarms. A warning is issued when a vital indicator reaches a predefined value. Threshold alarms are particularly effective at real-time detection of emergencies. However, this alarm technique creates a large number of alarms and a high percentage of false alarms, which contributes to caregiver exhaustion and may encourage caregivers to disregard or disable alarms. This has been demonstrated to have a negative influence on the standard of care. As a result, it is critical to implement a technique that reduces the number of false alarms.

3.6.9.2 Mechanisms

Automatic or manual control/actuation systems are available, as per the need and demand of the application. Three basic building blocks and requirements of a CPS are computation, communication, and physical entities it is essential to study and analyze the CPS interactions. The methodology is for building a forum and calculating systemwide results both design along with the implementation of real-time healthcare applications are handled by the mechanism.

Numerous attempts can be observed in healthcare to enhance the threshold accuracy warnings. However, they all pertain to the specific device. This rapid alarm generation rate in an independent threshold alarm device results in false alarms as well. False alarms exhaust caregivers. Given that the CPS in the healthcare setting will consider a variety of sensor styles, a strategy for ensuring the coexistence of heterogeneous sensors must be developed.

3.7 Conclusion

The CPS possesses the immense capacity for transforming all facets of life. Practical examples include self-driving cars, robotic operations, intelligent houses, smart power grids, intelligent manufacturing, and implanted medical devices. Each of these systems is based on a computer core that is inextricably linked to and coordinated with physical components. When systems grow, their reliance on human decision making takes on different, more strategic dimensions and increasingly relies on the use of artificial intelligence to operationalize human information. It can provide a variety of advantages, such as detecting and reacting to a computing core faster than humans, being more reliable and less fatigued by human operation, or expanding the system's capabilities beyond the operator's capabilities. The task is to build robust and dependable systems—systems in which we can place our confidence as our reliance on the CPS grows. The study serves as a call to action. Though progress has been made, numerous obstacles remain. Overcoming these obstacles creates exciting opportunities to place the United States as a global technology pioneer in the CPS sector.

Major issues are illustrated in this call to action:

- Robust, efficient system and infrastructure design and construction—essential for the growth, development, and cost-effectiveness of reliable systems;
- Improved quality and performance-critical for potential investment, adoption, and usage of revolutionary systems that revolutionize traditional practice.
- Multidisciplinary and diverse training and formation—will allow sustainable growth and creativity, spawning a new generation of businessmen and cyber-physical systems in the future.
- Increased efficiency and quality assurance—crucial for promoting potential investment in, recognition of, and use of groundbreaking systems that promise to revolutionize traditional practice.
- Effective and dependable system integration and interoperability—required for highly connected and networked components to function effectively as a complete system.

References

[1] A Roadmap to Industry 4.0: Smart Production, Sharp Business and Sustainable Development, 2020 Springer Science and Business,Switzerland, Media LLC.

[2] Michael S., 2020 Design of cyber-physical system architecture for industry 4.0 through lean six sigma: conceptual foundations and research issues, Production & Manufacturing Research, 8, 1, 158–181.

[3] Industrial Internet of Things, 2017 Springer Science and Business. Media LLC.

[4] Jeschke, S., Brecher, C., Song, H. 2017 Industrial Internet of Things. Cham, Springer.

[5] Zhang, Y., Qiu, M., Tsai, C-W. 2017 Health-CPS: healthcare cyber-physical system assisted by cloud and big data. IEEE Systems Journal, 11, 88–95

[6] Lee, J., Bagheri, B., Kao, H. A., 2015 A cyber-physical systems architecture for industry 4.0-based manufacturing systems. Manufacturing Letters, 3, 18–23.

[7] Colombo, A. W., Bangemann, T., Karnouskos, S. 2014 Industrial Cloud-based Cyber-physical Systems: The IMC-AESOP Approach. Cham, Springer.

[8] Haque, S. A., Aziz, S. M., 2013 False alarm detection in cyber-physical systems for healthcare application, AASRIProcedia, vol 5(1), 54–61.

[9] Zhang, Z., Wang, H., Wang, C., Fang, H. 2013 Interference mitigation for cyber-physical wireless body area network system using social networks. IEEE Transactions on Emerging Topics in Computing, 1(1), 121–132..

[10] Yilmaz, T., Munoz, M., Foster, R. N., Hao, Y. 2013 Wearable wireless sensors for healthcare applications. Proceedings of the International Workshop on Antenna Technology (iWAT '13), 1(1), 376–379.

[11] Haque, S. A., Aziz, S. M. 2013 Storage node based routing protocol for wireless sensor networks. Proceedings of the 7th International Conference on Sensing Technology (ICST '13) Wellington, New Zealand.

[12] Zhang, Z., Wang, H., Wang, C., Fang, H. 2013 Interference mitigation for cyber-physical wireless body area network system using social networks. IEEE Transactions on Emerging Topics in Computing, 1(1), 121–132.

[13] Avrunin, G. S., Clarke, L. A., Osterweil, L. J., Goldman, J. M., Rausch, T. 2012 Smart checklists for human-intensive medical systems Proceedings of the IEEE/IFIP 42nd

International Conference on Dependable Systems and Networks Workshops (DSNW '12). USA, Boston, MA.

[14] Lee, I., Sokolsky, O., Chen, S., Hatcliff, J., Jee, E., Kim, B., King, A., Mullen-Fortino, M., Park, S., Roederer, A., Venkatasubramanian, K. K. 2012 Challenges and research directions in medical cyber-physical systems. Proceedings of the IEEE, 100(1), 75–90.

[15] Tang, L. A., Yu, X., Kim, S., Han, J., Peng, W. C., Sun, Y., Leung, A., La, P. T. 2012 Multidimensional sensor data analysis in the cyber-physical system: an atypical cube approach. International Journal of Distributed Sensor Networks, 8(4), 724846.

[16] Huang, Q., Ye, L., Yu, M., Wu, F., Liang, R. 2011 Medical information integration based cloud computing. Proceedings of the International Conference on Network Computing and Information Security (NCIS '11), May.

[17] Wang, J., Abid, H., Lee, S., Shu, L., Xia, F. 2011 A secured health care application architecture for cyber-physical systems. Control Engineering and Applied Informatics, arXiv:1201.0213.

[18] Wu, F.-J., Kao, Y.-F., Tseng, Y.-C. 2011 From wireless sensor networks towards cyber-physical systems. Pervasive and Mobile Computing.

[19] Meng, W., Liu, Q., Xu, W., Zhou, Z. 2011 A cyber-physical system for public environment perception and emergency handling. Proceedings of the IEEE International Conference on High-Performance Computing and Communications.

[20] Taleb, T., Bottazzi, D., Guizani, M., Nait-Charif, H. 2009 Angelah: a framework for assisting elders at home. IEEE Journal on Selected Areas in Communications, 27(4), 480–494.

[21] Arney, D., Fischmeister, S., Goldman, J. M., Lee, I., Trausmuth, R. 2009 Plug-and-play for medical devices: experiences from a case study. Biomedical Instrumentation and Technology, 43(4), 313–317.

[22] Poon, C. C. Y., Zhang, Y.-T., Bao, S.-D. 2006 A novel biometrics method to secure wireless body area sensor networks for telemedicine and M-health. IEEE Communications Magazine, 44(4), 73–81.

[23] Kang, K.-D., Son, S. H., Stankovic, J. 2004 A managing deadline miss ratio and sensor data freshness in real-time databases. IEEE Transactions on Knowledge and Data Engineering, 16(10), 1200–1216.

[24] Nahvi, M., Ivanov, A. 2004 , Indirect test architecture for SoC testingIEEE Transactions on Computer-Aided Design of Integrated Circuits and Systems, 23(7), 1128–1142.

4

A Theoretical Framework for Deep Neural Networks over CPS: Vision, Application, Challenges

Azra Nazir, Roohie Naaz Mir, and Shaima Qureshi
Computer Science & Engineering Department, National Institute of Technology Srinagar, Hazratbal, Jammu & Kashmir, India

4.1 Introduction to CPS

The world around us is evolving due to the billions of interconnected devices. IoT is taking our favourite classics like *2001—A Space Odyssey* and *The Terminator*, and others to reality with smart homes, drones, and driverless cars. Refrigerators are placing an order on running out of an item, and a smart room is adjusting lights depending on a person's mood. As effective networking technology develops and becomes more widely available, our knowledge of the condition of the world and our capacity to affect it improve as well. The terms "cyber-physical systems," "Internet of Things," or "embedded systems" originate from distinct sources but have overlapping meanings, all pointing to developments in combining technologies by bringing distinct fields together. The standard definition of the CPS focuses on computation applied to physical systems with an information flow network. However, the physical and digital world data flow requires standard interfaces to control this transformation. Building the CPS over the underlying IoT architecture can essentially make it easy to understand and develop both concepts parallelly [1].

Many physical objects connected using wireless or wired media have facilitated communication of the physical and digital realms, resulting in the emergence of cyber-physical systems (CPSs; Figure 4.1). A cyber-physical system essentially combines a physical task with cyber components causing information flow through a closed communication system potentially networked and tightly interconnected. A CPS is typically a tightly coupled system in which the data from the physical environment is sensed via a diverse array of sensors, interpreted via a variety of software components, and the feedback from the cyber sub-system often drives mechanical components of the CPS such as actuators, motors, and so on [2].

IoT has proven that connectivity is where the future lies. IoT is a network of networks with devices, objects almost everything that can sense and interact in its core definition. The definition is not limited to the physical realm only but covers the virtual realm

DOI: 10.1201/9781003202752-4

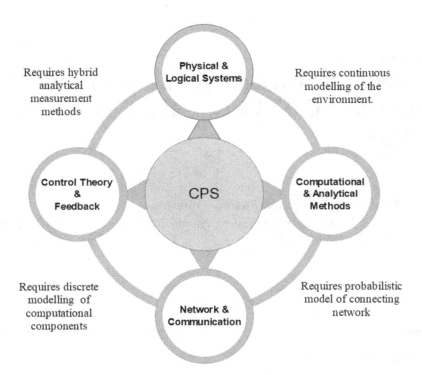

FIGURE 4.1
Refined View of CPS.

as well. With these overlapping definitions laying a boundary between IoT and CPS is difficult. However, the two fields can complement each other as the whole planet can be considered a huge CPS. Learning from vast IoT data is crucial in the CPS engagement process because it allows for the extraction of useful knowledge that enables intelligent decision making. Recent developments in machine learning and deep learning allow the extraction of useful knowledge from vast amounts of IoT data. Establishing deep learning tools in the computation engine of a CPS has become inevitable given the success of these tools in a wide variety of applications [3].

CPSs are present in every aspect of our lives, including our houses, transportation, medicine, agriculture, factory automation, and energy harvesting. Smart homes with voice command processors, facial expression readers, cleaning robots, driverless cars, and smart roads are all examples. Intelligent wearables can improve the standard of human lives and, at times, save them too. It is clear that CPSs are everywhere and are more futuristic and cannot be evaded as contenders for the next industrial revolution [4].

A unified perspective of CPS and IoT is considered critical to avoid duplication of efforts and exchanging best practices to pursue common interests. However, few underlying differences, like identifying participating entities, are essential in IoT but may not be so in the CPS. Also, CPSs vary in scale and form and are typically built for handling a specific task. Despite the differences, both CPS and IoT point to a common collection of developments involving integrating technologies with the physical world and structures to improve performance and functionality [5].

Deep learning techniques have become a powerful computational tool for applications ranging from spam detection to virtual assistants, fraud news detection, and self-driving cars [6]. Considering the CPS in particular, [7] have employed deep learning models for CPS security. [8] have explored the efficiency of deep learning models for the detection of anomalies in the CPS. Authors in [9] have employed various deep networks and machine learning tools for monitoring various CPS components. Deep learning models have been established only in limited scenarios due to their extensive resource demand and complex black-box functionality. This chapter explores these challenges and proposes a distributed framework for establishing deep neural networks in the CPS.

4.2 Need for DL-Enabled CPS

It is vital to incorporate intelligence in the computational module of a CPS, thus augmenting the systems' capabilities regarding protection, performance, and productivity. Intelligent energy systems can be more robust and secure by detecting various cyberattacks, and smart disaster management systems can significantly reduce economic costs and environmental impact. Smart houses can reduce economic costs and environmental impact by operating optimally in a variety of situations. The incorporation of deep learning algorithms has enormous scope in enhancing the popularity of the CPS. The classification networks like CNN can classify diseases in smart health and smart agriculture systems. More complex architectures like RNN and autoencoders can detect attacks in unusual environments or missing data required to control system behaviour in uncertain situations [10]. Most CPSs are placed in dynamic environments and need big data analytical tools instead of traditional computational tools. Deep learning techniques explore useful patterns and statistical distributions and overcome the limitations of classical computational techniques like manual feature extraction [11]. The incorporation of deep learning techniques favours optimization of a CPS, as in Figure 4.2, for a better understanding of physical components in a CPS [12].

4.3 Deep Learning Models

Growth in artificial intelligence led to the emergence of deep neural network models known to humankind today. Fascinated by the brain's working, this field has come far ahead, overcoming many of its initial limitations due to speedy, simultaneous development in hardware and the availability of massive data.

4.3.1 Feed Forward Neural Network

A deep neural network still has neurons as its basic processing unit. Like the human brain tends to have millions of interconnected neurons, a deep neural network also idealizes neurons and their interconnectivity along with novel learning algorithms to solve

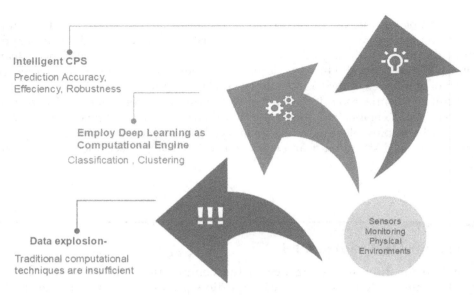

FIGURE 4.2
Scope of DL in CPS.

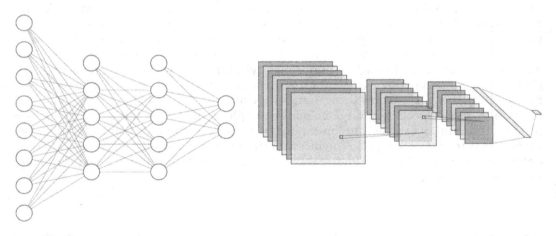

FIGURE 4.3
Feed Forward Network with Two Hidden Layers (left) Convolutional Neural Network (right).

real-world problems. A neuron sums up weighted inputs and then applies some non-linearity to this output to decide the final output. These neurons are arranged in layers in a feedforward network, as shown in Figure 4.3 (left). Such architectures are also known as multi-layer perceptrons. Hidden layers generally follow the input layer, and the last layer is the output layer. A simple feedforward network has no recursive or feedback connections and computes series of transformations that attribute to distinct patterns in the input, thus removing manual feature extraction. Feedforward networks have been employed extensively in regression and classification tasks when data is labelled [13].

4.3.2 Convolutional Neural Network

Convolutional neural networks (CNNs) prove that a regional interpretation of an image is sufficient for their interpretation. Rather than a fully connected network leading to parameter explosion, a CNN cuts both the time to learn and the data required to do the same. A CNN looks only at a part of the problem before covering the entire feature set, as shown in Figure 4.3 (right). Their popularity in a wide variety of tasks shows that the technique is more successful than initially presumed. A convolution operation takes an input image and transforms it into a stack of filtered images using filters/kernels. CNNs are by far the most commonly employed deep models used in a CPS. However, the massive size and computational demand of CNNs have made the task challenging until the appearance of fog-edge computing [14].

4.3.3 Recurrent Neural Network

A recurrent neural network (RNN), as shown in Figure 4.4 (left), possesses an internal memory that can generate current output concerning previous output. When generating output, it weighs both the current input and the output from the previous decision. RNNs come in various types, depending on the model's existence or lack of repetitive interactions. Long short-term memory (LSTM) [15] is rather popular with robotics and language processing applications. The function is controlled by specialized gates using the sigmoid and hyperbolic tangent function. LSTM performs pretty well for classifying and forecasting time series data of uncertain time lags. RNN has played a crucial role in the security of the CPS.

Small circles represent neurons connected by lines, a backward arrow from a layer to the layer before it represents the flow of information like a loop. Four circles in three vertical rows connected using lines represent a neural structure. The first circle in the first row is connected to all three circles in the second row. All other circles are also connected similarly until the last row from which no connections emerge.

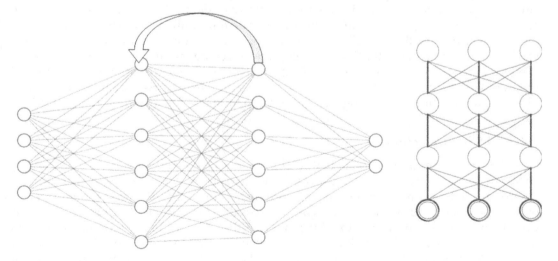

FIGURE 4.4
Recurrent Neural Network (left); Deep Boltzmann Machine (right).

4.3.4 Autoencoders

Autoencoders force input to a lower dimensionality before replicating it back with a decoder network. During this transformation, the network explores any coherent relationships in the data fed to its encoder part. Autoencoders have gained prominence in the tasks dealing with unlabelled data. The model must retain only the data variations necessary for reconstructing the input, thus discarding redundancies not essential. They are used in handling adversarial tasks, particularly in driverless automobiles [16, 17].

4.3.5 Restricted Boltzmann Machines

Restricted Boltzmann machines (RBMs), as shown in Figure 4.4 (right), are special architectures with only hidden and visible nodes capable of identifying patterns using a non-deterministic learning technique. The complex connections enable them to exchange knowledge and produce corresponding evidence on their own. They can identify all associations present in the data without involving a teacher or label [18].

4.3.6 Deep Belief Network

In a deep belief network, neurons inside a layer aren't connected to the neurons in the other layers. These networks engage both unsupervised and supervised training methods. Training is carried in a layerwise manner, making these models popular with probabilistic distributions [19].

4.4 CPS with Deep Learning Components

The CPS significantly improves the quality of living besides laying the groundwork for smart systems, goods, and services. Since the advent of the CPS, several applications have already come into play and are embedded into our daily lives. These applications leverage various artificial intelligence techniques for achieving autonomousness while staying safe and robust [20]. Deep learning and machine learning techniques are being used for perception and data analytics. Reinforcement learning is employed in the control module. However, there are numerous inherent complexities associated with the CPS. They require continuous sensing, real-time decision making, and high precision [21].

4.4.1 CPS in Production

The CPS streamlines production operations by integrating data from computers, the supply chain, manufacturers, corporate networks, and consumers. CPSs are used in industrial environments to self-monitor and manage production processes [22]. Intercommunication between various parts enables high visibility across the supply chain. It results in increased product traceability and protection. Integration of the CPS and IoT in various production lines at large industries lowers the cost of maintenance and improves the efficiency of the service. When production lines evolve into scalable production networks, the need for machine learning and deep learning–based CPS has become critical. Industries have adapted the CPS to stay in the automation race and compete with better yields [23].

4.4.2 CPS in Health Care

Healthcare CPS has made a huge difference and raised living standards with numerous wearable gadgets and remotely controlled robotic surgeries. A body-sensor network is an example of a CPS that utilizes a series of sensors to monitor vital body parameters such as heart rate and blood pressure. Sometimes these values are constantly tracked, resulting in data that falls into the banner of big data. ML and DL models often analyze the data to identify any anomalies and predict the overall health or make an emergency contact in case of any deviations. The success of deep learning models in healthcare CPS is entangled with data accuracy and diversity. Nonetheless, increased data volume entails increased noise and complexity associated with the operating environment, diverse data sources, and data transfer, both of which must be resolved. Additionally, when dealing with large industrial data sets, the problems associated with missing data, unbalanced classes, and unseen patterns become more severe and extreme [24].

4.4.3 CPS in Transportation

The CPS is transforming the transportation industry, with driverless vehicles and drone fighters already on the market. To avoid collisions and drive safely, vehicles are fitted with a real-time image processing module. Vehicles can connect and communicate with other vehicles and roadside units to share information and avoid congested routes. Commercially affordable partially or entirely autonomous vehicles will be available in the immediate future, highlighting the crucial need for security monitoring of CPS-based transportation. Methods to simulate the dynamics of physical and cyber parts of a transportation CPS are being researched extensively. Security vulnerability analysis to ensure safety and robust activity while finding solutions to counterattacks needs to be addressed. DL models are generalized for real-time task handling and intrusion detection in these use cases [25].

4.4.4 CPS in Farming

The CPS has played a vital role by increasing production with precision farming. Precision farming with suitable sensors, monitoring systems, and actuators can use resources like water and fertilizers in an optimized manner while also detecting disease or other issues timely. The system is based on an adaptive approach that considers various factors, including soil and ground moisture, temperature, drainage, and soil acidity. Data collected is passed to deep-learning models that are trained to maximize production. High-resolution cameras mounted on drones provide real-time farm data to image processing modules for disease detection and classification. A decision-oriented CPS system can provide feedback on a particular herbicide or pesticide needed by the plants in any specific situation. Remote locations can efficiently handle feedback through the use of network services. Cyber-enabled agricultural tools provide a unified vision of how CPS, IoT and networking can revolutionize old farming techniques with automation and better estimations [26].

4.4.5 CPS in Buildings

CPS- and IoT-based infrastructures like smart homes and smart buildings go complementary to each other. The CPS tags for automation, while IoT deals with efficient resource utilization like electricity and numerous comforts. A CPS-fitted building often controls and regulates functions as complex as monitoring security or thermostat reading or as simple as auto-adjusting the volume of music speakers based on surrounding noise. A smart home often has an array of sensors forming a small network of its own. The interface for a smart building is usually not as user friendly as that of a smart home. An associated CPS can tackle the heterogeneity of associated data and functions in smart homes. However, a trustworthy CPS requires a fail-safe network and better semantic handlers. Concurrent models can handle deadlines and are reliable models that can handle unseen situations and prevent system failure if a sub-module is not responding [27].

4.5 Challenges in Establishing Deep Learning in the CPS

DL algorithms have been favourable for various tasks in CPS such as anomaly detection, classification, and attribute identification [28]. These techniques can capture outliers and prevent disasters in smart buildings like a nuclear plant or electric grid power surge. However, due to a deep neural network architecture's inherent complexity, many challenges are associated with their CPS integration.

4.5.1 Data Management

A deep model's performance is heavily dependent on the accuracy and diversity of the data gathered. Increased data volume entails increased noise and complexity associated with the operating environment. The majority of approaches assume a relatively imbalanced situation and overlook the reality of substantially underrepresented data. Further, it is difficult to incorporate heterogeneous data into deep models without impairing training performance. In the CPS, where various sensors collect data, it is often unstructured and multimodal, complicating its processing by any DL architecture [29].

4.5.2 Hyperparameter Tuning

It is challenging to justify picking a particular deep learning architecture in a particular problem in the literature. Deep learning offers significant benefits in automated solutions, yet it is surprisingly dependent on a diverse set of hyperparameters to be tuned manually. There is a shortage of literature describing the optimization of hyperparameters [30].

4.5.3 Apprehension of DL Model

Another major challenge hampering the adaptability of deep learning models in businesses is their black-box nature. It isn't easy to trust a technique is working if it isn't transparent and can't be explained. In many cases, the DL community uses only experimental results to establish the superiority of the technique with little or no theoretical proof. However, explainable deep learning is a novel paradigm for dismantling the black box and increasing the model's accountability [31].

4.5.4 Resource Management

Deep learning models are resource-intensive; when training a model, a simple CPU is often not sufficient. These models generally require special hardware and complex GPUs for training. A CPS usually has a continuous stream of input data, and the attributes of the real world keep changing, thus complicating real-time inference. Also, most of these CPSs are inherently distributed in nature, thus requiring proper synchronization while being trained online [32].

4.5.5 Standardization

There is no benchmarking architecture that would allow a reasonable comparison in training time, inference time, and cost of the model. Due to the variety of models present, standardization in the field is needed for a particular model selection. Several scholars have recently compared various strategies, but there is no common evaluation metric system [33].

4.5.6 Generalization

A CPS isn't employed in ideal laboratory conditions. Deep learning frameworks are not designed to address delivery mismatches across several contexts, including actual manufacturing machinery and simulated laboratory faults. It is crucial to work on the generalization of deep learning models, to develop practicable models. Due to the model's black-box nature, selecting a particular regularization technique to generalize a model is challenging in itself. Some DL models perform well with one technique. However, the same approach may fail if the application of the model is changed [34].

4.6 Proposed Framework

A unified frame of reference for a CPS and IoT that can engage deep learning models for computation in the cyber sub-system is proposed in Figure 4.5. Understanding the modern standard three-layer IoT architecture is essential to understand the merged framework for CPS and IoT. Earlier IoT architectures used a physical layer to collect data and a cloud layer to interpret it. Cloud computing possessed sufficient compute power to manage the vast amounts of data generated by IoT with its limitless capacity. Cloud supported infrastructure and software as a service model, making it an ideal solution for emerging IoT applications. Over time, the drawbacks of centralized architecture became prominent, paving the way for a three-layered architecture. Fog bridges the computational gap by bringing a portion of cloud utilities closer to the end user. Fog can handle a part of the computation, thus reducing network traffic to the cloud [35]. A smart car collision avoidance system needs local information in real time; sending such requests to the cloud would render the system useless [36].

The earlier centralized architecture of IoT with two layers, a physical layer for data collection and a cloud for data processing is not suited to most CPS applications. For a smart car trying to avoid a collision, the response from the cloud may take long enough to have already resulted in an otherwise avoidable accident. Although the cloud, with its

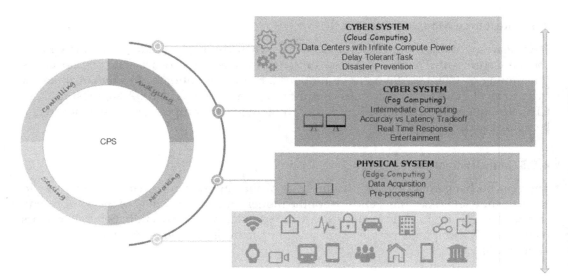

FIGURE 4.5
CPS-IoT Reference Architecture for Unification.

infinite resources, is the perfect layer for meeting a DL model's computational needs, latency and security remain a challenge. The addition of the fog layer with intermediate resources doesn't render the cloud layer useless. Instead, it enables both to execute activities in tandem. By overcoming their respective shortcoming, this architecture allows for DL as compute engine for IoT-CPS integration.

The physical system in CPS involves sensing the environment or world around us. As such, the things layer in IoT consists of an array of sensors meant to collect information. Often the data is collected from critical infrastructures or automation artefacts. A smart car has more than 15 different sensors for collecting information about various environmental conditions and the health of its various parts. Smart wearables monitor their users, the number of which has grown to millions in the past decade. The data generated by these devices is beyond the comprehension of the human mind. The volume of data generated goes beyond trillions of gigabytes, so traditional computational algorithms fail to handle such massive data. However, for data-hungry deep learning models, the physical layer becomes the best available data source. This also brings out the primary concern of employing these models, being data-hungry and resource-hungry. The processing power, memory, and battery provided by things in the physical layer are far beyond these models' demand. As such, deployment of DL models without optimization or distributed analytics in the physical layer is neither desirable nor achievable. In IoT, this layer is known as the edge layer as it forms the lower edge of the network [37].

Every DL model has two processing phases: training and inference. The training is carried using various learning techniques. If the data available is appropriately labelled, then a supervised technique is used otherwise unsupervised. A cost function evaluates the difference between the actual value and the predicted value. Training tries to minimize the difference between the two values by adjusting network parameters called weights. For every wrong prediction, weights are tuned to reduce the error rate. The training phase is tedious and requires substantial computational power; hence it is often limited to the cloud [38]. Every DL model is trained before it can be deployed for inference. When the model faces unseen data and takes a decision based on its training, it is referred to as inference. Another tedious task is selecting the optimal architecture, including the number of layers and their interconnection well suited to a particular application.

If a CPS requires a real-time response, the inference result should be available from the fog layer. Otherwise, the query can be sent to the cloud. This decision can be made at the edge layer itself. The edge layer involves devices that form the transducers in a CPS. A simple smartphone or a network-enabled interface receives data from the sensor array or receives a control command for an actuator. Generally, this layer has no processing power except for a small memory and an optional display unit. If the complexity of the problem is made available a priori, then a decision regarding the dissemination of the data should be taken at the network edge itself. Two solutions can be proposed for establishing deep learning models as compute engines in a CPS. The first solution would require splitting the model across the fog and cloud layer. The second solution is to utilize a device pool at the fog in a collaborative manner, forming a cluster [39, 40].

The DL model can be distributed across the fog and cloud layers for CPS –IoT integration. In this scenario, some model layers are stored on a fog device, and the rest are placed in the cloud (Figure 4.6). If the task at hand values latency over the accuracy, the

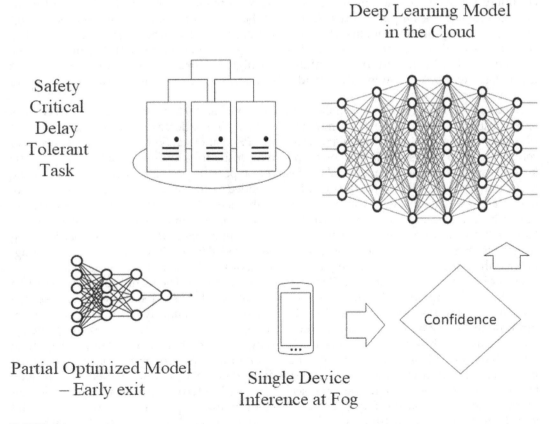

FIGURE 4.6
Splitting a Deep Learning Model across Fog – Cloud Hierarchy.

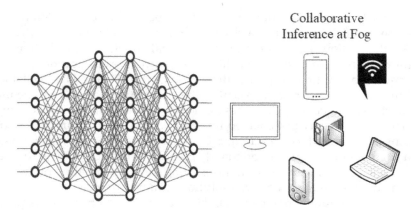

FIGURE 4.7
Collaborative Inference at the Fog Layer.

result obtained after executing only a portion of the model at the fog can be utilized. The fog layer can also compute the confidence for a particular solution and, based on the confidence, decide whether the remaining portion of the model in the cloud is required or not. Several studies support the distribution of the deep learning model across computing hierarchy to exploit the benefits of local computation and overcome latency issues. The confidence of the local result is calculated using various mathematical functions like entropy and log-likelihood. If the confidence is high, the process can terminate in the fog layer itself without involving the cloud. The distribution saves network resources and controls response time.

Another possible scenario for establishing a DL model at the fog is creating random clusters and distributing the inference task among the participating nodes, as shown in Figure 4.7. The possibility of this scenario would vary from one CPS to another. Some CPSs, like a swarm of robots, are inherently scalable and thus can form a cluster for executing an inference task. The swarm can work either in master-slave fashion or peer to peer for carrying a task. If the participating devices are static, they can be embedded with a portion of the DL model and, once the task is ready, they can coordinate with each other to arrive at a final decision. Similarly, in a smart building or a smart home, a device with intermediate processing power like a laptop can form a fog node and create a dynamic cluster for the rest of participating devices to enable a DL model over resource-restricted devices. The master device can aggregate the partial results from the participating nodes and deliver the final result.

The collaborative inference is still in its developing phase. The technique, when applied to CPS, brings out several critical issues. In the above-discussed scenario, it is assumed that devices are non-malicious and static. However, the majority of the real-world environments are dynamic. In a smart, collaborative vehicular network, nodes come and go dynamically. Such networks require establishing trust first before they can participate in any collaborative task. The framework built to handle these collaborations must handle internetwork communications and intermediate data in a manner suited to real-time tasks. Another issue is to address the scalability and heterogeneity of the dynamic networks. The devices at the fog layer vary in computational power and storage. This demands non-uniform partitioning of the employed deep learning model, which is a complex task requiring specialized algorithms.

4.7 Future Research Directions

4.7.1 Redundancy and Understandability of DL Models

Dark knowledge and explanable artificial intelligence are trying to open the black box mystery of deep learning. Adaptation of DL models in the CPS will be facilitated if the workings of such models become transparent. Several research articles suggest that more than 50% parameters of a DL model can be eliminated without affecting the model's accuracy. Techniques like pruning and quantization have reduced both the computational and storage requirements of DL models.

The generalization of deep learning models needs to be explored in depth to move from the research on paper to actual products in companies. Despite the large volumes of data generated each day, most of it can't be used by deep learning algorithms and needs preprocessing. Unsupervised techniques that support learning from unlabelled data should be encouraged. Although the human brain inspires the algorithm, it is far from reaching the human brain's abilities. A human brain takes only a few instances of an example object before generalizing it and classifying any variant of this object. On the other hand, a DL algorithm needs thousands of instances of a single object, and even after that, it can be fooled by intelligent variations [41].

4.7.2 Adjusting to Dynamic Environments

The real world is not static; hence, a model can't be trained once and deployed for a lifetime. Any deep learning model deployed in CPS–IoT-based systems would need timely updates to add new information and remove redundant ones. In these situations, the fluctuating load and changing user requirements demand the system should be scalable. There is a dire need for optimal resource handlers at every layer of the reference architecture [42].

4.7.3 Security and Privacy

Automation brings out new threats and challenges that were not seen before. A smart home or a smart car controlled over the Internet raises sensitive concerns regarding privacy and security. The DL models employed in compute engines are themselves liable to attacks like that of false data injection. Attackers and hackers collecting personal information and monitoring consumers have scaled to exponential target surfaces. The success of CPS is massively dependent on tackling the security challenges associated with these systems. Since deep learning models learn from data and are not explicitly programmed; hence another safety issue with such models is their unpredictable or undesired outcome that humans can't control. Several techniques like lightweight cryptography and secure frameworks need to be introduced as security-enhancing components in CPS. Their efficient implementation can aid in reaching the balance between the cost and performance of such systems [43].

A similar issue is defining an appropriate safety-driven response to inevitable unintended consequences defined as potentially dangerous. There is no such thing as a safe state for a driverless car in the context of present safety critical implementations. Understanding the deep learning–based control system's failure modes and their effects at the embedding CPS stage is essential. As a result, safety checks for the CPS relying on deep learning–based control must encompass both the deep learning–based control system and the embedded CPS as the operating environment. The challenge lies in the fact that deep learning is opportunity-driven, whereas the CPS is more technology-driven and integration of both requires adaptation of the conventional safety-driven culture [44].

4.7.4 Advanced Analytics

It is critical to automate the entire implementation of data collection, pre-processing, and analysis without requiring excessive human intervention. There is a long way to go before the system can handle heterogeneity, stream-processing and sudden data bursts. With the fluctuating input, the system should maintain its core services in case of any sub-system failure. Distributed data analytics should be promoted for increasing throughput and better resource utilization. To obtain a globally optimal solution, multiple input sources must be handled with real-time constraints and proper synchronization [45].

4.7.5 Convergence of CPS and IoT

Integrating the CPS and IoT principles will assist the research communities to determine the common ground to employ earlier findings and avoid repetition of effort and building frameworks from scratch [46]. A thorough understanding of the challenges faced in the development of IoT applications will assist the CPS community in ensuring that they are developing applications that cater to real-world needs. Creating applications that could incorporate existing setup would increase development and lead to trust establishment and reliability. Researchers need to focus on finding the balance between the physical and logical realm of CPS and IoT that can dramatically increase the opportunities for creativity, economic development, and advancement that this merger can provide. To exploit the full potential of the abilities of CPS, networking and computational abstractions would need to be united in their treatment of physical mechanics. Design procedures would need to be upgraded and verified formally and informally to form a sound basis for CPS–IoT integration.

4.7.6 CPS Application Domain

CPSs are spread over a wide variety of applications. However, research trends show that the popular ones include critical infrastructures dealing with various forms of energy like smart grids or smart windmills. The future of networking lies in the interoperability of various heterogeneous components of these crucial systems with a simple interface and a complicated control loop that can guarantee their resilience. The theoretical background used to build a CPS must evolve and fulfill requirements critically evaluated at the design stage to withstand the quality assurance test. The future CPS systems are believed to act as per the surrounding context, cooperate, handle failure gracefully, understanding their impact on the real world [47].

4.8 Conclusion

Deep learning has enormous potential in safety-critical applications like health care, production, and automobiles. These models can mitigate the scalability, reliability, and security issues in CPS-based smart infrastructures. Compared to traditional methods, DL models can achieve better resource utilization, increase throughput, and provide a better user experience, especially in a distributed environment. This chapter has provided a reference architecture for employing deep learning as a compute layer in CPS–IoT unified systems. However, some questions about the requirements and norms of DL models must be followed to ensure their safe employment in CPS. Emerging technologies, such as 5G, are expected to aid in integrating deep learning into CPSs. It is believed that the challenges identified will strongly motivate research in CPS–IoT unification.

References

[1] Pishdad-Bozorgi, P., Gao, X., Shelden, D. R., (2020) "Introduction to cyber-physical systems in the built environment,". *Construction, 4.0*, February, 23–41, doi: 10.1201/9780429398100-2

[2] Letichevsky, A. A., Letychevskyi, O. O., Skobelev, V. G., Volkov, V. A., (2017) "Cyber-physical systems,". *Cybern. Syst. Anal.*, 53, 6, 821–834, doi: 10.1007/s10559-017-9984-9.

[3] Tsai, C. W., Lai, C. F., Vasilakos, A. V., (2014) "Future Internet of Things: Open issues and challenges,". *Wirel. Networks*, 20, 8, 2201–2217, doi: 10.1007/s11276-014-0731-0.

[4] Lachenmaier, J. F., Lasi, H., Kemper, H., (2017) "Simulation of production processes involving cyber-physical systems,". *Procedia CIRP*, 62, 577–582, doi: 10.1016/j.procir.2016.06.074.

[5] Klumpp, M., (2018) "Innovation potentials and pathways merging AI, CPS, and IoT,". *Appl. Syst. Innov.*, 1–18, doi: 10.3390/asi1010005.

[6] Letichevsky, A., A., Letychevskyi, O. O., Skobelev, V. G., & Volkov, V. A. (2017). Cyber-physical systems. *Cybernetics and Systems Analysis, 53(6)*. 821–834.

[7] Wickramasinghe, C. S., Marino, D., Manic, M., (September 2019) *"Generalization of deep learning for cyber-physical system security: A survey,"*. 2018, doi: 10.1109/IECON.2018.8591773.

[8] Luo, Y., Xiao, Y. A., Cheng, L., Peng, G., (2021)"Deep learning-based anomaly detection in cyber-physical systems: Progress and opportunities," *arXiv: 2003. 13213v2 [cs. CR] 19 Jan 2021. 1, 1, 1–37.*

[9] Boursinos, D., Koutsoukos, X. (2020). Assurance monitoring of cyber-physical systems with machine learning components. arXiv preprint arXiv:2001.05014.

[10] Yoginath, S., Tansakul, V., Chinthavali, S., Taylor, C., Hambrick, J., Irminger, P., (2019) *"On the effectiveness of recurrent neural networks for live modeling of cyber-physical systems"*. No. ICII, 309–317, doi: 10.1109/ICII.2019.00062.

[11] Niggemann, O., (2016) *Machine Learning for Cyber Physical Systems*.

[12] Gunes, V., Peter, S., Givargis, T., Vahid, F., (2014) "A survey on concepts, applications, and challenges in cyber-physical systems". *KSII Trans. Internet Inf. Syst.*, 8, 12, 4242–4268, doi: 10.3837/tiis.2014.12.001.

[13] Khan, A., Sohail, A., Zahoora, U., Qureshi, A. S., (2020) *"A survey of the recent architectures of deep convolutional neural networks"*. Artif. Intell. Rev., 1–69, doi: 10.1007/s10462-020-09825-6.

[14] O'Shea, K., Nash, R., December, 2015 *"An introduction to convolutional neural networks,"* [Online]. Available: http://arxiv.org/abs/1511.08458.

[15] Sherstinsky, A., (2020) "Fundamentals of Recurrent Neural Network (RNN) and Long Short-Term Memory (LSTM) network". *Phys. D Nonlinear Phenom*, 404, March, 1–43, doi: 10.1016/j.physd.2019.132306.

[16] Baldi, P., (2012) "Autoencoders, Unsupervised Learning, and Deep Architectures". *ICML Unsupervised Transf. Learn*, 37–50, doi: 10.1561/2200000006.

[17] Pu, Y., *et al.*, (2016) *"Variational autoencoder for deep learning of images, labels and captions"*. *Adv. Neural Inf. Process. Syst., no. Nips*, 2360–2368.

[18] Hinton, G. E., (1989) "Deterministic Boltzmann learning performs steepest descent in weight-space". *Neural Comput.*, *1*, 1, 143–150, doi: 10.1162/neco.1989.1.1.143.

[19] Lee, H., Grosse, R., Ranganath, R., Ng, A. Y., (2011) "Unsupervised learning of hierarchical representations with convolutional deep belief networks". *Commun. ACM*, *54*, 10, 95-103, doi: 10.1145/2001269.2001295.

[20] Radanliev, P., De Roure, D., Van Kleek, M., Santos, O., Ani, U., (2020) "Artificial intelligence in cyber physical systems,". *AI Soc, 0123456789*. doi: 10.1007/s00146-020-01049-0.

[21] Wang, E. K., Ye, Y., Xu, X., Yiu, S. M., Hui, L. C. K., Chow, K. P., (2010) "Security issues and challenges for cyber physical system". *Proc. – 2010 IEEE/ACM Int. Conf. Green Comput. Commun. GreenCom 2010, 2010 IEEE/ACM Int. Conf. Cyber, Phys. Soc. Comput. CPSCom, 2010*, 733–738. doi: 10.1109/GreenCom-CPSCom.2010.36.

[22] Chang, Q., Gao, R., Lei, Y., Wang, L., Wu, C., (2015) *Cyber-physical systems in manufacturing and service systems. Mathematical Problems in Engineering, 2015*, 1–2.

[23] Gangopadhyay, T., (2019) *Deep learning for monitoring cyber-physical systems (Doctoral dissertation, Iowa State University).*

[24] Rezaeianjouybari, B., Shang, Y., (2020) "Deep learning for prognostics and health management: State of the art, challenges, and opportunities". *Measurement, 107929*. doi: 10.1016/j.measurement.2020.107929.

[25] Zhou, J., (2019) *"Lightweight Convolution Neural Networks for Mobile Edge Computing in Transportation Cyber Physical Systems"*, *1*, 1, 1–21.

[26] Mirkouei, A., (2020) *"Environmental science: Current research a cyber-physical analyzer system for precision agriculture"*. doi: 10.24966/ESCR-5020/100016.

[27] Manufacturing, T. S., (February 2020) *"Integration of Digital Twin and Deep Learning in Cyber-Physical Systems: Integration of digital twin and deep learning in cyber-physical systems: Towards smart manufacturing"*. doi: 10.1049/iet-cim.2020.0009.

[28] Cai, F., Li, J., Koutsoukos, X., *(2020). Detecting adversarial examples in learning-enabled cyber-physical systems using variational autoencoder for regression. In IEEE Security and Privacy Workshops (SPW), 208–214.*

[29] Elazhary, H., (2018) "Internet of Things (IoT), mobile cloud, cloudlet, mobile IoT, IoT cloud, fog, mobile edge, and edge emerging computing paradigms: Disambiguation and research directions". *J. Netw. Comput. Appl.*, *128*, October, 105–140, doi: 10.1016/j.jnca.2018.10.0212019.

[30] Lecun, Y., Bengio, Y., Hinton, G., (2015) "Deep learning". *Nature*, *521*, 7553, 436–444, doi: 10.1038/nature14539.

[31] *Beyerer, J., Kühnert, C., & Niggemann, O. (2019). Machine Learning for Cyber Physical Systems: Selected Papers from the International Conference ML4CPS 2018. Springer Nature.* 1–136.

[32] Shen, Y., Ferdman, M., Milder, P., (2017) *"Maximizing CNN accelerator efficiency through resource partitioning"*. *Proc. – Int. Symp. Comput. Archit*, vol. Part F1286, 535–547, doi: 10.1145/3079856.3080221.

[33] Han, S., Pool, J., Tran, J., Dally, W. J., (2015) "Learning both weights and connections for efficient neural networks". *Adv. Neural Inf. Process. Syst., 2015*, January, 1135–1143.

[34] Kukačka, J., Golkov, V., Cremers, D., (2017) *"Regularization for deep learning: A taxonomy"*. 1–23, [Online]. Available: http://arxiv.org/abs/1710.10686.

[35] Bonomi, F., Milito, R., Zhu, J., Addepalli, S., (2012) *"Fog computing and its role in the internet of things"*. *MCC'12 – Proc. 1st ACM Mob. Cloud Comput. Work.*, No. August 2012, 13–15, doi: 10.1145/2342509.2342513.

[36] Singh, S. K., Jeong, Y., Park, J. H., (2020) "A deep learning based iot oriented infrastructure for secure smart city". *Sustain. Cities Soc., 102252*, 10.1016/j.scs.2020.102252.

[37] Pereira, A., Thomas, C., (2020) *"Challenges of machine learning applied to safety-critical cyber-physical systems"*. 579–602, doi: 10.3390/make2040031.

[38] Alom, M. Z., *et al*, (2019) "A state-of-the-art survey on deep learning theory and architectures,". *Electronics, 8*, 3, 1–67, doi: 10.3390/electronics8030292.

[39] Disabato, S., Roveri, M., Alippi, C., (2019) "Distributed deep convolutional neural networks for the Internet-of-Things". [Online]. Available: http://arxiv.org/abs/1908.01656.

[40] Hadidi, R., Cao, J., Ryoo, M. S., Kim, H., (2019) "Collaborative execution of deep neural networks on internet of things devices". [Online]. Available: http://arxiv.org/abs/1901.02537.

[41] Cheng, Y., Wang, D., Zhou, P., Zhang, T., Member, S. (2017). A survey of model compression and acceleration for deep neural networks. arXiv preprint arXiv:1710.09282.110

[42] Mostafa, H., Wang, X., *"Dynamic parameter reallocation improves trainability of deep convolutional networks,"*, no. Nips 2018.

[43] He, H., *et al.*, (2016) *"The security challenges in the IoT enabled cyber-physical systems and opportunities for evolutionary computing other computational intelligence BT – 2016 IEEE Congress on Evolutionary Computation, CEC 2016, July 24, 2016 – July 29, 2016".* IEEE Internet Things J., 1015–1021, [Online]. Available: 10.1109/CEC.2016.7743900.

[44] Cabanes, Q., Senouci, B., Ramdane-cherif, A., (2021) *"Embedded deep learning prototyping approach for cyber-physical systems: Smart LIDAR case study".*

[45] Mohammadi, M., Al-Fuqaha, A., Sorour, S., Guizani, M., (2018) "Deep learning for IoT big data and streaming analytics: A survey". *IEEE Commun. Surv. Tutorials, 20*, 4, 2923–2960, doi: 10.1109/COMST.2018.2844341.

[46] Greer, C., *Burns, M., Wollman, D., & Griffor, E. (2019). Cyber-physical systems and internet of things.*

[47] Chen, H., (2017) "Applications of cyber-physical system: A literature review". *J. Ind. Integr. Manag., 02*, 03, 1750012, doi: 10.1142/s2424862217500129.

5

Hybrid Model for Software Fault Prediction

Sourabh Yadav and Pradeep Tomar

Department of Computer Science and Engineering, Gautam Buddha University, Greater Noida, Uttar Pradesh, India

Vibha Nehra

Department of Computer Science and Engineering, Amity University, Noida, Uttar Pradesh, India

Nonita Sharma

Department of Computer Science and Engineering, Dr B R Ambedkar NIT, Jalandhar, Punjab, India

5.1 Introduction

Predicting faulty modules early in the product development process is a time-consuming aspect of quality assurance in the modern environment [1]. Software fault prediction (SFP) can assist the process of testing effort optimization by identifying software modules that are vulnerable to a wide number of defects [2–4]. It also helps in the more effective delivery of quality management resources. The efficacy of various fault prediction learning algorithms varies depending on the application, rendering them unsuitable for use with uncertain software projects [5,6]. The early identification of flaws is critical because the cost of fixing these flaws increases as the software development life cycle (SDLC) progresses. Inspection and debugging are both time and effort intensive processes in software engineering [7]. In the last decade, there have been significant advancements in this field, with the aim of determining how to anticipate malfunctions in technological fields. The extraction of measurement metrics from the current data set is the most important aspect in determining the effectiveness of a malfunction detection approach. There are a variety of statistical features that can be used to determine whether a software case, class, or package is dysfunctional or not [8–11]. Furthermore, a number of meta-analyses have shown that some subtypes of system metrics can aid descriptive statistics in producing more effective results [12]. The practice of malware detection is bound to enhance the regulatory compliance procedure's reliability. It will aid in the production of impromptu products with little assets and in a limited time frame. Machine learning algorithms are considered to be a successful means of identifying program faults early in the SDLC by discovering a hidden pattern in the historical scheme.

DOI: 10.1201/9781003202752-5

Directed machine learning algorithms need pre-classified data for preparation (training data). During the training process, these approaches create instructions for identifying undisclosed data (test data) [13–20]. The generic databases are used in the study to allow other researchers to compare their estimated findings to their proposed methods, allowing them to assert a higher degree of accuracy from their analysis that can be confirmed by the entire science community. It also enables tech experts to refine monitoring practices proportional to the number of bugs and to identify the majority of faults earlier than usual and proficiently.

This research analyzes a structured hybrid predictive analytics and deep learning–based classifier for device fault classification using NASA data sets. NASA's clean software fault data sets, including PC1, PC2, and PC3, are included in the analyses. This research discusses the performance of common machine learning classification techniques in detail using an 80:20 combination of training and test data. Several baseline models are used in the hybrid classifier, including random forest and support vector machine. Each base model is an Ada-boosting and bagging ensemble.

This study aims to suggest various blended learning for labeling software faults that are dependent on machine learning and deep learning. There are seven sections in total in the research paper. The key goal of the first section is to provide a reinterpretation of the vulnerability predictor and the meta-analyses used to prepare such classifiers. The literature survey is outlined in the second section, and it attempts to justify the most prominent research in this area, as well as include a general idea for developing classifiers and suggesting methods for analyzing them. Section three aims to clarify the potential approach or algorithm for structuring the predictive model. In addition, the fourth section provides information about the planned research's execution. The fifth and sixth sections aim to show the derived findings and compare various trained classifiers briefly and see which one is the better match. This work's conclusion is outlined in the last section.

5.2 Related Work

Machine learning–based techniques are commonly used strategies to identify software bugs at a preliminary phase in the scrum; however just a few of the studies listed here are the strongest fit. There is a study [21] in which researchers gathered a database of at least 25 educational ventures, used supervised learning (six in total), and compared their performance. The researchers used principal component analysis (PCA) to separate parameters and extract specific features, and then trained the model using machine learning and deep learning approaches such as logistic regression, neural networks, and logical classification. The efficiency of each model was assessed using a variety of metrics, including the false recognition rate, true predictive rate, cost of authentication, and consistency attained. Scholars cite studies that show learned models are ineffective at estimating the precise number of defective units. The researchers in [22] used four readily searchable NASA data sets, KC3, KC1, CM1, and PC1, to train a SVM classifier. In addition, a number of statistical and stochastical machine learning methods (such as multilayer perceptron (MLP), radial basis function (RBF), decision tree (DT), K-nearest neighbour (KNN), logistic regression (LR), and others) were implemented and tested in reference to the SVM model's output. For evaluating the findings, a confusion matrix was created using these modeling or model learning strategies, and it has been proposed that SVM outclasses other training methods. By comparing complexity and change history metrics, the authors in [23] used a generic linear regression approach to decipher software flaws. This study was assessed using correlation coefficient, and the primary testing configuration was a massive telecommunication device. The findings show that the change history metric surpassed the complexity metric for detecting software faults.

Many regression-based approaches have been used in the past to estimate the number of glitches in software systems. Previous studies [24,25] find no clear winner among the various methodologies. Some of them have gone so far as to assemble a repository from several ventures together into single one for software fault diagnosis. Research [26] takes a similar approach in which a data set is assembled from several works and a predictive approach is formulated, which also identifies benefiting and majorly contributing factors in prediction tasks. In addition, [27] developed the Peter filter for modeling predictor models and choosing germane databases for testing. For estimating the number of flaws in the software kit, some of the researchers used genetic programming. Research [28] suggested a prediction model based on industrial software sets, which involves training process using weekly fault counts set. The findings obtained from genetic programming showed a substantial rise in deciphering software faults.

Many scholars have conducted comprehensive analyses of automated fault forecasting. Similarly, [29] suggested a concise summary of all the models, as well as a list of their dependent and independent variables that help forecast software faults. Three separate classifiers were used by researchers in [30] to distinguish flawed and non-faulty software models depending on multiple features. Furthermore, operating on the ensemble of these classifiers improves their performance. According to the study, an ensemble of decision trees combined with the apriori technique surpassed all other configured configurations and generated the best yield. Researchers in [31] used boosted and bagged learning strategies to train a classifier for predicting faulty modules, and then contrasted it to other classification algorithms. The ensemble-based classifier outstripped all other models with successful outcomes, according to the findings. For detecting software defective units, the scholars suggested two separate ensemble classifiers (CSForest and CSVoting) in [32]. To minimize classification misfortunes, the suggested ensemble method began with a compilation of decision trees and then combined them. In addition to the other six classifiers adequately prepared in the study, an ensemble classifier is illustrated and claimed the highest performing model by the scholars.

Scholars in over 30 published studies between 2000 and 2010 concluded that techniques such as logistic regression and Naive Bayes perform remarkably well when compared to SVM results. Furthermore, when it comes to software metrics, complexity, and LOC metrics are ineffective when opposed to object-oriented metrics for evaluating processed classifiers in a more stable and effective environment. In addition, researchers have suggested tangible and analytical algorithms for evaluating the accuracy of the forecasting scope and methodology. Furthermore, researchers claim that the accuracy of a predictor model can differ depending on the data set used. According to researchers, the performance of the predictor model will vary by up to 30% depending on the learning methodology used [33]. Several regression algorithms for estimating defect count have been used by a few other researchers [34]. A similar methodology was used here, in which the model was trained using several data sets from the PROMISE repository. The processed classification techniques are tested in both a cross-project and a project-specific environment. Furthermore, the decision tree regressor model was found to be the optimal model for estimation.

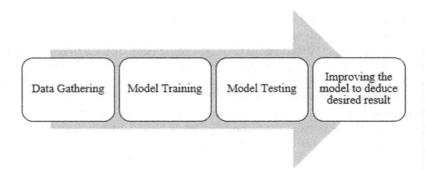

FIGURE 5.1
Proposed Methodology.

5.3 Proposed Approach for Efficient Fault Detection

The proposed study speculates the efficacy of many machine learning algorithms on predictive analysis using standard NASA databases. The data set used contains certain bulk data about software modules, as well as a subsequent feature. The resultant attribute is an attribute whose measurements are calculated based on the values of other parameters in the database. It is also known as dependent class or variable. The used data set has a contingent attribute of binary values, i.e., either 0 or 1, where 0 indicates that the item is not defective and 1 indicates that it is defective. The different steps followed in proposed approach has been demonstrated in Figure 5.1.

5.3.1 Data Preparation

By far the most important step is to gather insights that will enable one to quantify the target variable. In this process, the data is prepared for the training period. A data set in its true perspective can contain a variety of random facts as well as potentially false values. Consequently, the model's quality can be seriously hindered if input is not derived from a credible source.

5.3.1.1 Data Gathering

Data gathering is the process of gathering and analyzing unambiguous information in order to respond to relevant requests and assess the results [35]. There is also insufficient access to information for data scientists, and therefore restricted expertise that can be gathered. Irrespectively, the primary goal of knowledge collection is to put a researcher in a position where he or she can make intelligent assumptions about future opportunities and situations. The base configuration on which information is acquired must be primitive and strongly correlated. The first is put together by an investigator using oblique references, whereas the latter is put together by someone other than the consumer. Gathering data has a variety of purposes, most specifically for scholars. One of the most important motivations for gathering evidence, whether analytical or qualitative, is to ensure that the study issue's credibility is preserved. The possibility of an outcomes blend is eliminated when legitimate clustering methods are used properly. Furthermore, accurate evidence must be gathered to prevent the specialist from making missteps, reducing the risk of misjudgements in prominent positions. By integrating results, the analyst saves time and resources that would otherwise be squandered with little progress toward a better understanding of the subject matter or problem. Similarly, gathering evidence to verify these instances is critical in demonstrating the necessity for standard change or the introduction of widely accepted new data.

Data collection technique describes the process for gathering and analyzing data from diverse sources. To use the data for providing cutting-edge artificial intelligence (AI) and AI applications, it must be accessed and processed in a way that is useful to the business issue at hand. Data logging also allows for the creation of an archive of previous events, which can be used for data analysis to detect recurrent trends. AI computations can be used to predict future trends that search for patterns and forecast future improvements contingent on those instances. Effective and structured data collection approaches are vital for building high-performing systems because classification algorithms are just as effective as the data set they're based on. The final product should be error-free (trash in, trash out) as well as provide meaningful data for the job at hand.

5.3.1.2 Data Pre-processing

Preparing hard data for use of a configuration is referred to as data pre-processing. Often compact, well-structured data is used when working with a methodology. Pre-processing constructs the liquefied data set. The metadata is always disorganized. It almost always contains bugs, garbage values, anomalies, and other defects, making the data unfit for feeding applications. This involves a pre-processing phase in which details about the model's specific moment are produced, leading to increased productivity. The significant proportion of pre-processing mechanisms have been used, to detect conflicting characteristics, qualities that clash, and redundant values. The assembled data is pre-processed for the method by extracting relevant and non-relevant data elements that have a significant effect on forecasting and rendering the model inadequate for forecasting software flaws. This procedure will aid in the identification of influencing and non-contributing factors, as well as the preparation of the base, ensemble, and hybrid models. Additionally, it aids in the removal of garbage attributes that only add distortion to the data set during learning. Furthermore, structured data is divided into two parts: training and testing. The training data set is the information used to prepare the model (loads and predispositions due to neural network). This data is seen by the model, and it benefits from it. The testing set is used to ensure a high degree of accuracy, and it can also be used to validate the model. It's only used when a model has been fully trained. The testing set is used once in the whole study to compare competing predictor models.

5.3.2 Training Base, Ensemble, and Hybrid Learner Model

In terminologies, "machine learning" describes a set of operations that uses input data set to build or construct a new technique. Machine learning modelling techniques are at the root of the field. These algorithms primarily interact with the data, interpret it, and prepare the optimal technique. Machine learning algorithms are divided into two categories: supervised and unsupervised. The supervised algorithms use a labelled data set for estimations, while the unsupervised algorithms use the inverse of a labelled data set. Classification and regression are two types of supervised algorithms. The algorithms are used to prepare the appropriate model based on their requirements. In general, classification methods are used to classify or evaluate variations in the data and, in some cases, to ascertain the element based on the insight.

As part of the proposed approach, several classifiers are trained with the aim of identifying the defect-prone portion of software packages. The standard learning technique is a critical component of research involving classification enhancement. It provides a basic foundation for contrast. The aim of this paper is to create three distinct types of models: baseline, ensemble, and hybrid. As previously said, the base model would serve as a starting point for analyzing the data set's dynamics. After that, the ensemble model will be trained. Ensemble planning aims to improve the performance by using various machine learning algorithms. Last but not least, the hybrid model will be trained, which will aid in the preparation of the model with greater exactness, i.e., overall performance. Different methods, like both deep and machine learning algorithms, can be used in the hybrid model.

5.3.3 Comparison and Analysis of Results

Probably the most crucial move would be to examine the findings. The test portion of the data set is used for the subsequent computations. The test data set is used to thoroughly analyze all of the trained models. Their determining variables, such as classifier precision, are trained using a test data set, among other aspects, to select the optimal conducting and effective classifier. After slicing the data, a correlation coefficient is determined, in which attributes are classified as contributing or non-contributing contingent on the correlation score. In addition, based on the output of the base classifier, ensemble and hybrid models will be developed. The step wise approach for machine learning-based model training has been illustrated in Figure 5.2.

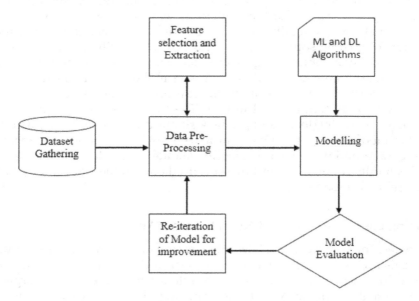

FIGURE 5.2
Step-wise Approach for Machine Learning–Based Model Training.

5.4 Design and Implementation

5.4.1 Data Set Elucidation

In this ongoing study, the proffered analysis uses 18 software fault data sets from a variety of fully obtainable software improvement methodologies that are available in the PROMISE data repository [36]. For computations, 3 of the 18 software defect data sets from the PROMISE data repository are retrieved. PROMISE was a publicly released directory that hosted defect databases from a wide range of fully accessible projects, which include Apache programs like PROP, Xalan, Ant, Camel, and others. The use of structured data as well as the ability to replicate trials are two main advantages to using fault data sets in analysis, which are collected using freely available software modules [37]. The research of M. Jureczko [38] includes information on both of these attribute sets, as well as a description of their variables. Table 5.1 lists the database that was used and is addressed further.

5.4.1.1 PC

The ground data for C-based project deployment is obtained from Halstead and McCabe function retrievers in the PC software fault diagnosis data set. It is a software for flights that are orbiting around earth.

As part of the pre-processing for the planned analysis, the data set was filtered and subsequently graded. Each data item is first examined for the existence of a null value. The data was prepared for baseline classifiers, and boosted and bagged ensemble training after the null values were deleted and modified. In addition, the data was pre-processed for hybrid training. The upper stage of pre-processing entails slicing the data or extracting the most significant and participating parameters based on a respective correlation coefficient with the predictive component. For each data set, a correlation matrix is generated in preparation for subsequent infusions and subdivides. In addition, SMOTE analysis is also performed, which is used to prevent the classifier from being overfit or underfit.

5.4.2 Measures for Evaluating the Performance of Trained Models

There are multiple separate output metrics used to evaluate the forecasted values of the prepared models in the proposed study. Accuracy is the criterion on which success is judged.

The term "accuracy" refers to a metric used to assess the classification model's results. Accuracy is characterized mathematically as the ratio of overall successful forecasts to the overall count of forecasts, as seen in equation 5.1.

$$Accuracy = \frac{Total\ Number\ of\ Correct\ Predictions}{Total\ Predictions} \tag{5.1}$$

TABLE 5.1

Data Set Elucidation

#	Total Attributes	Total Data Points	Total Defects Data Points	Total Non-Defect Data Points
PC1	22	1109	77	1032
PC2	37	5589	5566	23
PC3	38	1563	1403	160

True positives (TPs), true negatives (TNs), false positives (FPs), and false negatives (FNs) are all terms used to describe precision throughout the context of digital analysis (FN).

$$Accuracy = \frac{TP + TN}{TP + TN + FP + FN} \tag{5.2}$$

5.4.3 Insights of Implementation

The implemented approach is broken down into various implementation stages as depicted in Figure 5.3 . The first and most crucial thing of any research project is to collect a suitable and uniform data sets such that experiments and modeling techniques can be contrasted and universally adopted. As previously stated, the University of Ottawa publicized the PROMISE Archive, which was used to retrieve the relevant data sets, and the PC data set is chosen from the archive for the calculations.

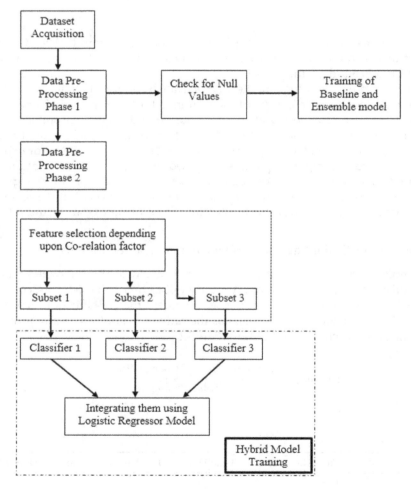

FIGURE 5.3
Flow Chart of Proposed Implementation.

Data pre-processing is the next stage after obtaining the necessary databases. Pre-processing in this case entails removing an anomaly, such as null values, which would undoubtedly influence the classifier and, therefore, predicting performance. As a result, it's critical to get them out and modify or delete them as required. In the proposed study, data pre-processing is conducted in two distinct stages: first, data is primed for training the baseline learners and ensemble models and then, after training the baseline learners and ensemble models, data is pre-processed again to build the hybrid model.

5.4.3.1 First Phase of Data Pre-Processing

Null values are modified and eliminated in the first pre-processing step so that anomalies impacting the learning of baseline and ensemble models can be quickly rebutted.

5.4.3.2 Second Phase of Data Pre-Processing

The data set is cleaved in the second stage. This divide is achieved using a correlation coefficient generated from the PC1, PC2, and PC3 data set. The PC2 and PC3 data set is divided into three data frames based on the correlation scale: one data frame comprises all parameters with a correlation coefficient substantially greater than 0.25, the second data frame includes parameters with a coefficient scale of [0.20, 0.25), and the third frame contains parameters with a coefficient scale of [0.15–0.25). The PC1 data set is similarly cleaved depending on the scales of more than 0.60, [0.50, 0.60), and [0.40, 0.50). For efficient feature learning, each data frame is inserted with a dependent variables at the top.

Furthermore, SMOTE analysis is used in each step of pre-processing because it helps to prevent inconsistencies in model fitting and thereby aids in the training of an accurate and consistent model. A data splitting is done before actual model fit, and the data is divided between training and test sets with an 80:20 ratio, i.e., 80% for training and the remaining percent for testing. Furthermore, the training data set is divided into two parts: training and validation, with a 9:1 ratio, i.e., 90% for training and 10% for validation.

After data pre-processing is completed successfully, the final data set is collected in order to prepare the classifier. The fitting of the model is the next step. As discussed in the previous section, three modeling techniques are prepared for the prospective study Baseline Learners, AdaBoosted Base Learners, Bagged Base Learners, Voting Based Base Learner, and Hybrid. Deep learning–based neural networks were developed with parallel machine learning techniques for efficient contrast and paramount precision and accuracy. Decision tree classifier (DTC), multi-layer perceptron (MLP), Naïve Bayes (NB), random forest (RF), and support vector machine are the baseline learner classifiers used in the proposed study. Model fitting is often performed in phases, analogous to data pre-processing, and each step is described below,

5.4.3.3 Training of Base Learners and Ensemble Models

The learning of baseline classifiers is used in the first step of model fit. To train the models, only the data configured during the first stage of data pre-processing is used. Model fit can be done with pre-defined Python libraries, namely the sklearn package in Python 3.8. After the base classifiers have been conditioned, the primed base models are forwarded on for AdaBoosting and Bagging.

5.4.3.3.1 AdaBoosting

The AdaBoost classification mostly emphasizes on correcting erroneous categorized findings so that the subsequent estimators can operate on more complex cases. It usually begins with the learning of a baseline model with the main data set, and then trains the same classifier with a replica of the original data set, with the aim of appropriately identifying occurrences that have been incorrectly identified.

5.4.3.3.2 Bagging

The cleaving-based methodology is the focal point of the Bagging classification. It splits the schema into subsets and applies the base classifier structural model to each subclass. The overall forecast is then derived by aggregating the specific forecasts, which can be centered on the aggregation of inferred forecasts or on polling.

This method is used to work with the effects of black-box estimation techniques, i.e., a reasonable method for reducing uncertainty. It primarily raises the anonymization in the creation algorithm, resulting in a stronger classification aggregate.

5.4.3.4 Training of Hybrid Model

The learning of the hybrid model is the main objective of the second step of model fitting. The data constructed in the second stage of pre-processing is used to develop the hybrid model. Multiple classifiers are used to prepare each one of the primed data frames. Furthermore, training the same classification model on three independent data frames is perfectly appropriate. For the suggested analysis a hybrid model is created by combining different approaches on each data sets. The PC1 data set's hybrid learner is built utilizing decision tree classifier (DTC) for a data set that contains parameters with the maximum correlation factors, random forest (RF) for data containing parameters with correlation coefficients between [0.20, 0.25), and support vector machine (SVM) for data containing parameters with correlation coefficients less than 0.20. For the PC2 data set, SVM is used for the first data set (which contains parameters with a strong correlation >= 0.25), RF is used for the second (which contains parameters with a correlations coefficient scale [0.20, 0.25), and DTC is used for the third (which contains parameters with a correlations factor <0.20). Analogously, again for PC3 schema, hybrid is created by using a random forest classifier to train each of the data frames. The obtained results from these three data frames are forwarded to logistic regression model for compilation.

The suggested approach ends by contrasting the inferred outcome and snags out the most appropriate classifier from the all primed classification models. Accuracy is the criterion used to assess the efficacy of classification model.

5.5 Deduced Results

The suggested approach is a systemic progression of analysis on the data sets PC1, PC2, and PC3 are used. The analysis begins with the collection of the data set, which was obtained from the University of Ottawa's authorized web service for the PROMISE Repository. Each extracted data set has its own parameters, which serve as the predictive variable's metadata.

The second phase of the approach is data pre-processing, which is conducted in two stages: one about base and ensemble models, and the other for the hybrid model. The elimination of null values is the very first step of data pre-processing. As a result, during the first stage of data pre-processing, all anomalies were eliminated. As a consequence, you'll have a configured data sets for base and ensemble model training. As a result, the data sets is transferred to the algorithm for model training after conducting SMOTE analysis and slicing the data set into training (training + validation) and testing. DTC, SVM, NB, MLP, and RF are the baseline models that were trained. Deep learning–based neural networks have also been learned alongside machine learning models. Convolutional neural network (CNN) and artificial neural network (ANN) are the neural network models that were trained (ANN). In addition to machine learning and neural network models, a voting-based ensemble is being created, with logistic regression, random forest classifier, Gaussian Naïve Bayes, multi-layer perceptron, support vector machine, and decision tree classifier as training methods. Table 5.2 shows the results derived after training the base and voting-based ensemble classifier models

Following the testing of the base models, the AdaBoosted model is trained on the same baseline models. Table 5.3 shows the AdaBoosted ensemble model's derived training effectiveness using DTC, SVM, NB, MLP, and RF base computations.

The next step in the approach is to build a Bagging-based ensemble focusing on the models built. Table 5.4 shows the derived training effectiveness from the bagging ensemble trained model on the same models built.

TABLE 5.2

Results Deduced after Training the Baseline and Voting-Based Ensemble Models

#	CNN	ANN	RF	SVM	Voting
PC1	61	78	70	69	73
PC2	90	47	57	50	48
PC3	85	62	85	62	75

TABLE 5.3

Results of AdaBoosted Ensemble Model

#	RF	SVM
PC1	74	50
PC2	59	58
PC3	68	50

TABLE 5.4

Results of Bagged Ensemble Model

#	RF	SVM
PC1	75	71
PC2	57	90
PC3	87	70

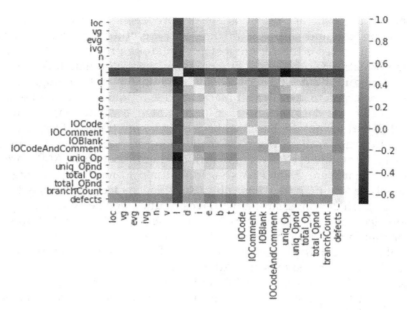

FIGURE 5.4
Heat Map of Correlation factors for PC1 Data Set.

Furthermore, the hybrid model is trained to obtain greater precision and performance, according to the proposed approach. However, the second step of data pre-processing must be completed before the hybrid concept can be trained. The data set is then cleaved based on the correlation coefficient in the second step of data pre-processing. The graphical representation shown in Figure 5.4 depicts correlation coefficients among the parameters of the PC1 schema.

A heat map of the correlation coefficient among the PC2 parameters is also shown in Figure 5.5.

Figure 5.6 depicts a heat map of feature correlation coefficients from the PC3 data set.

Following the analysis of the correlation factors, a subsection of each data set's parameters is prepared to be dependent on the correlation factors. Three subsets of the PC2 and PC3 data set are generated based on the scales of more than 0.25, [0.20, 0.25), and [0.15, 0.20). The PC1 data set is divided into three subsections based on the distribution of more than 0.60, [0.50, 0.60), and [0.40, 0.50). Table 5.5 shows the updated data configuration.

Following the preparation of the final cleaved numerous data frames, the next step is to train them individually using baseliners. Models who have been boosted or bagged are still practiced here. The best match among baseliner boosted and bagged classifiers is determined, and the results of that classifier are then used further in computations. As a result, three distinct forecasted outcomes for three distinct data frames will be obtainable. These distinct results are further passed on to a logistic regression model for final compilation. The ultimate forecast list is formatted in such a way that it can be contrasted to the test data set. Table 5.6 shows the final test results for the primed voting and hybrid models.

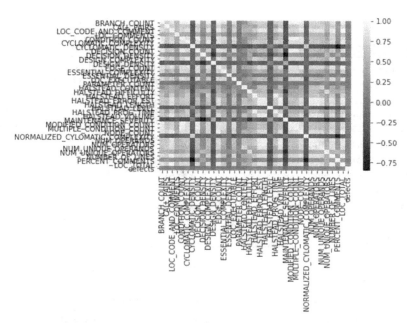

FIGURE 5.5
Heat Map of Correlation Factors for PC2 Data Set.

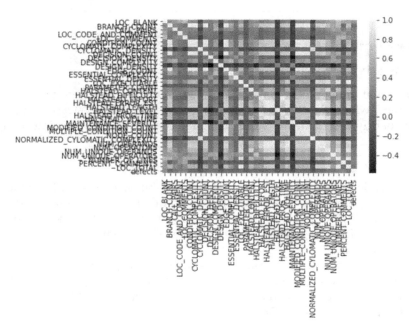

FIGURE 5.6
Heat Map of Correlation Factors for PC3 Data Set.

TABLE 5.5

Dataset Composition after Phase 2 Data Pre-Processing

#	Data Frames	Total Attributes	Total Data Points	Total Defects Data Points	Total Non-Defect Data Points
PC1	Data frame 1 (more than 0.60)	6	1109	77	1032
	Data frame 2 ([0.50, 0.60))	12	1109	77	1032
	Data frame 3 ([0.40, 0.50))	3	1109	77	1032
PC2	Data frame 1 (more than 0.25)	4	5589	5566	23
	Data frame 2 ([0.20, 0.25))	9	5589	5566	23
	Data frame 3 ([0.15, 0.20))	2	5589	5566	23
PC3	Data frame 1 (more than 0.25)	2	1563	1403	160
	Data frame 2 ([0.20, 0.25))	2	1563	1403	160
	Data frame 3 ([0.15, 0.20))	3	1563	1403	160

TABLE 5.6

Accuracy Obtained from Voting and Hybrid Classification Model

#	Baseliner	Boosted	Bagged	Voting
PC1	70	74	75	73
PC2	57	59	90	48
PC3	85	68	87	75

5.6 Comparative Analysis

Some of the classification model generated in the research project were well trained and be-haved admirably while others even resulted close to the worst-case category. In order to make an accurate analogy, the following sections include comprehensive statistical comparisons.

5.6.1 Comparison of Bagging, Boosting, and Base Learner

The general tendency is skewed towards the AdaBoosted ensemble model, which is doing well among the other base and bagged ensemble models, with a slight distinction in the case of the PC2 data set, predicated on the results of the baseline and ensemble (AdaBoosted and Bagged) models. Table 5.7 shows the contrast between the ensemble and baseline classifier.

The Bagged ensemble of the RF classifier is the highest-quality classifier for estimating the PC1 data set, according to the findings. Furthermore, the Bagged ensemble predictive model of SVM has the best accuracy for PC2. Finally, the optimal labelling paradigm for PC3 is the Bagged ensemble of RF.

5.6.2 Comparison of Base Learner and Neural Network Classification Models

The suggested study examined how the base learner and neural network detection per-formed on the same data set. Table 5.8 provides an outline of the contrast.

TABLE 5.7

Comparison of Ensemble and Baseline Classification Model

#		RF	SVM
PC1	Baseline	70	69
	AdaBoosted	74	50
	Bagged	**75**	71
PC2	Baseline	57	50
	AdaBoosted	59	58
	Bagged	57	**90**
PC3	Baseline	85	50
	AdaBoosted	68	50
	Bagged	**87**	70

TABLE 5.8

Comparison between Baseline and Neural Network Classification Model

#	Baseline		Neural Network	
	RF	SVM	CNN	ANN
PC1	70	69	73	**80**
PC2	57	50	48	**95**
PC3	85	50	75	**89**

When the findings from the base learner and neural Nnetwork classification models are compared, it is evident that neural network classifiers surpass base machine learning classification models.

5.6.3 Comparison of Hybrid Model, Voting, and Base Learner

A distinction of base learners, voting-based, and hybrid classification models is another sort of distinction. Logistic regression, random forest classifier, multi-layer perceptron, support vector machine, decision tree classifier, and Gaussian Naïve Bayes are sources of voting-based classification models. For each data set, the hybrid model is constructed by merging various algorithms. A combination of decision tree classifier (DTC), random forest (RF), and support vector machine were used to examine the PC1 data set (SVM). SVM, RF, and DTC are used for labeling on the PC2 data set. Likewise, for the PC3 data set, a hybrid is built by using the random forest classifier to train each of the data frames. Table 5.9 shows the final results obtained after training the above-mentioned.

TABLE 5.9

Comparison between Hybrid, Voting, and Base Learner

#	Baseline		Voting	Hybrid
	RF	SVM		
PC1	70	69	73	**80**
PC2	57	50	48	**95**
PC3	85	50	75	**89**

TABLE 5.10

Comparison between Hybrid Model and Ensemble (AdaBoosted and Bagged) Classification Models

#		RF	SVM	Hybrid
PC1	Baseline	70	69	**80**
	AdaBoosted	74	50	**86**
	Bagged	75	71	82
PC2	Baseline	57	50	**95**
	AdaBoosted	59	58	91
	Bagged	57	90	**95**
PC3	Baseline	85	50	89
	AdaBoosted	68	50	85
	Bagged	87	70	**90**

Among the baseliner and voting-based labeling methodologies it is clear that the hybrid classifier trained using base approach (without boosting and bagging) is the best for labeling.

5.6.4 Comparison of Hybrid Model and Boosted and Bagged Learner

In addition, the proposed examines and contrasts the proposed hybrid and ensemble classification models. Hybrid uses the same baseline models as the previous comparison and ensemble (AdaBoosted and Bagged) uses the same baseline models as the previous comparison. Table 5.10 summarizes the computed results.

The difference in Table 5.10 shows that the hybrid model does well in detecting unreliable software in the corresponding data set (PC1, PC2, and PC3).

5.7 Conclusion

The hypothesis proposed in this analysis is that the automated fault forecasting model varies greatly depending on the learning methodology used and the characteristics of faulty data sets. As a result of this consideration, it is clear that numerous fault predictive models are expected. The proposed study aims to prepare four different types of prediction models: baseline, ensemble (AdaBoosted and Bagged), voting, and hybrid. The proposed study began by removing null values from the data set in order to prepare it for training the baseline and ensemble (AdaBoosted and Bagged) classification models. The voting-based model, which incorporates the same baseline models, is used and learned to improve efficient scale. In addition, the hybrid model is optimized for more precise prediction. The data set needed to be pre-processed before it could be used to train the hybrid model. The data set is divided into three data frames for a hybrid classifier based on the correlation factor. After the data set has been sliced, each data frame is forwarded to the baseline models, and the results from three models are merged by averaging the results. The PROMISE archive is used to extract the original PC (PC1, PC2, and PC3) data sets.

The final results reached using the proposed approach are extremely beneficial and comparable. As a consequence, the proposed study's comparative analysis is the final part. Comparative analysis shows that the voting-based classifier surpasses nearly all baseline versions, while the ensemble (AdaBoosted and Bagged) prepared also yields optimistic outcomes as compared to the voting-based classification algorithm. However, the results show that in the cases of PC2 and PC3, the hybrid model developed using ensemble (Bagging) models is the most efficient of all the models evaluated and the hybrid model of ensemble (AdaBoosted) models is the highest quality match for the PC1 data set.

References

[1] Ma, Y., Luo, G., Zeng, X. and Chen, A. (2012). Transfer learning for cross-company software defect prediction. *Information and Software Technology*, 54(3), 248–256.

[2] Singh, Y. and Malhotra, R. (2012). *Object-oriented Software Engineering*. PHI Learning Pvt. Ltd.

[3] Moser, R., Pedrycz, W. and Succi, G. (2008, May). A comparative analysis of the efficiency of change metrics and static code attributes for defect prediction. In Proceedings of the 30th international conference on Software engineering (pp. 181–190).

[4] Giger, E., D'Ambros, M., Pinzger, M. and Gall, H. C. (2012, September). Method-level bug prediction. In *Proceedings of the 2012 ACM-IEEE International Symposium on Empirical Software Engineering and Measurement* (pp. 171–180). IEEE.

[5] Taba, S. E. S., Foutse K., Ying Z., Ahmed E. H. and Meiyappan N., (2013). Predicting bugs using antipatterns. In *2013 IEEE International Conference on Software Maintenance*, pp. 270–279. IEEE.

[6] Herzig, K., Just, S., Rau, A. and Zeller, A. (2013, November). Predicting defects using change genealogies. In *2013 IEEE 24th International Symposium on Software Reliability Engineering (ISSRE)* (pp. 118–127). IEEE.

[7] Moustafa, S., Mustafa Y. E., Nagwa E. M. and Mohamed S. A. (2018). Software bug prediction using weighted majority voting techniques. *Alexandria Engineering Journal* 57, 4, 2763–2774.

[8] Ahmad, M., Aftab, S., Ali, I. and Hameed, N. (2017). Hybrid tools and techniques for sentiment analysis: a review. *International Journal of Multidisciplinary Sciences and Engineering*, 8(3), 29–33.

[9] Ahmad, M., Aftab, S., Ali, I. and Hameed, N. (2017). Hybrid tools and techniques for sentiment analysis: a review. *International Journal of Multidisciplinary Sciences and Engineering*, 8(3), 29–33.

[10] Ahmad, M. and Aftab, S. (2017). Analyzing the performance of SVM for polarity detection with different data sets. *International Journal of Modern Education & Computer Science*, 9(10).

[11] Ahmad, M., Aftab, S. and Ali, I. (2017). Sentiment analysis of tweets using SVM. *International Journal of Computer Applications*, 177(5), 25–29.

[12] Ahmad, M., Aftab, S., Bashir, M. S., Hameed, N., Ali, I. and Nawaz, Z. (2018). SVM optimization for sentiment analysis. *International Journal of Computer Applications*, 9(4), 393–398.

[13] Shabib Aftab, M. A., Hameed, N., Bashir, M. S., Ali, I. and Nawaz, Z. (2018). Rainfall prediction in Lahore city using data mining techniques. *International Journal of Advanced Computer Science and Applications*, 9(4).

[14] Shepperd, M., Song, Q., Sun, Z. and Mair, C. (2013). Data quality: some comments on the NASA software defect data sets. *IEEE Transactions on Software Engineering*, 39(9), 1208–1215.

[15] "NASA – Software Defect Datasets [Online]. Available: https://nasasoftwaredefectdata sets.wikispaces.com. [Accessed: 01-April-2020].

[16] Menzies, T., Milton, Z., Turhan, B., Cukic, B., Jiang, Y. and Bener, A. (2010). Defect prediction from static code features: current results, limitations, new approaches. *Automated Software Engineering*, 17(4), 375–407.

[17] Xia, X., Lo, D., Shihab, E. and Wang, X. (2015). Automated bug report field reassignment and refinement prediction. *IEEE Transactions on Reliability*, 65(3), 1094–1113.

[18] Song, Q., Jia, Z., Shepperd, M., Ying, S. and Liu, J. (2010). A general software defect-proneness prediction framework. *IEEE Transactions on Software Engineering*, 37(3), 356–370.

[19] Khoshgoftaar, T. M., Allen, E. B. and Deng, J. (2002). Using regression trees to classify fault-prone software modules. *IEEE Transactions on Reliability*, 51(4), 455–462.

[20] Ostrand, T. J., Weyuker, E. J. and Bell, R. M. (2005). Predicting the location and number of faults in large software systems. *IEEE Transactions on Software Engineering*, 31(4), 340–355.

[21] Lanubile, F., Lonigro, A. and Vissagio, G. (1995, June). *Comparing Models for Identifying Fault-prone Software Components*. In SEKE (pp. 312–319).

[22] Elish, K. O. and Elish, M. O. (2008). Predicting defect-prone software modules using support vector machines. *Journal of Systems and Software*, 81(5), 649–660.

[23] Graves, T. L., Karr, A. F., Marron, J. S. and Siy, H. (2000). Predicting fault incidence using software change history. *IEEE Transactions on Software Engineering*, 26(7), 653–661.

[24] Khoshgoftaar, T. M. and Gao, K. (2007). Count models for software quality estimation. *IEEE Transactions on Reliability*, 56(2), 212–222.

[25] Chen, M. and Ma, Y. (2015, July). *An empirical study on predicting defect numbers*. In SEKE (pp. 397–402).

[26] Zimmermann, T., Nagappan, N., Gall, H., Giger, E. and Murphy, B. (2009). "Crossproject defect prediction: A large scale experiment on data vs. domain vs. process," in Proc. 7th Joint Meeting Eur. Softw. Eng. Conf. ACM SIGSOFT Symp. Foundations Softw. Eng., 91–100.

[27] Zimmermann, T., Nagappan, N., Gall, H., Giger, E. and Murphy, B. (2009, August). Cross-project defect prediction: a large scale experiment on data vs. domain vs. process. In Proceedings of the 7th joint meeting of the European software engineering conference and the ACM SIGSOFT symposium on The foundations of software engineering (pp. 91–100).

[28] Afzal, W., Torkar, R. and Feldt, R. (2008, December). Prediction of fault count data using genetic programming. In *2008 IEEE International Multitopic Conference* (pp. 349–356). IEEE.

[29] Hall, T., Beecham, S., Bowes, D., Gray, D. and Counsell, S. (2011). A systematic literature review on fault prediction performance in software engineering. *IEEE Transactions on Software Engineering*, 38(6), 1276–1304.

[30] Twala, B. (2011). Predicting software faults in large space systems using machine learning techniques. *Defence Science Journal*, 61(4), 306.

[31] Aljamaan, H. I. and Elish, M. O. (2009, March). An empirical study of bagging and boosting ensembles for identifying faulty classes in object-oriented software. In *2009 IEEE Symposium on Computational Intelligence and Data Mining* (pp. 187–194). IEEE.

[32] Siers, M. J. and Islam, M. Z. (2014, December). Cost sensitive decision forest and voting for software defect prediction. In *Pacific Rim International Conference on Artificial Intelligence* (pp. 929–936). Springer, Cham.

[33] Ghotra, B., McIntosh, S. and Hassan, A. E. (2015, May). Revisiting the impact of classification techniques on the performance of defect prediction models. In *2015 IEEE/ACM 37th IEEE International Conference on Software Engineering* (Vol. 1, 789–800). IEEE.

[34] Chen, M. and Ma, Y. (2015, July). *An empirical study on predicting defect numbers*. In SEKE (pp. 397–402).

[35] Devers, K. J. and Frankel, R. M. (2000). Study design in qualitative research--2: Sampling and data collection strategies. *Education for health*, 13(2), 263.

[36] Boetticher, G. (2007). The PROMISE repository of empirical software engineering data. http://promisedata.org/repository.

[37] Gyimóthy, T., Ferenc, R. and Siket, I. (2005). Empirical validation of object-oriented metrics on open source software for fault prediction. *IEEE Transactions on Software engineering*, 31(10), 897–910.

[38] Jureczko, M. (2011). Significance of different software metrics in defect prediction. *Software Engineering: An International Journal*, 1(1), 86–95.

6

I-ACTIVE: A Low-Cost, Efficient, End-to-End Cyber-Physical System for Ubiquitous Real-Time Human Activity Recognition

Soumen Moulik, Amrit Raj, and Arun Kumar Verma

Department of Computer Science and Engineering, National Institute of Technology Meghalaya, Shillong, India

6.1 Introduction

We are living in a time when the elderly population in the world is facing a steep rise. Worldwide, the total number of persons aged 65 years or above in 2010 was 524 million, which was nearly 8% of the then total world population. Until 2019, it increased to 703 billion, which was nearly 9% of the then total world population. This share was 6% in the year 1990. It is expected that by the year 2050 this elderly population will reach 1.5 billion, i.e., nearly 16% of the projected world population. As per the projection drawn by UN Department of Economic and Social Affairs in their report titled *"World Population Ageing 2019: Highlights,"* 1 in 6 people in the world will be aged 65 years or more by 2050, in place of the present ratio of 1 in 11. Moreover, the overall life expectancy of human being is in a growing phase. The chance of surviving at the age of 65 was less than 50% in 1980s. However, it has become more than 90% in countries with very high life expectancy. At present, in 17 countries, older people account for more than one-fifth of the population. As per the projection, this will be the case for 155 countries by the end of this century, covering a majority (approximately 61%) of the world's population. In less developed countries, the elderly people will increase more than 250% between the years 2010 and 2050. In the same span, there will be 71% increase of elderly population in the developed countries. In another report titled "World Population Prospects 2019: Highlights" prepared by the same department, it was revealed that in 2018 persons aged 65 years or more outnumbered the children under age five worldwide for the first time in history. By 2050, it will be more than twice of the latter and will globally surpass the number of adolescents and youth aged 15–24 years. Interestingly, it was also realized in this report that the population above the age of 80 years is growing even faster than the number above age 65. This population nearly tripled in 2019 in comparison with 1990 and, as per the projection, it will again become nearly triple by 2050 [1,2].

The statistical summary gives us immense pleasure because it shows that due to enormous technological advancement in various fields the average life expectancy has

DOI: 10.1201/9781003202752-6

reached this phase and will continue to be in a better position in the future. However, at the same time, it has also become a challenge to maintain the quality of life for the elderly population, who spend most of their time alone in his/her home or outdoors. Along with the ageing, naturally the problems associated with ageing like mortality risk, health status, type and level of activity, etc. are also following a steep rise. Researchers across the globe are looking for innovative technological solutions for these problems. The recent developments in Internet of Things (IoT) and cyber-physical systems (CPSs) are envisioning a safe and secure life for this elderly population through innovative e-health applications. In this regard, development of easy-to-use, cost-effective, ubiquitous, and real-time human activity recognition (HAR) systems will be a great help to this elderly population and to the society at large [3]. Any kind of movement produced by our skeletal muscles with the help of energy is known as physical activity. When a person works, travels, or does regular household work then he/she undergoes different such physical activities such as walking, sitting, going upstairs and downstairs, running, and many more like this. The HAR methods can help the major chunk of the elderly population by assisting individuals with the interface of tracking, monitoring, and recognizing the physical activities, and furthermore, will be able to classify them and send alarm notifications to near and dear ones in case of any unwanted activities. Especially for the patients suffering from diabetes, heart diseases, and obesity, HAR plays a vital role in modern IoT and CPS-based health care. Moreover, every individual, especially elderly persons, develop patterns in their daily livings. Monitoring such daily routines can be very helpful, especially in post medical-operation scenarios. Moreover, the rapid development of high-end smartphones with built-in sensors and constant miniaturization of sensing modules enables them to be easy to carry or wear and has made it possible to develop low-cost wearable HAR systems [4]. The proposed I-ACTIVE system is an attempt in that direction.

6.2 Background and Motivation

The efforts of human activity monitoring and recognition have been in place for the last two decades, more specifically since the emergence of ubiquitous and mobile computing [5]. The developments in sensing and communication technologies, and in data analysis methods, throughout the period, have made it possible to recognize human activities in real time. The HAR systems can be broadly categorized into two groups, such as video based and sensor based [6]. Video-based approaches deal with the understanding of the detailed localization of body parts. Such systems take images such as inputs and analyze pixel coordinates of the body's key points such as neck, left and right shoulder, chest, left and right wrist, left and right elbow, left and right knee, left and right hip, left and right ankle, etc. Then the regression problem can be formulated and modeled through various classification algorithms. However, the primary drawback of video-based systems is its closed nature, i.e., these systems are only able to recognize human activities inside a room where cameras can be installed. Secondly, they are computationally complex and resource-extensive in nature. For ubiquitous real-time activity, recognition of such systems is not at all suitable. Thirdly, the privacy of the end users is an inseparable problem in these video-based approaches.

The sensor-based approaches can be further divided into two groups, such as smartphone sensor based, and wearable sensor based. In both cases, they are effective for outdoor activity recognition. Accelerometers and gyroscopes are the two most used sensors in this regard. However, starting from sensor calibration to recognition accuracy, everything varies from one smartphone to another. In order to get an accurate recognition result, one must spend a significant amount of money and buy a high-end smartphone, which off course will come with several other features.

Evidently, if we are only concerned about HAR, then smartphones are not a cost-effective solution. Rather, it is better to use an accelerometer and gyroscope sensors directly, and then develop a wearable system. Such systems will also be cost-effective. The most popular approach among is activity recognition using wearable sensors. The accelerometer measures the acceleration for the body movements in three dimensions, whereas the gyroscope measures the attitude and rotational rate in three dimensions. As such systems are wearable, multiple sensors (both homogeneous and heterogeneous) can be used in different places on the human body for a precise recognition of human activities. Gradually, such sensors are becoming small and multi-functional, thus making the whole system lightweight and comfortable for a person to wear. Therefore, from all points of view, such wearable systems are the best choice for ubiquitous real-time HAR.

All of the previous types of HAR use either offline or online modes of activity classification. In the online mode, the classification is done in real time. This approach needs a server where real-time processing can be done, and also it is bandwidth consuming. But in the offline mode, the activity classification is done offline, which means there is no need for an online server to do the processing. The generated data set is stored in a system, and the classification algorithms are applied to them. The proposed I-ACTIVE system is an effort towards developing an online mode of activity classification. Before explaining the proposed system, let us discuss a few research works and their performances, relevant to the proposed work.

6.3 Related Works

A few recent works in the field of HAR are briefly described below.

Ermes et al. attempted to recognize daily activities and sports performed by different subjects by using a hybrid classifier. Activity data was collected from 12 subjects with the help of tri-axial accelerometers placed on the hip and wrist. The different activities considered in this work were lying down, sitting, standing, walking, running, cycling, rowing, playing football, etc. The authors used four different classifiers, such as artificial neural network, automatically generated decision tree, custom decision tree, and a proposed hybrid model in which best qualities of the custom decision tree model and neural networks are combined. The authors achieved 89% accuracy while using both supervised and unsupervised data [7].

Hong et al. proposed a HAR system with accelerometer and RFID sensors. The daily living activities were divided into "body state" and "hand activities." To detect the user's body state, two accelerometers were attached to the thigh and waist, and another accelerometer was attached to the wrist to classify hand movements. The system achieved an overall 95.53% accuracy in the case of hand activities. In recognition of body states, 93.79% accuracy was achieved. It was also noted that in this work the "walking" activity showed a little bit of low accuracy, which may be because of the different walking speed of different people [8].

Elvira et al. presented a feature extraction method for HAR using a magnetic, angular rate and gravity (MARG) sensor. The authors considered the acceleration quaternion (AQ) method to represent 3-D orientations and rotations. The proposed method processes the sensor's signals to excerpt the orientation of a person with respect to the earth frame and the acceleration in the person frame. The proposed AQ algorithm exhibits a lower error rate in comparison with the acceleration angular rate (AAR) method. In terms of F-measures, the AQ method outperforms AAR, with a mean F-measure of 0.89 [9].

Wang proposed a model for HAR, where a sensor module, consisting of a tri-axial accelerometer, a tri-axial gyroscope, and a tri-axial magnetometer, is used in different subjects in their different body locations such as left and right arms, left and right legs, and the body torso. The authors used the time and frequency domain feature Extract (TFFE) method to extract features from original signals and extracted four-dimensional time domain features such as mean value, mean absolute deviation, skewness, and correlation between axes. Similarly, frequency domain features such as fast fourier transform (FFT) and cepstrum coefficient are extracted from the original signals. For feature reduction, the author used the principal component analysis (PCA) method. The author tried to recognize 19 different activities that included several complex ones apart from basic activities such as standing, walking, and running. Finally, the author compared different traditional learning methods and showed that the deep belief network (DBN) performs best, with a 99.3% differentiation rate. The author also concluded that the combination of accelerometer and magnetometer gives the most accurate result [10].

Davila et al. presented a data classification model for HAR based on an iterative learning framework. The framework proposed in this work classifies human daily living activities such as standing, walking, sitting, and lying down. The data set used in this work was prepared by acquiring data from 12 tri-axial accelerometers and 7 inertial measurement units. The authors used a two-stage consecutive filtering approach combining a band-pass finite impulse response (FIR) and a wavelet filter. Principal components and other kinematical features were extracted from the data set. The number of samples was minimized by the interactive learning procedure. The processed data set was then applied to train an SVM multi-class classifier. The proposed iterative learning framework used only 6.94% of the samples for training but achieved an average accuracy of 74.08%. However, in the case of the supervised method, the average accuracy is 81.07%, where training and testing samples are considered as an 80:20 ratio. Therefore, the minimization of the number of samples, without hampering the accuracy much, is an important contribution in this work [11].

Nandy et al. proposed a framework for detailed activity recognition, where a total of 12 activities, involving both static (such as standing and sitting, with and without weight) and dynamic activities (such as walking and climbing, with and without weight), were considered. The authors collected three axes of acceleration data and heart rate data from a smartphone, which was kept in the subjects' pant pocket. Traditional classifiers such as decision tree, linear regression, bagged trees, support vector machine, K-nearest neighbor, etc. were used to validate the experimental results, and a 10-fold cross validation was considered. The authors proposed an ensemble classifier, based on a weighted majority voting, which recognizes the test data set with less error than other classifiers and with a 94% accuracy [12].

Asim et al. proposed a context-aware human activity recognition, which deals with activity recognition enigma by classifying different activity of daily livings (ADLs) in a different context. They incorporated a public data set, *ExtraSensory* [13], which has the data of 60 subjects and contains the raw sensor data from smartphones and smartwatches. They used only the smartphone-based raw sensor to perform their experiment, which is acquired at a 40 Hz sampling rate. The main advantage of the incorporated data set is that it has extra labelled data about the primary and secondary activities in paired form, which describes the user's presence. To prepare a context-aware data set, they mixed data of 6 primary activities and 10 secondary activities, and carried the classification on them. To make the data usable, they did the data pre-processing using a time-domain smoothing filter to eliminate noise and then extracted 18 features that will efficiently separate the different user activities. They exploited different learning models for activity classification and finally achieved an accuracy of 84% [14].

Tang et al. introduced a lightweight CNN-based model to handle different HAR systems' challenges. The proposed model supplanted the conventional CNN filters with Lego-based filters, which are more diminutive in size and autonomous of the CNN unique network construction. The model reduces the total computational overhead by an outstanding value because of the smaller Lego filters' efficient memory (less memory) utilization. Since the computational time is decreasing, they saw a small trade-off between model performance and time, which was further handled with the help of local loss function while training the model. They experimented with four publicly available data sets and managed to achieve the highest accuracy of 98.92% [15].

Chen et al. proposed an ensemble extreme learning (ELM) method with Gaussian random projection (GRP) to improve speed and accuracy while recognizing different human activities. The GRP was employed to implement input weights to the raw sensor data to make it more distinct. They extracted 11 additional time-dependent features and 6 frequency-dependent features, which helped them make their raw sensor data less noisy and a bit more compliant for the classification task. The ELM method is learning with every phase because of the support of different sequential learners. Because of this, they managed to classify human activities with the highest accuracy of 98.74% [16]. In one previous work, the authors presented multiple handcrafted features for the human activity recognition system by referring to different state-of-the-art HAR papers. They conveyed that the raw sensor data cannot be immediately given to the shallow learning algorithms as it is tough to associate human activity with them. To solve this problem, they extracted multiple statistical features and made the various human activity more separable to classify. They extracted 10 time domain and 4 frequency domain features for their experiment and used both shallow and deep learning classifiers for activity recognition. The proposed model manages to achieve better performance by incorporating the different handcrafted features than using only the raw sensor data [17].

Zhu et al. proposed a novel semi-supervised deep learning method that uses DLSTM with temporal ensembling for human activity recognition. Their approach helps in improving the performance of the recognition results with significantly less labelled data as well. Their model used both labelled and unlabelled data at a time, and by using data augmentation, they generate similar rules for unlabelled data. Once the data is augmented, they extracted statistical features for creating separability between different classes. The list of features they used is the handcrafted features laid out by in their work [16]. The loss is calculated using the randomness and regularization applied to the deep learning layers, which helps identify the labelled data loss (supervised loss) and unlabelled data loss (unsupervised loss). Then the total loss is calculated for determining the different parameters of the neural network. Then they tested their proposed model using the set of neural network layers and different percentage of unlabeled data. They managed to achieve the highest accuracy of 87.67% with just 1% labelled data and an accuracy of 97.21% with 100% labelled data [18].

Vallathan et al. proposed a deep learning and IoT-based suspicious activity detection system. The primary target audience is children who are left alone for doing daily activities and need constant monitoring from a third party for their continuous monitoring care. They used a deep learning method to detect abnormal activities from the series of images captured from a video surveillance camera. They also incorporated a multi-classifier model, which is used for is used for input classifications from the sequence of frames of videos. In order to detect, they first pre-process the data and make sure that the camera is continuously capturing the images. Once the data is pre-processed, the random vectors are generated and using a random forest classifier; multiple decision trees are generated. The results which are generated for the numerous decision trees are then combined and, using the deep learning approach, the static and dynamic activities are detected [19].

Khokhlov et al. laid out the foundation design implementation for an efficient human activity recognition system. They introduced four basic parameters that are tightly coupled with each other and directly dependent on each other. The first parameter of the data collection technique is the sensor choice . For the sensor platform choice, they identified the sensor and mounting choice in which they are deciding what kind of sensors to be used and in which location that sensor has to be mounted. The mounting location has to be done on a specific human body areas to get the best data for specific human activity. Also, the number of sensors are identified in this step. Then in the machine learning technique choice, the designer has to decide what features from the sensor data is to be extracted and what machine learning model fits best for those features. The final parameter, model design choice, is where the classifiers and mounting position dependency is checked. Using these parameters, they collected the data from different smartphones and did the data pre-processing and feature extraction. For feature extraction, they extracted features of fundamental frequency, average frequency, maximum frequency and minimum frequency, and many more. Finally, using different shallow and ensemble learning algorithms, they achieved the higest accuracy of 97.9% with the KNN (K=1) classifier [20].

Dehzangi et al. proposed a robust human activity recognition system where an inertial measurement unit (IMU) is used. They focused on three major components such as feature extraction, feature selection, and different classification algorithms for activity recognition. They used different feature extraction models that are based on time and frequency. Extracting too many features hampers the classifiers in terms of time and space complexity. To solve this, they also used feature selection, where they select only necessary features, which will help them in recognising the various human activities without affecting much accuracy. Finally, when they applied different classifiers, they managed to achieve an overall accuracy of 96.3% with only nine features [21].

Choudhury et al. did the basic human activity recognition using a wearable sensor module that consists of a tri-axial accelerometer, analog-digital converter, and a NodeMCU microcontroller. They used an open-source cloud platform called ThingSpeak for data collection, where they collect the data from an accelerometer using an Wi-Fi module. The data is written to the cloud using a WriteAPI key, which helps in identifying the particular channel and filed it for data collection. The pre-processing of the data is done on the cloud itself where the noisy and duplicate data is removed for the data set. As the data collected by them has limited number of features (three features from an accelerometer) they extracted a few more features like maximal, minimal, and average

3-D accelerometer features. This helps them create a more efficient data set for activity classification. Finally, to recognise the various human activity, they used the K-nearest neighbor (KNN) machine learning classifier (K=1) and managed to achieve an average accuracy of 93% [22]. In another work, Choudhury et al. proposed an approach of physique-based HAR in order to consider physical attributes such as height and weight while performing the recognition. The authors observed that the physique-based approach performs better than the traditional approach, both in case of publicly available data set and the data set generated by the authors, with a maximum accuracy of 99.88% [23].

Synthesis: For data analysis and classification, the researchers have applied various machine learning algorithms that are computationally expensive. We can make a quick summary of the steps involved in these works, such as 1) data acquisition from wearable sensors, 2) reduction of sample size, 3) feature extraction, and then 4) classification. Theoretically, for research purposes, this flow is fine to come to a comparative analysis of various algorithms in terms of their classification accuracy. However, where the execution of these algorithms is taking place, how much time they are taking, how they are recognizing a sequence of activities in real time, these questions are not addressed in the existing works. In a nutshell, we witness the lack of urge to develop an end-to-end location-independent ubiquitous real-time HAR system that does not involve complex algorithms, and thus, able to provide recognition results in real time. In this regard, we attempt to fill this gap through the proposed I-ACTIVE system.

6.4 The Proposed I-ACTIVE System

The proposed I-ACTIVE IoT-based HAR system can be attached with a wearable belt that any human being can wear comfortably. When a person wears this belt and starts the battery-powered system, then all his/her movement acceleration data are transmitted over an Internet connection and stored in a remote server or cloud for further analysis. The system may directly connect to a Wi-Fi access point, or the person may turn the Wi-Fi hotspot on his/her smartphone and use a mobile SIM card based 2G/3G/4G Internet. The I-ACTIVE prototype system transmits data to the Google cloud platform or, more precisely, to a Google spreadsheet in real time, and the spreadsheet acts like a remote cloud server. All kinds of computations responsible for precise recognition of activities are done in this spreadsheet. No machine learning algorithms or computationally extensive mechanisms are involved in the process. This makes the system low-cost, user-friendly, and very fast, without compromising the performance of the system. The system is also able to send automatic e-mail notifications based on the results of the analysis.

6.4.1 Components

The I-ACTIVE system prototype is developed using the following primary components: 1) accelerometer, 2) development board with Wi-Fi module, 3) analog-to-digital converter. We also used a beadboard, a few connecting wires, and a 9 V battery as a power supply. Figure. 6.1(a) illustrates the system prototype and its various components. The connections between the primary components are depicted in Figure 6.1(b). Below, we provide brief details about the primary components of the I-ACTIVE prototype.

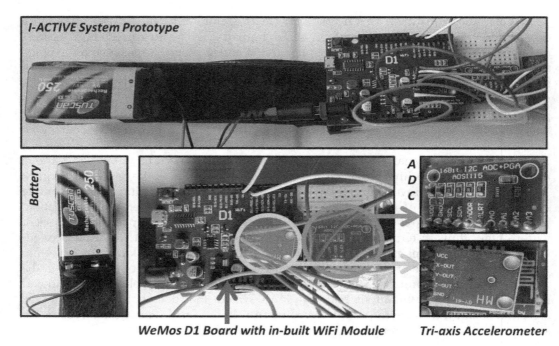

WeMos D1 Board with in-built WiFi Module   **Tri-axis Accelerometer**

FIGURE 6.1
System Prototype and Its Components.

Accelerometer: This is an electromechanical device that measures acceleration forces. Such forces may be static, like the continuous force of gravity or dynamic to sense movement or vibrations. Acceleration is the rate of change in velocity. In the case of an accelerometer-based wearable device, it measures the acceleration of body movements in three directions or three axes, such as X, Y, and Z. The I-ACTIVE prototype system uses ADXL335, which is a small, thin, low-power, complete tri-axis accelerometer sensor. This sensor works on the piezoelectric effect, which is the ability of certain materials to generate an electric charge in response to applied mechanical stress. Here, in this application, the body movement of an end user is the applied mechanical stress and we get a corresponding analog signal due to the generated electric charge. It works on the input voltage of 1.8 V to 3.6 V and has 10,000 g shock survival. This sensor has three analog output pins that deliver the 3-D accelerometer measures and has a self-test (ST) pin for the self-testing feature.

Development Board with Wi-Fi Module: The I-ACTIVE prototype system uses WeMos D1 as the development board, which has a built-in ESP8266 12E Wi-Fi module. This built-in module is a self-contained system-on-chip (SOC) with an integrated TCP/IP protocol stack that can give any microcontroller access to a Wi-Fi network. The functioning of the WeMos D1 board is similar to that of NodeMCU, except that the hardware is built resembling Arduino Uno. It has 11 digital I/O pins and only 1 analog input pin. However, we need three analog input pins since the ADXL335 sensor has three analog outputs. This forces us to use one analog-to-digital converter with at least three analog input pins.

Analog-to-Digital Converter (ADC): Neither the NodeMCU nor the WeMos D1 module has enough analog input pins. For this reason, the proposed I-ACTIVE system prototype uses ADS1115, which is a precise 16-bit ADC with four multiplexed analog inputs. It also has a digital comparator and a programmable gain amplifier (PGA), which allows precise measurements of both small and large signals. It has a data rate of 860 samples per second with an I2C compatible serial interface. In our system, the ADS1115 takes three analog outputs from ADXL335, converts them into digital data, and sends it to WeMos D1.

6.4.2 Operational Framework

The operational framework of the proposed I-ACTIVE system is illustrated in Figure 6.2. It is also depicted in this figure that I-ACTIVE system transmits sensed raw data, i.e., accelerations of the end user in three axes to a Google spreadsheet, which acts like a remote cloud server, where real-time data is stored and is analyzed to finally trigger an event, like sending notifications to the end user. The spreadsheet must be ready with different feature values corresponding to each activity that the system is able to re-cognize. These feature values are already calculated from the training data stored in the spreadsheet. The training data are generated corresponding to each activity with the help of the I-ACTIVE system and then the data are stored in separate sheet tabs within that spreadsheet. Outliers in the training data sets are also detected and removed before storing them.

In this work, we consider seven feature types, such as maximum values, minimum values, average values, standard deviation, mean of absolute values of first difference, mean of absolute values of second difference, and energy, for each axes. The mathema-tical expressions of the features are summarized in Table 6.1. Therefore, we have 21 features for three axes. These features are represented in Figure 6.2 as F1 to F21. These feature values are calculated for each activity with the help of corresponding training data and stored separately. For example, when the training data for *"walking plain"* is acquired, then at first the raw acceleration data of three axes are stored separately, and then the values of different features are calculated and stored in the spreadsheet in an organized manner.

The detailed description of all the features we have used and mentioned in Table 6.2 in our experiment are as follows.

Maximum: This feature calculates the maximum value between the x-, y-, and z-axis of a particular instance.

Accelerometer ADXL335	ADC ADS1115	WeMos D1 Board
VCC	VDD	3.3 V
X-OUT	A0	
Y-OUT	A1	
Z-OUT	A2	
GND	GND	GND
	SCL	D7
	SDA	D6

FIGURE 6.2
Pin Connections between the Primary Components.

TABLE 6.1

Features and Their Mathematical Expressions

Feature	Mathematical Expressions
Maximum	$A_{max} = \max(a(n))$
Minimum	$A_{min} = \min(a(n))$
Average	$A_{avg} = \text{avg}(a(n))$
Standard deviation	$\sigma = \sqrt{\frac{1}{N}\sum_{n=1}^{N}(a(n) - \bar{\mu})^2}$
Mean of absolute values of first difference	$\mu_{fd} = \frac{1}{N}\sum_{n=1}^{N}|a(n) - a(n-1)|$
Mean of absolute values of second difference	$\mu_{sd} = \frac{1}{N}\sum_{n=1}^{N}|a(n+1) - 2a(n) + a(n-1)|$
Energy	$e = \frac{1}{N}\sum_{n=1}^{N}(a(n))^2$

a(n) represents acceleration values along the x/y/z-axis of the accelerometer, and N represents the length of the
    data set.

TABLE 6.2

Summary of Experimental Results (with fine division of activities: Avg. Acc. = 97.71%)

Actual Activity	Recognized Activity							Performance Metrics			
	WP	WU	WD	ST	SI	JG	RN	P	R	F	A
WP	17	–	3	–	–	–	–	100	85	92	98
WU	–	20	–	–	–	–	–	80	100	89	96
WD	–	3	17	–	–	–	–	81	85	83	97
ST	–	–	–	20	–	–	–	91	100	95	99
SI	–	–	–	2	18	–	–	100	90	95	99
JG	–	–	1	–	–	17	2	100	85	92	98
RN	–	2	–	–	–	–	18	90	90	90	97

WP = Walking Plain, WU = Walking Upstairs, WD = Walking Downstairs, W = Walk (Any Type), ST = Standing, SI =
    Sitting, JG = Jogging, RN = Running, P = Precision, R = Recall, F = F-1 Score, A = Accuracy.

Minimum: This feature calculates the minimum value between the x-, y-, and z-axis of a
particular instance.

Average: Average calculates the mean of the x-, y-, and z-axis of a particular instance.
This feature is widely used by most of the researchers as it manages to segregate the
different human activities successfully.

Standard Deviation (SD): Standard deviation measures the amount of dispersion
between the accelerometer's three axes. A low standard deviation value for the same
activity indicates the value is closer to the mean value of that activity. A high standard deviation value indicates it is far away from the mean. It is always good to have
a low SD value within the same activity and a high SD value among different
activities.

Mean of Absolute Values of First Difference: It is a measure of dispersion that is
equal to the mean of absolute difference of two randomly chosen independent values.
Unlike standard deviation, it is not defined in terms of the specific measure of central
tendency.

Mean of Absolute Values of Second Difference: It is also a measure of variation that measures the degree of separability between the same class and among different classes as well and uses statistical modelling of means and differences.

Energy: The energy feature calculates the overall capacity (in terms of acceleration) required for exerting an activity from a human body.

We also prepared a sheet with a similar structure, where the I-ACTIVE system is dumping the tri-axial accelerometer data in real time. Unlike the training data sheet tabs for corresponding to different activities, this sheet tab is dynamic. If we do not stop the system, it will continue dumping the data and calculation of feature values and will not be possible in this way as some of the features need some static inputs. Thus, we consider a fixed number of rows, and we program the Google script editor in a way such that whenever the incoming real-time data index cross a particular threshold row, the old data will be deleted, and fresh data will start filling up the sheet from row number 1. In between, steps like calculation of feature values corresponding to the real-time test data, subsequent analysis, and then conditional notification sending will be performed.

As illustrated in Figure 6.2, the features value set of the test data generated in real time are compared with the pre-calculated feature value set corresponding to each activity. For each activity, the absolute difference (AD) between F_i of training data and F_i of test data are calculated, where $i \in [1,\ldots, 21]$. Then the summation of these absolute differences (AD_SUM) are calculated for each activity, in parallel. Finally, the minimum AD_SUM value is selected, and the corresponding activity is recognized as the performed activity. The minimum AD_SUM value ensures that the feature-wise difference between the training data and test data is minimum for that particular activity. With the help of the *sendEmail* function available in Google script editor, e-mail notifications are also sent to the end user.

6.5 Experimental Results

We tested the proposed I-ACTIVE system with seven different activities, such as walking plain (WP), walking upstairs (WU), walking downstairs (WD), standing (ST), sitting (SI), jogging (JG), and running (RN). We have performed a total of 140 experiments (20 for each activity) involving a total of 5 subjects. The actual and recognized results, along with four performance metric values, Precision (P), Recall (R), F1-Score (F1), Accuracy (A), are depicted in Table 6.2. It is evident from the result that the I-ACTIVE system yields an average accuracy of 97.71% when the activities are categorized into fine divisions (for example walking is further divided into walking plain, walking upstairs, and walking downstairs). In Table 6.3, results and corresponding performance metric values are illustrated by removing the fine divisions between activities, i.e., by considering different types of walks together into a single walk activity, jogging and running together into running. With such considerations I-ACTIVE achieved an average accuracy of 98.5%.

Figures 6.3–6.5 illustrate comparative analysis with few existing benchmarks. The benchmarks are not fully similar in terms of considered activities and performance metrics. That is why we considered only the overlapping parts in which comparison is possible. For example, recall is the performance metric considered in Nandy's work (Nandy et al., 2019) and the overlapping activities are basically the standard activities such as *sitting, standing, walking,* and *running*. Figure 6.3 compares the performance of

TABLE 6.3

Summary of Experimental Results (without fine division of activities: Avg. Acc. = 98.5%)

Actual Activity	Recognized				Performance Metrics			
	W	**ST**	**SI**	**RN**	**P**	**R**	**F**	**A**
W	60	–	–	–	100	100	100	98
ST	–	20	–	–	100	100	100	99
SI	–	2	18	–	100	90	95	99
RN	3	–	–	37	100	93	96	98

W = Walk (Any Type), ST = Standing, SI = Sitting, RN = Running, P = Precision, R = Recall, F = F-1 Score, A = Accuracy.

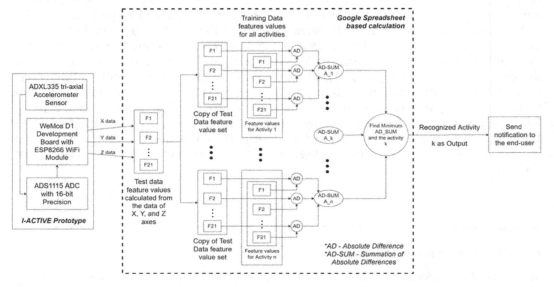

FIGURE 6.3
Operational Framework of the Proposed I-ACTIVE System.

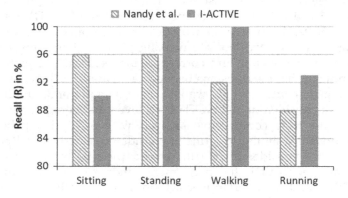

FIGURE 6.4
Comparison of Recall Values with Nandy et al. [12].

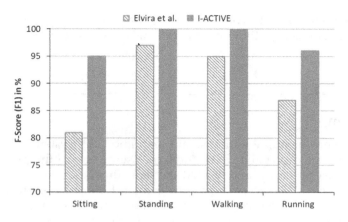

FIGURE 6.5
Comparison of F1-Score Values with Elvira et al. [9].

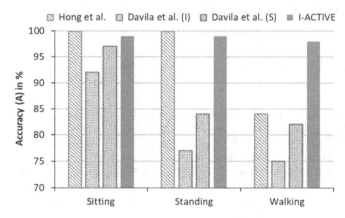

FIGURE 6.6
Comparison of Accuracy Values with Hong et al. [8] and Davila et al. [11].

I-ACTIVE with Nandy's work in terms of recall. It is evident from this figure that the performance of I-ACTIVE is better than Nandy's work in all standard activities, apart from *sitting*. The reason is, in two experiments I-ACTIVE confused sitting with standing. The performance of the proposed I-ACTIVE system is also compared with Elvira's work (Elvira et al., 2014) [9], as illustrated in Figure 6.4. Here also the overlapped activities are the same. However, the performance metric in this case is F-Score, as considered in Elvira's work, and as depicted, the performance of I-ACTIVE significantly overpowers Elvira's work for all standard activities (Figure 6.5). Figure 6.6 compares the accuracy of I-ACTIVE with Hong's work (Hong et al., 2008)[8] and Davila's work (Davila et al., 2017) [11]. Davila proposed two variants: Iterative (I) and Supervised (S). Both of these two are considered in this comparison. However, we found only three overlapping activities. It seems that I-ACTIVE provides significantly better accuracy than the benchmarks in a dynamic activity like *walking*. For static activities like *standing* and *sitting*, I-ACTIVE performs better than Davila's work. However, for these two activities the recognition accuracy of I-ACTIVE is slightly lower than Hong's work. Figure 6.2, Figure 6.3

6.6 Conclusion

In this work, an end-to-end, ubiquitous, and real-time HAR system is proposed. Simple components and a simple analytical method are used to make the proposed I-ACTIVE system low cost, user-friendly, and fast. At the same time, the proposed system does not compromise the recognition accuracy, as it is evident from the experimental results. The system is able to recognize complex human activities with 97.71% accuracy, and in case of more standard activities, the accuracy is 98.5%. In the future, the proposed I-ACTIVE system will be experimented with more complex activities such as cycling and walking upwards and downwards on a slope, which are difficult to distinguish from their other variants. In addition, the I-ACTIVE system will be extended in the future by incorporating other relevant sensors without hampering its simplicity.

References

[1] World Population Ageing 2019: Highlights (2019). Department of Economics and Social Affairs, United Nations, Population Division, New York.
[2] World Population Prospects 2019: Highlights (2019). Department of Economics and Social Affairs, United Nations, Population Division, New York.
[3] Schrader, L., Toro, A.V., Konietzny, S., Ruping, S., Schapers, B., Steinbock, M., Krewer, C., Muller, F., Guttler, J., and Bock, T. (2020). Advanced sensing and human activity recognition in early intervention and rehabilitation of elderly people. *Journal of Population Ageing, Springer, 13,* 139–165.
[4] Lentzas, A. and Vrakas, D. (2020). Non-intrusive human activity recognition and abnormal behavior detection on elderly people: a review. *Artificial Intelligence Review, Springer, 53,* 1975–2021.
[5] Chen, L., Hoey J., Nugent C.D., Cook D.J., and Yu Z. (2012). Sensor-based activity recognition. *IEEE Transactions on Systems, Man, and Cybernetics, Part C (Applications and Reviews), 42*(6), 790–808.
[6] Gupta A., Gupta K., Gupta K., and Gupta K. (2020, July 28–30). A Survey on Human Activity Recognition and Classification (pp. 0915–0919). International Conference on Communication and Signal Processing (ICCSP), Chennai, India.
[7] Ermes, M., PÄrkkÄ J., MÄntyjÄrvi J., and Korhonen I. (2008). Detection of daily activities and sports with wearable sensors in controlled and uncontrolled conditions. *IEEE Transactions on Information Technology in Biomedicine, 12*(1), 20–26.
[8] Hong, Y., Kim, I., Ahn, S.C., and Kim, H. (2008, December 13–15). Activity recognition using wearable sensors for elder care (pp. 302–305). Second International Conference on Future Generation Communication and Networking, Hainan, China.
[9] Elvira, V., Nazábal-Rentería, A., and Artés-RodrIguez, A. (2014, June 29–July 2). A novel feature extraction technique for human activity recognition (pp. 177–180). 2014 IEEE Workshop on Statistical Signal Processing (SSP), Gold Coast, QLD, Australia.

[10] Wang, L. (2016). Recognition of human activities using continuous autoencoders with wearable sensors. *MDPI Sensors*, *16*(189), 1–19.

[11] Davila, J.C., Cretu, A.M., and Jaremba, M. (2017). Wearable sensor data classification for human activity recognition based on an iterative learning framework. *MDPI Sensors*, *17*(1287), 1–18.

[12] Nandy, A., Saha, J., Chowdhury, C., and Singh, K.P.D. (2019, March 18–20). Detailed human activity recognition using wearable sensor and smartphones (pp. 1–6). 2019 International Conference on Opto-Electronics and Applied Optics (Optronix), Kolkata, India.

[13] Asim, Y., Azam, M.A., Ehatisham-ul-Haq, M., Naeem, U., and Khalid, A. (2020). Context-Aware Human Activity Recognition (CAHAR) in the wild using smartphone accelerometer. *IEEE Sensors Journal*, *20*(8), 4361–4371.

[14] Vaizman, Y., Ellis, K., Lanckriet, G., and Weibel, N. (2018). *ExtraSensory App: Data collection in-the-wild with rich user interface to self-report behavior* (pp. 1–12). Proceedings of the 2018 CHI Conference on Human Factors in Computing Systems (CHI 18), Association for Computing Machinery, New York, USA.

[15] Tang, Y., Teng, Q., Zhang, L., Min, F., and He, J. (2021). Layer-wise training convolutional neural networks with smaller filters for human activity recognition using wearable sensors. *IEEE Sensors Journal*, *21*(1), 581–592.

[16] Chen, Z., Jiang, C., and Xie, L. (2019). A Novel ensemble ELM for human activity recognition using smartphone sensors. *IEEE Transactions on Industrial Informatics*, *15*(5), 2691–2699.

[17] Chen, Z., Zhang, L., Cao, Z., and Guo, J. (2018). Distilling the knowledge from handcrafted features for human activity recognition. *IEEE Transactions on Industrial Informatics*, *14*(10), 4334–4342.

[18] Zhu, Q., Chen, Z., and Soh, Y.C. (2019). A novel semisupervised deep learning method for human activity recognition. *IEEE Transactions on Industrial Informatics*, *15*(7), 3821–3830.

[19] Vallathan, G., John, A., Thirumalai, C.S., Mohan, S., Srivastava, G., and Lin, C.-W. (2021). Suspicious activity detection using deep learning in secure assisted living IoT environments. *The Journal of Supercomputing, Springer*, *77*, 3242–3260.

[20] Khokhlov, I., Reznik, L., Cappos, J., and Bhaskar, R. (2018, March 12–14). Design of activity recognition systems with wearable sensors (pp. 1–6). 2018 IEEE Sensors Applications Symposium (SAS), Seoul, Korea (South).

[21] Dehzangi, O., and Sahu, V. (2018, August 20–24). IMU-based robust human activity recognition using feature analysis, extraction, and reduction (pp. 1402–1407). 2018 24th Int. Conf. on Pattern Recognition (ICPR), Beijing, China.

[22] Choudhury, N.A., Moulik, S., and Choudhury, S. (2020, September 28–30). Cloud-based real-time and remote human activity recognition system using wearable sensors (pp. 1–2). IEEE Int. Conf. on Consumer Electronics – Taiwan (ICCE-Taiwan), Taoyuan, Taiwan.

[23] Choudhury, N.A., Moulik, S., and Roy, D.S. (2021). Physique-based human activity recognition using ensemble learning and smartphone sensors. *IEEE Sensors Journal*, *21*(15), 16852–16860.

7

Efficient Compression Algorithms for Bandwidth- and Memory-Constrained Cyber-Physical Systems

Mohd Rafi Lone
SRM Institute of Science and Technology, Kattankulathur, Chennai, India

Najeeb-ud-Din Hakim
National Institute of Technology, Srinagar, J&K

7.1 Introduction

With the advent of a new media age, the advancements in digital imaging systems in every sphere of life have revolutionized the world. Almost every enterprise is currently dependent upon image and video information. Digital image processing includes a broad spectrum of applications ranging from stock market reports to medical diagnostic reports and from low-resolution Internet images to high-resolution remote sensing applications. The development in high-quality and less expensive image acquisition devices has resulted in exponential increase in digital information. There is an increased demand for high-resolution devices, due to advancement in display technology. With the arrival of 4K and 8K resolution, the demand for high definition and full high definition TVs has been dropping by 3% for the past four years [1]. This has not only increased the challenge to maintain high bandwidth, but also high throughput as the frame size and the frame rate has increased. Although the storage capacity and network bandwidth has increased over time, there is still a need for data compression. Figure 7.1 shows the information available worldwide, optimally compressed, from 1986 to 2018 [2,3]. The graph would surely have been steeper, had there not been compression at all.

Compression standards are improving on performance; however, this comes at the expense of increased computational complexity. An increase in computational complexity gives rise to more execution time and more power dissipation.

The rest of the paper is organized as follows. Section 2 provides the motivation and the contribution of this work. The importance of compression and how much compression is currently achievable, is presented in Section 3. Section 4 provides the coding principle. The image transformation schemes are presented in Section 5. The information about entropy encoding is presented in Section 6. Section 7 presents the information regarding transform-based image compression schemes. Section 8 provides the insight regarding

DOI: 10.1201/9781003202752-7

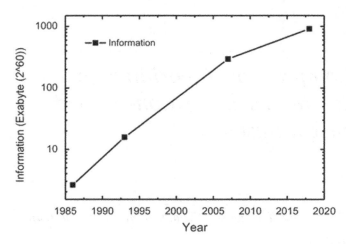

FIGURE 7.1
Information Content Generated from 1986 to 2018.

the image coders that can be the good candidates for CPS. The results and discussion are provided in Section 9. Section 10 concludes the paper.

7.2 Motivation and Contribution

Cyber-physical systems (CPSs) are more than visual sensor networks (VSNs) and Internet of Multimedia Things (IoMT). In VSNs and IoMTs, the sensor nodes acquire information, process it, and then transmit it to the other nodes. There is no feedback or closed-loop control on these processes. In cyber-physical systems, there is complete control and continuous monitoring of the processes. The devices used in the CPS are mainly micro-controllers. These microcontrollers are constrained with resources, including on-chip RAM. Also, most of the processes require acquisition of images and their processing. Compression of these images is needed in order to transmit the information seamlessly without any delay on bandwidth limited networks. Compressing the information requires on-chip RAM to be sufficiently high. The image coders require a significant amount of on-chip RAM to compress the images. However, in the last decade, many image coders have been proposed that thrive to be used in low-memory devices.

In this study, a complete analysis of the low-memory and low-complexity image coders is presented. The aim is to come up with those image coders that can be good candidates for cyber-physical systems.

7.3 How Much Compression Is Needed?

The question that arises at this stage is: why is compression needed? To answer this question, let's consider an example. If we have to store an uncompressed 1080p resolution color video of one hour, each color pixel represented by 24 bits and 30 frames per second, we need a storage of 625.71 GB. When compressed at a fair quality, we need less than 1 GB of storage for the same resolution. There is a trade-off between rate of compression and quality of recovered image. One must understand that the essence of video compression lies in image coding. Video can be understood as a sequence of image frames, captured at a very rapid rate (minimum 25 frames per second). It is evident that storing and transmitting such a large amount of uncompressed media is unrealistic at present despite the improvement in storage capacity and bandwidth. The words compression and coding are analogous and are used in this thesis interchangeably.

Image compression refers to the process of removing redundant information present in digital images. There are three forms of redundancy that can be classified: inter-pixel, psycho-visual, and coding redundancy. The inter-pixel redundancy refers to the correlation among pixels within a single image frame (spatial redundancy) or a sequence of image frames (temporal redundancy). The coding redundancy refers to the redundancy within the output sequence of symbols. The psycho-visual redundancy exists because the human visual system (HVS) does not pay attention equally to all the information captured in a scene. The human eye captures only a fraction of the unlimited information available in the environment at any given instance. About 10^{10} bits/sec are deposited on the retina, out of which only 10^4 bits/sec reach the layer IV and VI of the brain [4,5]. This is because HVS does not show the same sensitivity to all the content in the scene. As an example, HVS is more sensitive to brightness in comparison to color information [6].

7.4 Coding Principle

Image compression system consists of an encoder and a decoder. An encoder is used to compress an input image, while a decoder decompresses the compressed data to reconstruct the original image. A typical image compression system is shown in Figure 7.2. Compression can sometimes be carried out more efficiently in any other domain than the original spatial domain [7]. The discrete transforms, cosine [8], sine, and wavelet, are few examples. The bulk of the information in the transformed image is carried by fewer coefficients. Most of the coefficients carry less information, which can be easily quantized or discarded [9]. This discarded information is lost permanently and cannot be recovered. Finally, the coding redundancy present in the quantized sequence is removed by entropy encoding [10]. This is achieved by assigning each symbol with a fixed or variable length code. Variable length coding is more efficient, and works by mapping fewer bits to more frequent symbols and vice versa. Huffman [11] and arithmetic coding [12] are popular examples of entropy coding. This is a completely reversible process. Shannon's entropy theorem [13] gives the lower limit on the average number of bits required to represent the source symbols without any loss of information. The Shannon entropy is measured in terms of bits/symbol. Given an input source S consisting of symbols s1, s2, s3,..., sn with a probability of occurrences p1, p2, p3,..., pn, respectively, according to Shannon, the entropy of the source S is given by (1):

$$H(s) = -\sum_{i=1}^{n} p_i log_2 p_i \tag{7.1}$$

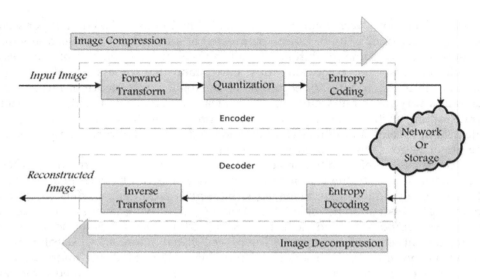

FIGURE 7.2
General Image Compression Scheme.

A compression system in which the reconstructed image is an exact replica of the input image is known as error-free or lossless compression algorithm. If the reconstructed image is distorted, the compression system is called lossy. Lossless compression is mainly based on entropy encoders and may also use any transform coders that are fully reversible in nature. Lossy compression schemes usually use some irreversible steps like quantization and inter-domain transformation to reduce the size of the output bitstream. For applications like medical image processing where a small loss of information may lead to erroneous diagnosis, a lossless compression is usually preferred. This may result in more encoding/decoding time, more power dissipation, and high bandwidth requirement, but quality is of prime importance. Applications like remote sensing where high quality needs to be maintained, lossless or near-lossless compression is used. On the other hand, the applications where quality is not of prime importance, like internet videos and images, lossy compression is usually preferred. In lossy compression applications, high quality may be appreciated, but the available bandwidth plays a prime role. For such applications, a progressive coding control mechanism is often appreciated to maintain best possible quality at a certain available bandwidth. Youtube is one such example.

7.5 Image Transforms

There are many transforms available that can be used for energy compaction of an image. But mostly the use of these transforms is application dependent. For lossy compression, the two very popular transform coding schemes are discrete cosine transform and discrete wavelet transform. The developments in these two transforms are discussed here.

7.5.1 Discrete Cosine Transform

The one-dimensional discrete cosine transform (DCT) was introduced in 1974 [14]. The aggregate of finite cosine functions various frequencies can be specified as DCT. The DCT transform is a Fourier transform that is similar to the DFT but only works for real numbers. DCT has a variety of applications ranging from compression to analysis of mathematical equations. Typical applications include joint photographic experts group (JPEG) [15] still image compression standard, H.261 and H.263 video compression standards. These standards are so simple in design that despite providing lower performance in comparison to some state-of-the-art compression standards, they still dominate in many fields in practical applications. DCT is a unitary transform which preserves the energy of a signal. The 2-D DCT for an image with block size N1 × N2 is given by the following equation:

$$X(k_1, k_2) = C(k_1)C(k_2) \sum_{n1=0}^{N1-1} \sum_{n2=0}^{N2-1} x(n_1, n_2) \cos\left[\frac{k_1\pi}{2N_1}(2n_1 + 1)\right] \cos\left[\frac{k_2\pi}{2N_2}(2n_2 + 1)\right] \tag{7.2}$$

where

$$C(k_i) = \begin{cases} \frac{1}{\sqrt{Ni}}; \text{ for } ki = 0 \\ \left(\frac{2}{Ni}\right)^{1/2}; \text{ for } ki = 1, 2, \ldots, N - 1 \end{cases} \tag{7.3}$$

The result is a transform coefficient array for a block of typical size 8 × 8. The DC (zero frequency) component is represented by the top-left element (0,0). The resulted transformed coefficients are arranged in increasing order of frequency as we move away from the DC component. The higher the coefficient frequency, the smaller the information it carries. In this manner, the energy is concentrated towards the top-left corner. The coefficients with higher frequencies can be easily discarded.

7.5.2 Discrete Wavelet Transform

In image compression and other applications, discrete wavelet transform (DWT) has completely replaced DCT. DWT provides many significant advantages over DCT. The main benefit of DWT over the other transforms has been that it allows for multi-resolution signal processing with localization across time-frequency spectrum [16]. Other significant advantages include progressive coding, region of interest coding, elimination of blocking artifacts, etc. The DWT constructs a multi-resolution analysis (MRA) time-frequency plane using filter banks. Special wavelet filters are used for analysis and synthesis of signals [17]. The analysis filter and filters H(z) and L(z) are applied on the discrete input signal, as shown in Figure 7.3. The filter bank produces

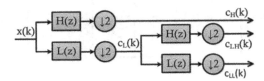

FIGURE 7.3
Two-Level Analysis Filter Bank.

two signals with different frequencies and equal bandwidth. L(z) is known as a low-pass filter while H(z) is called a high-pass filter. The output of analysis filter bank contains double the number of samples applied at the input. Half of the output samples are discarded by down-sampling by a factor of two. A synthesis filter bank initially up-samples by a factor of two by inserting zeros into the input sequence, as shown in Figure 7.4. The synthesis filters H'(z) and L'(z) are then used. The synthesis filters are based on the analysis filters. The sequence is then added to reconstruct the signal y(k). The outputs obtained from the filter bank are referred to as sub-bands and the process of filtering is known as sub-band coding. The aliasing can be eliminated by designing the synthesis filters so that:

$$L'(z) = H(-z) \tag{7.4}$$

$$H'(z) = -L(-z) \tag{7.5}$$

For perfect reconstruction, a product filter of L'(z) and L(z) is defined so that:

$$P_o(z) - P_o(-z) = 2z^{-N} \tag{7.6}$$

where N is the filter bank's total delay.

The low-frequency sub-band ($C_L(k)$) is further subjected to analysis filter bank to further decompose the signal into two more sub-bands, as shown in Figure 7.3. An L-level decomposition of the input signal can be achieved by extending the analysis filter bank L times. A 2D-DWT of an image is obtained by applying the analysis filter on row and column directions, respectively. The two-level 2D-decomposition of an image is shown in Figure 7.5. The first level results in four sub-bands, computed via low-pass and high-pass filters in row and column directions. The low-frequency sub-band is further decomposed in the second level of decomposition.

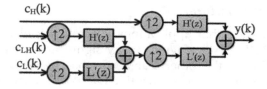

FIGURE 7.4
Two-Level Synthesis Filter Bank.

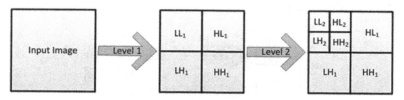

FIGURE 7.5
Two-Level 2D DWT Decomposition.

7.6 Entropy Coding

Entropy coding is the final step of the general coding scheme. The final sequence of symbols that has been obtained after quantization is further compressed in a lossless manner. The entropy encoders are mainly based on the statistics of the occurrence of each symbol to be encoded. Shannon's entropy theorem gives the lower limit on the needed bit count on average to represent the source symbols without any loss of information. The number of bits needed to encode a symbol decreases as its probability of occurrence increases. Two famous entropy encoders are Huffman [11] and Arithmetic [12]. Huffman makes a probability table before it starts encoding, and the table and encoded bits need to be transmitted so that the decoding can take place. Arithmetic coding, however, does not build the table beforehand. The encoder adapts to the statistics as it encodes the symbols. The most significant drawback of Arithmetic coding is that it is slow.

7.7 Transform-Based Image Coding Algorithms

7.7.1 DCT-Based Algorithms

One of the most extensively used image compression formats is JPEG, based on DCT. The baseline encoder and decoder for JPEG still image compression standard are shown in Figures 7.6 and 7.7, respectively. The image is first partitioned into blocks of size 8 × 8.

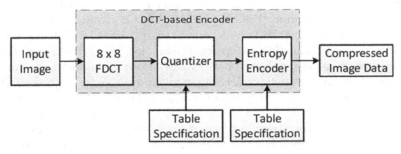

FIGURE 7.6
Steps Involved in a DCT-Based JPEG Encoder.

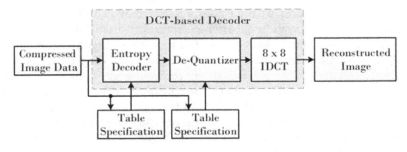

FIGURE 7.7
Steps Involved in a DCT-Based JPEG Decoder.

Each block is then DCT transformed into 64 coefficients. A maximum of 64 levels are needed to represent information carried by any coefficient. The quantizer is used to round off each integer value to one of these 64 levels. The amount of information carried by the coefficients reduces as we move away from the DC coefficient. Further compression can be achieved by discarding certain coefficients carrying less information. The coefficients are then scanned in a zig-zag manner starting from the DC coefficient. Finally, an entropy coder is used to compress it further. Two variable length entropy encoders are specified by JPEG: Huffman Coding and Arithmetic coding.

An embedded quadtree-based DCT algorithm is proposed in [18]. It uses adaptive quadtree splitting method in DCT for set partitioning. Every block of pixels with value zero are represented using only one symbol. The performance has improved in comparison to JPEG. A sorting method, based on prediction of DCT coefficients, is proposed in [19]. The decoder uses the reconstructed magnitudes of neighboring coefficients to predict the magnitude of each coefficient using linear prediction. Context-based arithmetic coding is used to optimally encode the symbols. The performance of this method is close to that of JPEG2000.

7.7.2 DWT-Based Algorithms

The wavelet transformed image is inherited with some features that are utilized by the encoder to compress optimally the transformed image. Different wavelet-based image compression schemes and their FPGA implementations are presented in this section.

After the success of JPEG standard, the JPEG committee launched an effort in 1996–97 in order to develop a new coding algorithm based on DWT. The ISO 15444/ITU–T Recommendation T.800, also recognized as the JPEG2000 standard, is the product of this endeavor [20]. JPEG2000 is established on the image coder, namely, Embedded Block Coding with Optimal Truncation (EBCOT) [21]. In EBCOT, from the most significant bit (MSB) to the least significant bit (LSB), each code block is encoded individually, bit plane by bit plane. The bit plane coding aids the creation of an embedded bit-stream. The encoding process consists of three passes. Each pass collects information about the context before encoding a primitive. An arithmetic coder is then given the objects. At present, JPEG2000 is considered as the state-of-the-art compression standard. However, the issue with JPEG2000 is that it utilizes a context-based arithmetic coder, which is exhaustive and computationally complex [22,23]. Also, improvement in throughput is very difficult to achieve.

In the year 1993, the embedded zerotree wavelet algorithm was introduced by JM Shapiro (EZW) [24], which marked a stepping stone in the field of image coding based on wavelets. The EZW is based on four key steps. These are: 1) DWT decomposition, 2) prediction of a lack of significant data, 3) quantization of successive approximations encoded with entropy coder, and 4) data compression that is universally lossless using Arithmetic coding. Besides providing better performance than DCT-based compression algorithms, EZW provides embedded coding. The bits are arranged in decreasing order of their importance and embedded coder can terminate the encoding (and decoding) at any desired bit rate. This is also called rate scalability or progressive coding. When an image is decomposed into many levels, the sub-bands are spatially correlated in a hierarchy. For example, LH1 is correlated to LH2, LH3, LH4, and so on. Each coefficient in a sub-band is correlated to four coefficients of sub-band in the next lower level. Such a spatially correlated tree with its roots (parent coefficient) in the highest level and the leaves (terminal coefficients) in the first (lowest) level is termed a spatial orientation tree (SOT). EZW exploits the correlation and predicts that the chances of an offspring node to be insignificant is more if its parent node is also insignificant. Such a tree with its parent node being insignificant (zero), followed by insignificant descendant nodes is termed a zerotree.

Another compression scheme was proposed in 1996 by Said and Pearlman, namely set partitioning in hierarchical trees (SPIHT) [25]. SPIHT can be viewed as an improved version of EZW. Three lists are used by SPIHT to store dynamically the addresses of significant/insignificant pixels and sets at any time. Like EZW and JPEG2000, SPIHT encodes bit plane by bit plane starting from MSB to LSB. It provides coding performance very close to that of the state-of-the-art JPEG2000 standard. The demerit of SPIHT however is that it needs a large memory to store the lists, which becomes impracticable for high-resolution images. As the performance of SPIHT is very close to JPEG2000, and has the ability to improve on throughput and memory reduction, a number of SPIHT variants have been proposed.

Set partitioned embedded bloCK (SPECK) coder [26,27] is one such variant. It reduces the complexity of SPIHT by using only two linked lists and considering only a single sub-band at a time. The performance of SPECK is less than, but close to that of SPIHT. Subband block hierarchical partitioning (SBHP) [28] is a low complexity coder of SPECK, using three lists as in SPIHT. Embedded zero block coding (EZBC) [29] is a high complexity coder of SPECK. It has the same coding procedure as SPECK; however, it takes advantage of node dependency within and throughout sub-bands at the individual quadtree stage. To efficiently encode the quadtree structure, EZBC also employs a sophisticated background modelling scheme. The memory issue remains with all the three algorithms: SPECK, SBHP, and EZBC, as all of these are based on dynamic lists. No list SPIHT (NLS) [30] is the first algorithm that has successfully reduced the memory requirement by conventional SPIHT. NLS has used state table markers instead of dynamic lists. A fixed storage of four bits per coefficient is needed to store the state table. In addition to this, two more arrays are needed to store maximum descendant and grand-descendant magnitudes. NLS shows a similar compression performance as SPIHT.

Memory requirement has also been reduced by strip-based encoding. In [31], multilevel DWT is taken on the input image and then the descendants in SOT trees are flattened into strips. A strip consists of all nodes of a SOT and can be encoded independently. Its FPGA implementation is given in [32]. In [33], the image is partitioned into line stripes that are then DWT-transformed and encoded. A few lines are buffered and then encoded in pipelined manner. ZainEldin, in [33] has presented the hardware implementation as well. wavelet block tree coding (WBTC) [34] takes blocks of coefficients as the nodes of SOT, unlike SPIHT, which has coefficients as nodes. WBTC merges the block and tree features to minimize the memory to some extent. A listless block tree coding (LBTC) algorithm, working on the listless implementation of WBTC with varying root block sizes, has also been proposed [35]. The state information is kept in a fixed size array requiring four pixels per coefficient. Special markers are placed on lower-level insignificant blocks and are updated during tree partitioning. This algorithm combines DWT and DCT to take advantage of the data organization results of DCT. The FPGA implementation of NLS [30] is proposed in [36]. An array structure is used to store the coding states instead of list structure. The NLS has succeeded in reducing SPIHT memory; however, it does not process coefficients in parallel, therefore throughput is less. A modified SPIHT architecture is proposed in [37], that processes 4×4 bit plane in one cycle. It processes multiple sequential steps in one cycle, thereby increasing the critical path delay significantly. The overall throughput is not high enough. A bit plane parallel SPIHT architecture is proposed in [38]. The DWT is processed bit plane by bit plane and then process multiple bit planes independently in parallel. High throughput is reached by processing four pixels in a single cycle. The encoded bits are then merged into a single bitstream. The main drawback lies in the fact that the decoding cannot be processed in parallel, because it is impossible to predict the length of each bitstream. The decoder needs to be faster than encoder, for the reason that encoder is needed only once to compress an image, while decoder is used again and again to reconstruct the image from the bitstream. The area consumed by this architecture is very high in comparison to NLS. A block-based pass-parallel SPIHT (BPS) architecture is proposed in [39]. BPS decomposes wavelet trans-formed image into 4 × 4 blocks of a bit plane and processes a 4 × 4 block in one cycle. It encodes in three passes, which can be processed in pipelined or parallel manner. Parallel processing is possible because the passes remove the data dependency and pre-calculates the bit length before the pass begins. The coding performance is degraded to a slight extent because of the parallel execution. Also, large memory and hardware logic is needed to implement the design. A one-dimensional SPIHT (1D SPIHT) is proposed in [40]. 1D SPIHT has the advantage of requiring less memory than 2D SPIHT. The inter-dependencies among the parallel frequency bands that are being processed are resolved in this architecture. A hardware efficient architecture has been designed at the cost of compression efficiency.

7.8 Image Coders for Cyber-Physical Systems

Cyber-physical systems are equipped with sensor nodes with imaging capabilities that find a wide range of both civilian as well as military applications. The imaging sensor nodes are severely constrained in terms of resources (memory, processing power, and battery life), and transmit images to more resourceful base station or hub through wireless link. These wireless channels are bandwidth limited and error prone; therefore, an embedded image coding is desirable over these channels, so that maximum in-formation image can be decoded with correct bits received before occurrence of error. The high cost of providing large on chip memory, and limited battery power put severe constraints on image coding algorithm for cyber-physical systems.

There has been a significant improvement in image coders in the last two decades. A number of low-memory and low-complexity image coders have been proposed in due course of time. These coders can be classified based on their parent image coder. The image coders are classified as 1) SPECK-based and 2) SPIHT-based. The image coders in each of these categories are discussed in some detail here. The list of image coders with their relationship with parent image coders is shown in Figure 7.8.

7.8.1 SPECK-Based Image Coders for CPS

Many image coders, based on SPECK, have been proposed, that aim at lowering the memory and computational complexity. Two main image coders are described here.

7.8.1.1 Listless SPECK

LSK [41] is based on SPECK, in which partitioning is done as per SPECK principles. Unlike SPECK, LSK does not use lists. The information regarding the states is maintained in fixed-sized arrays. Only two bits per coefficient are stored in these arrays in order to

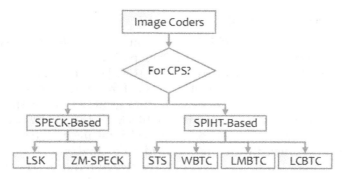

FIGURE 7.8
Image Coders That Qualify for CPS Applications.

get rid of the computational complexity of SPECK and make the algorithm faster. At partitioning, the markers used in LSK are updated. The coefficients are scanned using Z-scanning or linear indexing method. The blocks which are not significant are skipped using the status reflected in the arrays. The static memory used for storing the status information is used to keep track of the significance of each coefficient. The advantage of using static memory over dynamic memory is that it results in increased speed or reduction in computational complexity. However, static memory can only be used to occupy maximum memory required by the algorithm. The memory requirement of this algorithm is still very large for memory-constrained devices.

7.9 Zero-Memory SPECK

Zero-memory SPECK (ZM-SPECK) [42] is an efficient image coder based on SPECK. It eliminates the need for the lists. Only a few registers are required to perform basic operations (logical and arithmetic). The encoder itself does not require any memory for its implementation. However, the lower limit of memory needed in the overall image coder is set by the transform stage.

7.9.1 SPIHT-Based Image Coders for CPS

A number of image coders based on SPIHT have been proposed that have targeted the reduction of memory and complexity requirement. Four important such image coders are given below.

7.9.1.1 State Table–Based SPIHT

The state table–based SPIHT (STS) algorithm [43] has eliminated the need for large lists that are needed in SPIHT. STS has used two static memories to hold the significance status of blocks of size 2 × 2. Also, two small lists have been used in this algorithm to temporarily hold the coefficients needed in a depth-first search while encoding. The overall memory requirement has been significantly reduced. Also, the computational complexity and power consumption has been lowered significantly.

7.9.1.2 Wavelet Block Tree Coding

The wavelet block tree coding (WBTC) algorithm [34] is bit-plane-wise encoding the wavelet coefficients, beginning with the largest bit plane. The redundancy of sub-bands at various levels is targeted in the same way as SPIHT. Unlike SPIHT, however, the coefficients are packed into (m × n) coefficient groups before being encoded using block trees. Multiple SPIHT spatial orientation trees (SOT) are grouped into a single block tree in WBTC. All of the descendant blocks of a parent block, that is placed at the top sub-band, make up a block tree. When m=n=1 in set in WBTC, it results in SPIHT algorithm. WBTC is able to partially leverage the similarity inside the sub-bands due to the block tree encoding. WBTC stores significance data in three structured lists. The algorithm has reduced the memory requirement only to a certain extent. For CPS, the memory requirement is still high.

7.9.1.3 Low-Memory Block Tree Coding

An efficient image coder has been proposed in [44]. The algorithm has aimed at reducing the memory and complexity of the WBTC image coder. It has used a fractional wavelet filter (FrWF) [45] instead of the conventional DWT. FrWF is a low-memory implementation to achieve DWT. The wavelet transformed coefficients are then quantized and encoded using low-memory block tree coding (LMBTC) algorithm. The LMBTC is a listless version of the WBTC algorithm. During the encoding process, a small static memory is used to keep a record of the block-tree partitioning. This image coder has resulted in a significant decrease in the memory requirement and is a good candidate for memory-constrained devices.

7.9.1.4 Low-Complexity Block Tree Coding

A low-complexity block tree coding (LCBTC) algorithm has been proposed in [46]. The algorithm has aimed at reducing the computational complexity of the WBTC algorithm. The algorithm is targeted for the memory-constrained devices that happen to have a minimum memory of 64 kbytes. In order to achieve low-memory implementation, four coefficients (2 × 2) are grouped together. Block-based SOT trees are encoded with each node consisting of a block of fixed size. Two static memories are used to keep record of significance status of SOT trees. In order to reduce the complexity, fixed sized blocks are used and the depth-first approach has been used. Two small lists are used to keep record of the blocks of just one SOT tree, while encoding that SOT tree. The image coder has used modified fractional wavelet filter (MFrWF) [47] instead of FrWF or conventional DWT. The memory needed for MFrWF is slightly more than that of FrWF; however, it results in reduced computational complexity. The overall algorithm can be seen as a good candidate for memory-constrained devices that are used in delay intolerant networks like a CPS.

7.10 Results and Discussion

The state-of-the-art image coding algorithms have been compared here. The following coders have been compared: LCBTC, LMBTC, WBTC, ZM-SPECK, LSK, SPECK, and

SPIHT. The test images were obtained from widely available standard databases: The Centre for Image Processing Research (CIPR) Database and The USC-SIPI Image Database. The images of the clock, airplane, cameraman, and goldhill are all 256 × 256 pixels in size. The airport, male (aka pirate), metal, and pentagon are the images with a resolution of 1024 × 1024 pixels. All of the photographs are monochrome and have a bit depth of 8 bits per pixel. The wavelet filter CDF–9/7 is used in up to five decomposition stages for all of the coders. The encoding and decoding of each codec take place on the same machine. All coders are simulated in Matlab 2014 and run on an Intel Core i5–4210U processor with 1.70 GHz and 8 GB RAM to ensure a reasonable comparison.

7.10.1 Compression Efficiency

The compression efficiency indicates how closely the reconstructed image resembles the original image. It is often assessed in terms of the image distortion that has resulted. The rate-distortion relation is often used to assess an image coder's coding quality. The number of bits per pixel (bpp) needed to achieve a certain level of image quality is referred to as rate distortion (or maximum distortion). The peak-signal-to-noise ratio (PSNR) is a measure used to assess the reconstructed image's accuracy.

Figure 7.9 shows a comparative analysis of image coders based on their compression quality. The findings are summed through all images of the same scale. It can be seen from the graph that such coders, such as WBTC and LSK, have poorer quality for lower bit rates than other image coders. In contrast to other image coders, such as ZM-SPECK and LMBTC, LCBTC performs poorly at lower bit rates. At higher bit rates, though, LCBTC outperforms all other image coders in terms of PSNR.

7.10.2 Memory Utilization

CPS devices usually have 64 kB of RAM or less. As a result, the on-chip RAM specifications of various image coders are revealed in this study. The maximum file size that can be acquired and analysed is determined by the allowable on-chip memory for a given

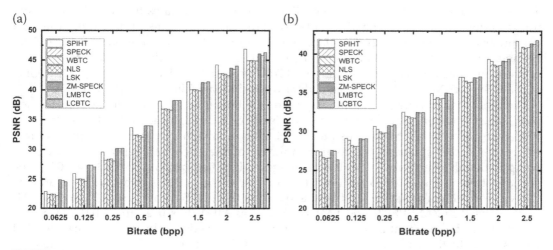

FIGURE 7.9
PSNR vs Bit Rate for Images with Size (a) 256 × 256 and (b) 1024 × 1024.

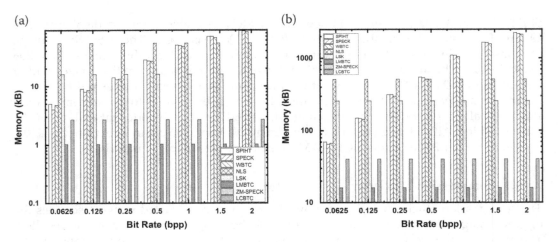

FIGURE 7.10
Memory Requirement of Image Coders at Image Sizes (a) 256 × 256 and (b) 1024 × 1024.

image codec. As a consequence, the maximum RAM for CPS nodes is 64 kB for the purpose of this chapter.

The memory requirements of different algorithms are compared to the corresponding bitrate in Figure 7.10. The memory requirements for SPIHT, SPECK, and WBTC are all dependent on the bit rate. The memory requirements of all other algorithms are constant across all bit rates because they are listless. LCBTC uses two small lists, but they are completely exploited even at very low bit rates, so they behave as though they have a fixed size for a specified image size and transform level. On the other hand, LMBTC needs less memory than LCBTC. ZM-SPECK does not need any memory since it does not use lists or state tables.

7.10.3 Computational Complexity

The time it takes to encode and decode the bitstream, determines the complexity of any image coder. The computational complexity is measured in terms of how long it takes a computer to encode and decode data. A comparison of the computational costs of state-of-the-art image coders is made. To make it a fair comparison, all of the coders were run on the same machine. On an Intel Core i5–4210U processor with a clock speed of 1.70 GHz and 8 GB of RAM, all of the image coders were simulated in MATLAB 2014.

The time it takes to transform an image plus the time it takes to encode the transformed coefficients into a bitstream is the total complexity of the image encoder. While as the time it takes to decode a bitstream plus the time it takes to take the inverse transform to obtain the reconstructed image is the total complexity of the decoder. Figure 7.11 shows the computational complexity of different image coders for image sizes 1024 × 1024. The encoder time (a) and decoder time (b) for the image coders are given separately. Conventional DWT is applied in the image coders LSK, NLS, WBTC, SPECK, and SPIHT. FrWF is used in ZM-SPECK and LMBTC. While as MFrWF is used in LCBTC. From the results, it can be seen that LCBTC outperforms all other coders. The next image coder that comes close to the encoder + decoder times of LCBTC is NLS. However, the memory requirement of NLS is way too high to be used for CPS devices.

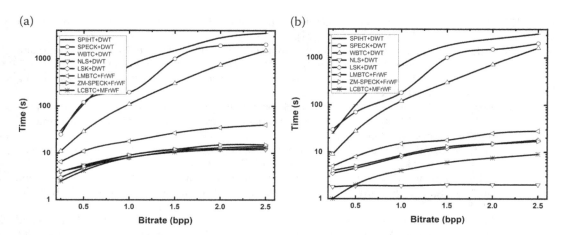

FIGURE 7.11
(a) Encoding and (b) Decoding Times of Image Coders for Image Size 1024 × 1024.

Two line graphs comparing the encoding and decoding times (seconds) with bit rates (bpp) for images with sizes 1024 x 1024. The image coders under consideration are SPIHT, SPECK, WBTC, NLS, LSK, ZM-SPECK, LMBTC, and LCBTC. The first five coders are based on conventional DWT while the last three coders are based on FrWF.

7.11 Conclusion

A detailed analysis has been presented in this chapter regarding the low-memory and low-complexity image coders for cyber-physical systems. The main parameters in consideration are the compression efficiency, memory utilization, and computational complexity. The on-chip memory of the bulk of the devices used in cyber-physical systems is limited. In this study, the image coders with on-chip RAM of 64 kB and less have been considered for a CPS. From the simulation results, it was seen that the image coders, LMBTC, ZM-SPECK, and LCBTC, are better candidates for the CPS applications. These coders not only require less memory, but also have good compression efficiency and lower computational complexity.

References

[1] Putman, "Display Technology: The Next Chapter | SMPTE Conference Publication | IEEE Xplore.". [Online]. Available: https://ieeexplore.ieee.org/document/7399644. [Accessed: 28-Jun-2021].

[2] Hilbert, M. and López, P., (Apr. 2011) "The world's technological capacity to store, communicate, and compute information". *Science (80-.), 332*, 6025, 60–65, doi: 10.1126/science.1200970.

[3] "Bernard Marr." [Online]. Available: https://www.forbes.com/sites/bernardmarr/?sh= 2e312e3e30c8. [Accessed: 28-Jun-2021].

[4] Anderson C.H., Van Essen D.C. and Olshausen B.A., (2005) "Directed visual attention and the dynamic control of information flow". *Neurobiology of Attention*, Elsevier Inc., pp. 11–17.

[5] Raichle M.E., (01-Apr-2010) "Two views of brain function". *Trends in Cognitive Sciences, 14*, 4, 180–190, doi: 10.1016/j.tics.2010.01.008.

[6] "Image quality of 4:2:2 and 4:2:0 chroma subsampling formats | IEEE Conference Publication | IEEE Xplore.". [Online]. Available: https://ieeexplore.ieee.org/document/ 5342868. [Accessed: 28-Jun-2021].

[7] Pratt, W.K., (1971) "Spatial transform coding of color images". *IEEE Trans. Commun. Technol., 19*, 6, 980–992, doi: 10.1109/TCOM.1971.1090769.

[8] Brebner, G.E. and Ritchings, R.T., (1988) "Image transform coding: A case study involving real time signal processing" *IEE Proc. E Comput. Digit. Tech., 135*, 1, 41–48, doi: 10.1049/ip-e.1988.0005.

[9] Curry, R.E., Velde, W.E.V. and Potter, J.E., (1970) "Nonlinear estimation with quantized measurements—PCM, predictive quantization, and data compression". *IEEE Trans. Inf. Theory, 16*, 2, 152–161, doi: 10.1109/TIT.1970.1054436.

[10] Tzannes, N.S., Sarantakis, A.J., Sarantakis, A.J. and Farr, E.H., (1970) "Entropy and data compression". *IEEE Trans. Inf. Theory, 16*, 1, 74–75, doi: 10.1109/TIT.1970.1054391.

[11] Huffman, D.A., (1952) "A method for the construction of minimum-redundancy codes". *Proc. IRE, 40*, 9, 1098–1101, doi: 10.1109/JRPROC.1952.273898.

[12] Langdon, G.G., (1984) "Introduction to arithmetic coding". *IBM J. Res. Dev., 28*, 2, 135–149, doi: 10.1147/rd.282.0135.

[13] Shannon, C.E., (1948) "A mathematical theory of communication". *Bell Syst. Tech. J., 27*, 4, 623–656, doi: 10.1002/j.1538-7305.1948.tb00917.x.

[14] Ahmed, N., Natarajan, T. and Rao, K.R., (1974) "Discrete cosine transform". *IEEE Trans. Comput., C–23*, 1, 90–93, doi: 10.1109/T-C.1974.223784.

[15] Wallace, G.K., (1992) "The JPEG still picture compression standard". *IEEE Trans. Consum. Electron., 38*, 1, xviii–xxxiv, doi: 10.1109/30.125072.

[16] Mallat, S.G., (1989) "A theory for multiresolution signal decomposition: The wavelet representation". *IEEE Trans. Pattern Anal. Mach. Intell., 11*, 7, 674–693, doi: 10.1109/34.192463.

[17] Vetterli, M. and Herley, C., (1992) "Wavelets and filter banks: Theory and design". *IEEE Trans. Signal Process, 40*, 9, 2207–2232, doi: 10.1109/78.157221.

[18] Hou, X.S., Liu, G.Z. and Zou, Y.Y., (2003) "Embedded quadtree-based image compression in DCT domain". *ICASSP, IEEE International Conference on Acoustics, Speech and Signal Processing - Proceedings, 3*, 277–280, doi: 10.1109/icassp.2003.1199226.

[19] Song, H.S. and Cho, N.I., (2009) "DCT-based embedded image compression with a new coefficient sorting method". *IEEE Signal Process. Lett., 16*, 5, 410–413, doi: 10.1109/LSP.2 009.2016010.

[20] "ISO – ISO/IEC 15444-1:2019 - Information technology — JPEG 2000 image coding system — Part 1: Core coding system". [Online]. Available: https://www.iso.org/standard/78321. html. [Accessed: 28-Jun-2021].

[21] Taubman, D., (Jul. 2000) "High performance scalable image compression with EBCOT". *IEEE Trans. Image Process, 9*, 7, 1158–1170, doi: 10.1109/83.847830.

[22] Belyaev, E., Liu, K., Gabbouj, M. and Li, Y., (Aug. 2015) "An efficient adaptive binary range coder and its VLSI architecture". *IEEE Trans. Circuits Syst. Video Technol., 25*, 8, 1435–1446, doi: 10.1109/TCSVT.2014.2372291.

[23] Liu, K., Zhou, Y., Song Li, Y. and Ma, J.F., (Jun. 2010) "A high performance MQ encoder architecture in JPEG2000,". *Integr. VLSI J., 43*, 3, 305–317, doi: 10.1016/j.vlsi.2010.01.001.

[24] Shapiro, J.M., (1993) "Embedded image coding using zerotrees of wavelet coefficients". *IEEE Trans. Signal Process, 41*, 12, 3445–3462, doi: 10.1109/78.258085.

[25] Said, A. and Pearlman, W.A., (1996) "A new, fast, and efficient image codec based on set partitioning in hierarchical trees". *IEEE Trans. Circuits Syst. Video Technol.*, 6, 3, 243–250, doi: 10.1109/76.499834.

[26] Pearlman, W.A., Islam, A., Nagaraj, N. and Said, A., (Nov. 2004) "Efficient, low-complexity image coding with a set-partitioning embedded block coder". *IEEE Trans. Circuits Syst. Video Technol.*, 14, 11, 1219–1235, doi: 10.1109/TCSVT.2004.835150.

[27] Islam, A. and Pearlman, W.A., (1998) "Embedded and efficient low-complexity hierarchical image coder". *Visual Communications and Image Processing '99*, 3653, 294–305, doi: 10.111 7/12.334677.

[28] Chrysafis, C., Said, A., Drukarev, A., Islam, A. and Pearlman, W.A. (2000) "SBHP-a low complexity wavelet coder". In *ICASSP, IEEE International Conference on Acoustics, Speech and Signal Processing - Proceedings*, 4, 2035–2038, doi: 10.1109/ICASSP.2000.859233.

[29] Shih-Ta, H., "Embedded image coding using zeroblocks of sub-band/wavelet coefficients and context modeling". *Proceedings DCC 2001. Data Compression Conference*, 83–92, 10.1109/ DCC.2001.917139.

[30] Wheeler, F.W. and Pearlman, W.A., (2000) "SPIHT image compression without lists". *ICASSP, IEEE International Conference on Acoustics, Speech and Signal Processing - Proceedings*, 4, 2047–2050, doi: 10.1109/ICASSP.2000.859236.

[31] Chew, L.W., Ang, L.M. and Seng, K.P., (2008) "New virtual SPIHT tree structures for very low memory strip-based image compression". *IEEE Signal Process. Lett.*, 15, 389–392, doi: 10.1109/LSP.2008.920515.

[32] Chew, L.W., Chia, W.C., Ang, L.M. and Seng, K.P., (Jan. 2009) "Very low-memory wavelet compression architecture using strip-based processing for implementation in wireless sensor networks". *Eurasip J. Embed. Syst.*, 2009, 16, doi: 10.1155/2009/479281.

[33] ZainEldin, H., Elhosseini, M.A. and Ali, H.A., (Nov. 2016) "A modified listless strip based SPIHT for wireless multimedia sensor networks". *Comput. Electr. Eng.*, 56, 519–532, doi: 10.1 016/j.compeleceng.2015.10.001.

[34] Moinuddin, A.A., Khan, E. and Ghanbari, M., (2008) "Efficient algorithm for very low bit rate embedded image coding". *IET Image Process*, 2, 2, 59, doi: 10.1049/iet-ipr:20070162.

[35] Senapati, R.K., Pati, U.C. and Mahapatra, K.K., (Dec. 2012) "Listless block-tree set partitioning algorithm for very low bit rate embedded image compression". *AEU – Int. J. Electron. Commun.*, 66, 12, 985–995, doi: 10.1016/j.aeue.2012.05.001.

[36] Corsonello, P., Perri, S., Staino, G., Lanuzza, M. and Cocorullo, G., (Jan. 2006) "Low bit rate image compression core for onboard space applications". *IEEE Trans. Circuits Syst. Video Technol.*, 16, 1, 114–128, doi: 10.1109/TCSVT.2005.856925.

[37] Cheng, C.C., Tseng, P.C. and Chen, L.G., (Feb. 2009) "Multimode embedded compression codec engine for power-aware video coding system". *IEEE Trans. Circuits Syst. Video Technol.*, 19, 2, 141–150, doi: 10.1109/TCSVT.2008.2009250.

[38] Fry, T.W. and Hauck, S.A., (Sep. 2005) "SPIHT image compression on FPGAs". *IEEE Trans. Circuits Syst. Video Technol.*, 15, 9, 1138–1147, doi: 10.1109/TCSVT.2005.852625.

[39] Jin, Y. and Lee, H.J., (2012) "A block-based pass-parallel SPIHT algorithm". *IEEE Trans. Circuits Syst. Video Technol.*, 22, 7, 1064–1075, doi: 10.1109/TCSVT.2012.2189793.

[40] Kim, S., Lee, D., Kim, J.S. and Lee, H.J., (Mar. 2016) "A High-Throughput Hardware Design of a One-Dimensional SPIHT Algorithm". *IEEE Trans. Multimed.*, 18, 3, 392–404, doi: 10.11 09/TMM.2015.2514196.

[41] Latte, M.V., Ayachit, N.H. and Deshpande, D.K., (Nov. 2006) "Reduced memory listless speck image compression". *Digit. Signal Process. A Rev. J.*, 16, 6, 817–824, doi: 10.1016/ j.dsp.2006.06.001.

[42] Kidwai, N.R., Khan, E. and Reisslein, M., (Apr. 2016) "ZM-SPECK: A fast and memoryless image coder for multimedia sensor networks". *IEEE Sens. J.*, 16, 8, 2575–2587, doi: 10.1109/ JSEN.2016.2519600.

[43] Lone, M.R. and Hakim, N. ud D., (2018) "FPGA implementation of a low-power and area-efficient state-table-based compression algorithm for DSLR cameras,". *Turkish J. Electr. Eng. Comput. Sci.*, *26*, 6, 2927–2942, doi: 10.3906/elk-1804-208.

[44] Tausif, M., Kidwai, N.R., Khan, E. and Reisslein, M., (Nov. 2015) "FrWF-based LMBTC: Memory-efficient image coding for visual sensors". *IEEE Sens. J.*, *15*, 11, 6218–6228, doi: 10.1109/JSEN.2015.2456332.

[45] Rein, S., Lehmann, S. and Gühmann, C. (2008) "Fractional wavelet filter for camera sensor node with external flash and extremely little RAM". *MOBIMEDIA 2008 – 4th International ICST Mobile Multimedia Communications Conference*, doi: 10.4108/ICST.MOBIMEDIA2008.4026.

[46] Lone, M.R. and Khan, E., (Dec. 2020) "Low-complexity block tree image coder for visual sensor networks". *IET Image Process*, *14*, 16, doi: 10.1049/iet-ipr.2020.0124.

[47] Tausif, M., Khan, E., Hasan, M. and Reisslein, M., (2019) "SMFrWF: Segmented modified fractional wavelet filter: Fast low-memory discrete wavelet transform (DWT)". *IEEE Access*, *7*, 84448–84467, doi: 10.1109/ACCESS.2019.2924490.

8

Novel Encryption Framework: HEA for IoT and Fog Network Data Transmission

Sameer Farooq and Priyanka Chawla
Lovely Professional University

8.1 Introduction

Cloud computing is a novel approach of computing based on demand, where the administrator shares data, processing, and storage resources with other cloud users via the Internet. This model is enabled worldwide on-appetite shared pool access of organized computing resources. Users and enterprises are provided with cloud computing and storage solutions having various capabilities like storing and processing their data in third-party data centers. Cloud computing provides cloud users and enterprises the ability to store and process their data inside data centers of some other third party. Cloud computing is aimed to be next-generation computing where users will move their data and resources from old client-server architecture to giant cloud architecture. Nowadays, the growing area is cloud computing in distributed computing in which adaptable services are delivered on-demand dynamically through hardware and software virtualization over the Internet. Leasing and releasing resource flexibility are the most significant advantages in cloud computing as per the user requirement. Furthermore, the two types of plans offered by the cloud service provider, namely on-demand short-term plan and long-term preservation plan, also make it attractive. The intelligent infrastructure, transparency, scalability, monitoring, and security also makes it the users' choice as shown in Figure 8.1.

The cloud user who is going to use the cloud services can pay per usage. He/she has the option to choose plans and services as per his/her need. The more significant advantage of the cloud is that the user who will use the cloud has neither to install any software nor to do any data analytics on his local system; everything will be done by the cloud service provider and these resources in the backend. Transparently, the storage, retrieval, and sharing with other users is offered by these cloud providers to their clients. The responsibilities of the cloud user are only installation and maintenance of hardware, and the rest of the jobs like storing, retrieval of data, or computational analytics of data are done by the cloud itself in remote data storing and data processing centers. The application stack of higher levels and administration sharing and customer responsibility remain intact.

DOI: 10.1201/9781003202752-8

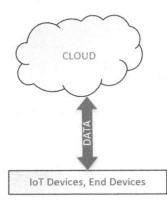

FIGURE 8.1
Cloud and IoT Architecture.

The key characteristics that are exhibited by cloud computing and that make it more exciting and attractive are:

- On-demand service
- Resource pooling
- Rapid elasticity
- Pay as you go
- Homogeneity
- Low-cost software
- Virtualization
- Advanced security

Recent rapid growth in pervasive mobile devices and cloud computing, which the Internet witnessed in past decades, motivated the researchers to focus on these radical changes. Today, lots of research is going on in mobile computing that bridges mobile devices with the cloud. The researchers try to effectively offload complex computational tasks from less-powered mobile devices to the cloud, where they can be executed rapidly. The centralized conventional cloud computing is facing several barriers, some of which include the following:

- High communication latency
- Low spectral efficiency
- Non-adaptive machine-type communication

The growing network of IoT devices generate enormous amounts of data and handling of this data is becoming resource exorbitant and challenging to transmit over networks. Another issue is the frequent unpredictable network latency, especially in mobile computing environments; this cloud computing cannot meet the precise privacy and security requirements in geographically constrained and latency-sensitive applications. It is motivated to solve conventional centralized computing and meet the new challenges of emerging technology: the "Internet of Things." IoT is the solution to shift the function of centralized cloud computing towards edge devices of the network. Until now, we have had three types of edge computing technologies:

- Fog computing
- Mobile edge computing
- Cloudlets

Internet of Things, or IoT, refers to the network of physical objects accessed through the Internet that contains embedded technology to sense or interact with their internal states or external environment. Thus, IoT is a network of billions and billions of electronic devices interacting and communicating with each other, which produces vast amounts of data related to real-world objects. The features of IoT include:

- Ultra-large-scale network of things
- Device and network-level heterogeneity
- The large number of events generated by these services

These features of IoT make the development of services and applications for it an arduous and daunting task. The vast amount of data generated by IoT devices needs to be handled for analytics and processing regularly. In order to handle this vast repository of data, there is only one solution, and that is big data. Big data may be the solution. However, data transmission for analytics or processing to the cloud via networks will require enormous bandwidth, whose availability is logically impractical. In order to solve this problem, the recent effort includes fogging and edge computing. All the noisy data is removed, and processing is done at these edges to minimize the data sent to the cloud.

Cloud computing with IoT forms the future Internet network, consisting of all types of heterogeneous devices interconnected for data transmission, storing, and processing. The future networks became wireless day by day. The cables are being replaced with wireless hotspots and chips. The IoT primarily consists of wireless devices. The broadcasting nature and remote environment add more to its vulnerabilities. The IoT mainly consists of sensors and other low-powered devices distributed in remote locations.

Similarly, cloud computing also has infrastructure distributed remotely. IoT devices like sensors have constraints that include low-powered CPUs, low battery capacity, and small storage capabilities. All of this makes data stored or generated by these devices prone to security risks. Encryption is the best possible mean that may avoid risks or threats related to data. Nevertheless, encryption still has issues like complexity, resource consumption, and feasibility. The traditional encryption algorithms are not feasible when dealing with IoT, fog, and cloud networks, as they are more resource-sensitive. Whether it is the cloud or IoT, both require such encryption algorithms that are less complex, less resource consumable, but more secure.

The size of ciphertext generated is directly related to battery consumption as the processing of each bit consumes energy. Therefore, if we reduce the size of generated ciphertext, we are eventually reducing the battery consumption. Not only battery saving but less ciphertext means less requirement of memory that is good when it comes to data saving or data transmission in IoT or cloud networks. Another factor is the execution time of the algorithm in CPU, and more execution time means more battery drainage. Therefore, if we reduce the execution time of encryption and decryption, we are reducing processing time and saving battery consumption. Many cryptosystems and algorithms were proposed to achieve security parameters like confidentiality, integrity, and authenticity. All of them work well, but they face the issue when they have to deal with IoT and cloud networks are they are resource-sensitive networks. The cryptosystems are of two types: asymmetric and symmetric. The symmetric is also known as private key cryptosystems because they use the same key for encryption and decryption. At the same time, the asymmetric is also known as public-key cryptosystems because they use public and private keys for encryption and decryption, respectively. Both types of crypto algorithms are pros and cons; for example, symmetric algorithms are cost-effective and provide reasonable security for data protection, but the problem is key sharing (sharing the secret key). The asymmetric algorithms overcome this key sharing problem as there is no requirement of the secured channel, but they are too resource costly, complex, and slow.

In the cloud and IoT, all the devices are on a public network of mostly the broadcasting type. Any person, whether user or non-user, can access the network. Therefore, all the devices, services, and resources are under threat of malicious attack. Thus, there is the requirement of such a security framework that is less complex, less resource cost-effective, fast but more secure when it comes to security parameters. The solution to this problem is to use the hybrid cryptosystem to merge the pros of both asymmetric and symmetric cryptosystems and remove the cons of both. This also traps the cryptanalyst as it adds more confusion in cryptanalysis. It also balances the complexity, resource utilization, and execution time. The hashing with MD5 (Message-Digest 5) is done [1]. MD5 produces fixed size 128-bit (16-byte) hash code. MD5 is a widely used hash in all cryptosystems. In the proposed system, the algorithm inherits the attributes of ECC-128 (Elliptic-Curve Cryptography-128) bit and AES-128 (Advanced Encryption Standard-128). The proposed system includes an encryption phase and a decryption phase. The data is enciphered or deciphered with both symmetric, AES-128 bit and asymmetric, ECC-128-bit algorithms in both phases. MD5 hashing is used for integrity checks.

8.1.1 Issues and Challenges

Regarding the current issues and challenges that we face with newly emerged cloud, fog, and mobile computing technologies, it includes issues and challenges in the security of data and security of the network. The security of data includes security of it while:

- Data is in rest (Cloud Data Centers)
- Data in transit (Cloud Network)
- Data in processing (Cloud Application)

The network's security includes preventing any intrusion or hacktivism activity on the cloud network while data centers are connected with the external world via the Internet. It includes preserving integrity, confidentiality, and availability of data while data is moving inside the network. The other network issues that we face in the cloud network include delays in data transmission between IoT devices and cloud servers. The requirement of the enormous amount of bandwidth of the backbone network that moves data to cloud servers from IoT devices is another issue. Another issue is in the case of storing data generated by IoT devices. The challenge is the requirement of huge data storage capacity, which could save billions of bytes of data generated from IoT devices worldwide. The last but not least issue is who will access data stored in cloud data centers and how to authenticate the actual user and prevent fraudulent ones. In order to solve all these issues, we are proposing a novel framework that can solve all these issues (Figure 8.2).

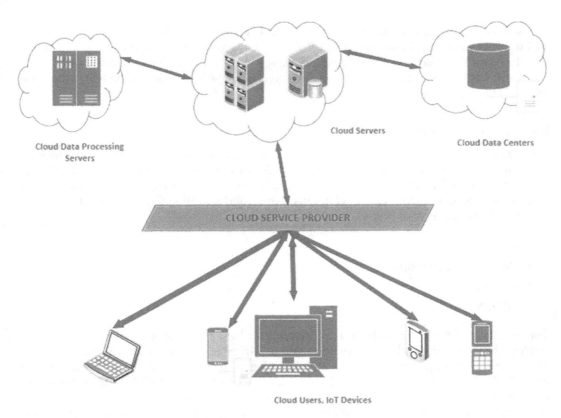

FIGURE 8.2
Cloud and IoT Framework.

There are both security and privacy issues in cloud computing because cybercriminals can target the data stored inside cloud data centers at any time, and security may be compromised. This is not a myth; this happened many times. The best example is the leakage of confidential e-files of NSA related to U.S. wars. Another issue is, another person may use the cloud storage space that a user previously used for their private data after closing the service user account of the former. The latter may scan the memory to retrieve the previous data.

The solution to all of these security and privacy issues is only encryption of information. The person who will use the cloud for their data storage or processing should never send unencrypted data to the cloud; rather, the data must be encrypted as soon as it leaves the user's system. The challenges we face in the cloud are also related to connecting IoT devices with the cloud. The following challenges that we face after merging of the cloud with the IoT are:

- Latency
- Bandwidth
- Data volume

In order to send the huge amount of unprocessed data to the cloud generated by IoT devices, it will consume a lot of bandwidth, which may eventually not be possible at all times. Imagine the data generated by 50 billion IoT devices, each with data, and sending this unprocessed data to the cloud for analytics. How much bandwidth will it consume? Another problem that it will create is the latency in communication, and storage of these huge amounts of data is not possible. Therefore, the question is can we do better than the cloud? The answer is YES, and it is FOG.

8.1.2 Fog Computing

CISCO introduced the fog concept. It is also known as fogging or fog computing. The idea of the fog is to extend cloud services near IoT devices (edges). The main aim of the fog is to solve the problem faced by IoT devices during data processing or data transmission. The fog acts as an intermediate level between the cloud and the IoT devices as depicted in Figure 8.3. As we already know, the IoT devices vary in:

- Bandwidth
- Processing capabilities
- Memory
- Energy

The handling of huge amounts of data for analytics and processing is not possible on IoT devices. We have to send it further to the cloud. In order to cope with the data security issues and challenges of the cloud and IoT, fog is the best solution. Fog computing bridges the IoT with the existing computer infrastructure. It will distribute networking, storage, advanced computing, and management services closer to the end systems along the continuum from the cloud to the end user's devices. The fog computing offers many key advantages desired by today's application, such as:

- Real-time processing
- Rapid and affordable scaling
- Local content and resource pooling

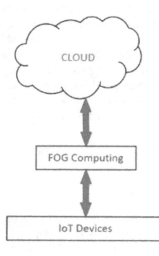

FIGURE 8.3
Fog and Middleware between IoT and Cloud.

The applications that we are using currently and the new upcoming ones that demand fog computing services in order to overcome the existing security issues and the challenges are the following:

- Connected or autopilot vehicles
- WSN and actuator networks
- Smart grids, smart home, smart cities
- Connected manufacturing
- Connected oil and gas
- Mobile health care

It is being estimated that 40% of world data will alone come from sensors by 2020, and 90% of world data will only be generated only during the last two years, which is 2.5 quintillion bytes of data per day. According to another estimation, the total expenditure on IoT devices will be $1.7 trillion by 2020. The inability of the current cloud model to handle the requirements of IoT gave birth to fog computing. In fog computing, the cloud services are extended near the IoT devices through the fog. The data generated by the IoT devices are processed in the fog before it is sent to the cloud. This reduces latency, saves bandwidth, and saves storage of the cloud.

The issue that we are facing in fog computing today is the security of data. At the same time, it is being transmitted from IoT devices to fog systems via a local area network (LAN). The data may be compromised while in transmission from IoT devices to fog nodes or while it is stored in, the cloud and thus whole security framework of the cloud system may go in vain. To address these issues, we are proposing the "novel hybrid encryption framework" for data encryption, mutual authentication, and access control of data that is generated by IoT devices, then sent via the network, and stored in the cloud.

8.1.3 Motivation for Research

Data security is the hotspot area of research in cloud computing because data is the most important entity that organizations may have. The future generations of computer networks that will be IoT, Bigdata, Cloud computing, Block chain technology, and AI will be integrated into one platform. Therefore, the administration of the whole network that includes handling communication delays and moving a huge bulk of data from IoT devices to the cloud for data analytics will be cumbersome. Moreover, solving difficult tasks is an interesting motivation for research.

Another problem is the increase in day-by-day attacks on data by cybercriminals, which uses different tactics to compromise data security, making it troublesome to secure data, particularly when dealing with small IoT devices like sensors. Moreover, we know it is impossible to implement complex data security algorithms on low-powered IoT devices like sensors due to limited storage and battery power. Thus, there is a need for a small-sized but powerful encryption algorithm that can stand with security attacks. Developing a proper framework to guard the system is like a challenge. Thus, this challenge is another motivation for the research.

The main motivation for researching this field is the growth of information systems in day-to-day business and commerce applications. The business giants like Amazon, Google, Flipkart, etc. all are moving their data and services into the cloud. The other organizations, both governmental and non-governmental, are also moving from paper-based systems towards digitalization, moving their data and services into the cloud (e.g., Digital India). Therefore, we have to go too far in cloud research areas like security, load balancing, resource utilization, etc. It will be more economically beneficial for organizations and users. The paper is organized into different sections, viz, introduction, literature review, proposed system, simulation results, and conclusion.

8.2 Literature Review

The IoT cloud network mainly consists of low resource devices with limited memory size, low-power backups, and low-performance processors, so using traditional algorithms for data protection and security is not a good option. The algorithm should be less complex and generating limited size ciphertext, as the processing of each bit consumes battery power, memory storage, and CPU cycles. The key size and ciphertext should be reduced by Faye et al. in [2]. So many cryptographic algorithms were proposed, but none of them truly suits the network that consists of resource constraint devices like IoT cloud networks.

Ren et al. [3] proposed the hybrid algorithm; the algorithm uses the DES algorithm to encrypt the given plain text. The keys of this DES are encrypted via the RSA algorithm. The DES algorithm is efficient among block encryption algorithms, and the RSA algorithm is known for better key management. However, the algorithm inherits weakness due to the low-security level of DES and RSA. The RSA is susceptible to prime factorization attacks.

Subasree et al. [4] proposed an encryption algorithm that uses the ECC encryption algorithm to encrypt plain text. For integrity checks, the MD5 algorithm is used. The DUAL_RSA algorithm is used to encipher the hash values generated with MD5. After that, these hash values, together with ciphertext, are transmitted to the receiver. The asymmetric algorithms ECC and DUAL RSA make it too complex, thus too slow and more prone to processing in resource-limited networks.

Zhu et al. [5] proposed a hybrid encryption algorithm; the algorithm uses AES to encrypt plain text. The key and digital signature used by the algorithm are protected with the asymmetric encryption algorithm. The algorithm suffers a low-security level due to single-phase encryption of a message with a single key that yields less complexity.

Dubal et al. [6] proposed the encryption architecture that encrypts plain text with the DUAL RSA algorithm. The key used by the DUAL RSA algorithm is generated with the ECDH key generation algorithm. For more authentication, the ECDSA algorithm is used to generate a digital signature. The MD5 hashing algorithm is used for hash value generation of encrypted text. The generated digital signature, hash code along with cipher text, is sent to the destination. The asymmetric algorithms used like ECDSA, ECDH, and DUAL RSA increase complexity, making the algorithm slow and more resource consumable.

Kumar et al. [7] proposed a hybrid algorithm for data encryption. The algorithm uses the AES encryption algorithm to encrypt plain text. The generated ciphertext is again encrypted with the ECC encryption algorithm to make it more secure from cryptanalysis. For integrity, MD5 algorithm is used. The ciphertext is sent to the destination along with generated hash values. The algorithm is too secure; but, in addition, complex, as it uses two asymmetric algorithms in serial to encrypt data, so resource utilization and execution time is too much. Another issue is that if a private key is disclosed during transmission, the attacker can decrypt the message easily.

Rawya Rizik et al. [8] proposed a hybrid encryption algorithm. The algorithm divides the plain text into two equal parts. The algorithm later uses AES to encrypt one part and DUAL RSA to encrypt another part. The key used by AES is encrypted with ECC. For integrity checks, the MD5 algorithm is used. The algorithm traps the intruder by making it more difficult to do cryptanalysis. The proposed system is complex, too, as it uses DUAL RSA, ECC, and AES. Another problem is that DUAL RSA inherits weakness of prime factorization attack.

Nur Afifah et al. [9] proposed a 3D-AES algorithm to protect cloud data. The algorithm 3D-AES is a block cipher algorithm. The algorithm has a rotating function that performs key mixing operations with iterating round functions. The issue is sharing the private key with the destination (server). Another issue is data decryption on the destination (server), which is later sent to various clients; the attacker may access the message while transmitting it to the client.

The cloud security alliance (CSA) [10] has given rise to seven security dangers to cloud information stockpiling: abuse of distributed computing, weak application programming interfaces (APIs), vindictive substance insider, shared innovation security issues, data spillage, record or administration getting to/by an ill-conceived client, and so forth.

Louai et al. [11], Singh et al. [12], and Yu et al. [13] have distinguished numerous issues, escape clauses, and attacks to information's security, respectability, and secrecy over the cloud information stockpiling. The attacks contemplated incorporate denial of service (DOS) assaults, cloud malware infusion assaults, side channel attacks because of shared foundation, verification attacks, and man-in-the-middle attacks.

Yu et al. [13] have said that information uprightness can be found out by the just SSL convention during transmission.

Karthik et al. [14] have recommended another half-and-half calculation utilizing some notable cryptographic calculations in a positive cluster, to upgrade and advance cloud information security.

Li et al. [15] have introduced a mixture encryption calculation that contains a straightforward encryption calculation, which improved to the Vigenere encryption calculation; and at last, came out with a half-and-half encryption calculation with a Base64 encoding calculation. The proposed half-and-half encryption calculation essentially improved the information insurance.

Tweney et al. [16] have referenced an occurrence, back in 2007, from the finish of CSP Salesforce.com, which sent a letter to every one of its great many supporters illustrating how the client messages, locations, and rest points of interest had been taken by cybercriminals.

Authors in [17–21] have featured the weakness of the information security in the cloud, one of the significant elements confining the development of distributed computing and assessed the dangers to security and protection of cloud information warehousing.

Divya et al. [22] have proposed a protected distributed storage calculation utilizing elliptic bend cryptography. The proposed work additionally focuses on online alert strategy, which shows the information proprietor when an assailant endeavors to change the information or any misbehavior occurs during information sending.

Kumar et al. [23] have explored elliptic bend cryptography (ECC) encryption method specifically utilized for securing cloud information documents, which confirm the genuine client and decline the information getting to by naughty programmer or cloud capacity supplier.

Fu et al. [24] have zeroed in on safe information cancellation on the record frameworks. The report proposed a document framework, which supports secure erasure of information. This paper proposed the possibility of mystery code text-strategy quality-based encryption procedure (CP-ABE), which supports fine-grained admittance strategy to scramble documents.

Tan et al. [25] have proposed a cloud information security calculation utilizing completely homomorphic encryption to guarantee information insurance during both during transmission furthermore, capacity. The full homomorphic encryption calculation can measure the encoded information also.

Sinha et al. [26] has thought about the working of two topsy-turvy key encryption calculation among RSA and ECC tentatively; and inferred that ECC performs better in numerous regards required key sizes, data transmission saving, encryption time, little gadget's effectiveness, just as security when contrasted with RSA calculation.

Authors in [27,28] have executed six most utilized symmetric key encryption calculations: DES, 3DES, AES (Rijndael), Blowfish, RC2, and RC6 what's more, correlation was directed dependent on a few boundaries. The report closed that the AES calculation is cutthroat with the remainder of calculation on being quick and adaptable.

Marshall et al. [29] have planned a half-breed encryption model by utilizing RSA and AES calculations to guarantee cloud information insurance. Since only the client possesses the private key, the data will not be readable to anyone who does not has private key and hence data may be preserved.

Tripathi et al. [30] have given a relative work between two notable uneven encryption calculations between elliptic bend cryptography and the RSA cryptography calculation in regard of the cloud data security parameter. The paper erupted with exploratory outcomes, which demonstrate the predominance of elliptic bend–based public key cryptography contrasted with RSA public key cryptography.

Mohamed et al. [31] have recommended Amazon EC2 cloud clients, to should utilize an AES symmetric calculation, which guarantees the most noteworthy security with least an ideal opportunity to code. Dinadayalan et al. [32] have proposed all the essential information security issues and their answers.

From the above-proposed system, it is clear there is a need for such a system that should be less complex, more secure, and resource-efficient.

8.3 Proposed Methodology

The proposed framework consists of IoT devices that generate data. This generated data is not stored locally due to various constraints of IoT devices. Instead, it is sent to the cloud for storage via the fog system. The stored data can be accessed by its owner or by any authorized user after verifying various validation parameters properly. The data generated by IoT devices is not sent to cloud in plain text form. Instead, the devices that generate it before it leaves it encrypt it. The IoT devices using the proposed algorithm to provide higher efficiency and higher security encrypt the data. If any time a user wants to access the data, he/she can decrypt it using the proposed decryption algorithm.

The proposed framework utilizes the novel technique for encryption and decryption. The algorithm is using both asymmetric and symmetric cryptosystems. This method avoids disadvantages of both provides higher efficacy with minimization of disadvantages of both. The algorithms work in parallel phases. This reduces overall time consumption by the system. The proposed framework consists of the following sections:

Section I: Encryption phase
Section II: Decryption phase

8.3.1 Section I: Encryption Phase

In this phase, the data "*Pi*," which is in plain text, is converted into binary equivalents. After that, the data is arranged into 128-bit sized "*n*" blocks. The blocks are then divided into two sets: "*Set A*" and "*Set B*," each of which consists of an equal number of blocks. If it is a fraction, then padding bits are appended in the end block to make it 128-bit size.

The first set of blocks, *Set A* that consists of *Bi* (1: n/2) blocks, is encrypted with an ECC encryption algorithm. ECC requires less memory. The keys used by it are also less in size than other algorithms [33]. Asymmetric ECC needs more power than symmetric algorithms, but using it with AES balances this consumption [34]. Using AES and ECC jointly, we save power consumption with a 25% and 20% increase in speed for encryption and decryption, respectively [35].

$$\text{Bi} = \sum_{i=1}^{n/2} (Pi)\ 1 \le i \le \frac{n}{2} \tag{12.1}$$

After this, the ciphertext "*Xi*" is generated from the first *Set A* "*Bi*" using the *ECC_Encryption()* function and key "*K*" that is generated in the ECDH algorithm.

$$Xi = ECC\_Encryption(Bi, K) \tag{12.2}$$

Another encryption phase is performed in parallel to save execution time and improve security uses the symmetric algorithm AES. This phase encrypts the remaining *Set B* "*bi*" using *AES_Encryption()*; function and key "*k*" generated in the ECDH_AES algorithm.

$$\text{bi} = \sum_{i=\frac{n}{2}+1}^{n} (Pi)\quad \frac{n}{2} + 1 \le i \le n \tag{12.3}$$

$$xi = AES\_Encryption(bi, k) \tag{12.4}$$

xi is another part of the ciphertext that is generated from *Set B'* "*bi*" blocks. For integrity checks, the MD5 algorithm is used. MD5 algorithm calculates hash codes of both Xi and xi separately. The final hash code "*H*" is obtained by concatenation to calculated hashes.

$$Qi = MD5(Ci) \tag{12.5}$$

$$qi = MD5(ci) \tag{12.6}$$

$$H = (Qi + qi) \tag{12.7}$$

The final ciphertext "*C*" results in merging the "*Xi*"+ "*xi*."

$$C = (Xi + xi) \tag{12.8}$$

After calculating C and H, both are sent to the destination side.

8.3.2 Section II: Decryption Phase

When the receiver fog system receives the encrypted data sent by the IoT device, the received ciphertext is split into "*n*" blocks, each 128-bit sized. These blocks are then divided into sets "*A*" and "*B*." Set *A* consists of "*Xi*" (1: n/2 blocks) while Set *B* consists of "*xi*" (n/2+1: n blocks). To check whether the received data is original as sent by the user, the hashing is done with the MD5 algorithm. If calculated and received hashes are the same, the data is further processed for decryption; if they are not the same, received data is discarded. In decryption, the set A "*X*" is decrypted with *ECC_Decryption()* function.

$$Xi = \sum_{i=1}^{n/2} (Ci) \quad 1 \le i \le \frac{n}{2} \tag{12.9}$$

$$Mi = ECC\_Decryption(Xi, K) \tag{12.10}$$

The remaining Set B "*xi*" that consists of n/2+1: n blocks are decrypted with *AES_Decryption()* function.

$$xi = \sum_{i=\frac{n}{2}+1}^{n} (Ci) \quad \frac{n}{2} + 1 \le i \le n \tag{12.11}$$

$$mi = AES\_decryption(xi, k) \tag{12.12}$$

The final plain text P is obtained by concatenating decrypted texts *Mi* and *mi*.

$$P = (Mi + mi) \tag{12.13}$$

8.4 Algorithms

8.4.1 Encryption Algorithms

0Input:

    P = Plain text.
    S = Block size (128-bit).
    K = Key generated via ECDH.
    k = Key generated with ECDH_AES.

Output:

    Xi = ciphertext produced with ECC.
    xi = ciphertext produced with AES.
    Qi = Hash value of first part of the cipher text.
    qi = Hash value of second part of the cipher text.

STEPS:

1. $n = P/S;$
2. $set\ i = 1;$
3. $do\{Bi = \Sigma_{i=1}^{\frac{n}{2}}(Pi)\quad 1 \le i \le \frac{n}{2}$
4. $Ci = ECC\_Encryption(Bi, K)$
5. $Qi = MD5(Ci);$
6. $i{+}{+};\ \}$ while (i<=n/2);
7. $i = (n/2 + 1)$
8. $Do\{bi = \Sigma_{i=\frac{n}{2}+1}^{n}(Pi)\quad \frac{n}{2} + 1 \le i \le n$
9. $ci = AES\_Encryption(bi, k)$
10. $qi = Md5(ci);$
11. $i{+}{+};\ \}$ while (i <= n);
12. $C = Xi + xi;$
13. $X = Qi + qi;$

8.4.2 Decryption Algorithms

Input:

S = Block size (128-bit).
Hi′ = Calculated hash of Xi.
hi′ = Calculated hash of xi.
K = Key generated via ECDH.
k = Key generated with ECDH_AES.

Output:

Mi = Decrypted text produced with ECC.
mi = Decrypted text produced with AES.
P = Plain text.

STEPS:

1. $n = C/S;$
2. $set\ i = 1;$
3. $do\{Xi = \Sigma_{i=1}^{n/2}(Ci)\quad 1 \le i \le \frac{n}{2}$
   $\quad xi = \Sigma_{i=\frac{n}{2}+1}^{n}(Ci)\quad \frac{n}{2} + 1 \le i \le n$
4. $Hi' = MD5(Xi);$
5. $hi' = Md5(xi);$
6. If (Qi = Hi′) & (qi = hi′){
7. $Mi = ECC\_Decryption(Xi, K)$
8. $i{+}{+};\ \}\}$ while (i < =n/2);
9. $i = (n/2 + 1);$
10. $do\{xi = \Sigma_{i=\frac{n}{2}+1}^{n}(Ci)\ \frac{n}{2} + 1 \le i \le n$

11. $mi = AES\_decryption(xi, \ k)$
12.   i++;}} while (i <= n);
13. $P = Mi + mi;$

8.5 Results and Discussions

The proposed algorithm is implemented in MATLAB 2016. The time for encryption, decryption, and the size of ciphertext generated is noted down and represented graphically. The generated outcomes of the algorithm are compared with the various parameters of the existing algorithms. The complexity of the algorithm is also calculated numerically. The algorithm's complexity is directly related to resource consumption and security, so it needs to be balanced. There is no good testing toolkit or simulation framework available except a few for fog computing because of the field's novelty. The existing simulation frameworks do not have modules for testing encryption and decryption. Another problem is that the cloud service providers and fog service providers do not allow external third parties to test various tools and parameters in their networks due to security concerns. MATLAB is rich with various types of external libraries and toolkits. The implementation and testing requirements for our proposed algorithm are all available in MATLAB. The MATLAB encourages advanced calculation and code development methods due to the availability of various advanced mathematical tools. The execution of the command is fast, and code can be compiled and recompiled easily from CLI or execution section. Due to all these reasons, we are using MATLAB instead of other simulation tools.

After the registration phase, if the user wants access to the cloud via fog, the fog will first authenticate the IoT device via mutual authentication; if it is genuine, it will access the key generation phase. After keys are generated successfully on both sides, the same keys are used to encrypt and decrypt the contents using a novel hybrid encryption algorithm (HEA) proposed by the author. The figures below show the graphical results obtained on MATLAB simulation.

Figure 8.4 shows the time taken by the ECC algorithm for encryption and decryption of plain text. The graph shows a gradual increase in encryption and decryption time with the increase in plain text size. However, in our case, we are dealing with the IoT devices like sensor nodes, which are sensing real-time data, which it regularly sends after frequent intervals of time. The IoT devices (nodes) encrypt data from small chunks due to limited memory capacity, processing hardware, and the need for real-time data transmission to the cloud.

Figure 8.5 shows encryption and decryption time taken by AES algorithms. The graph shows the gradual increase in encryption and decryption time, with an increase in plain text size. The graph also shows the decryption process of AES takes more time compared to its encryption time.

Figures 8.4 and 8.5 show that the ECC algorithm takes more time for encryption and decryption because it is asymmetric compared to AES, which is symmetric, thus taking less time. ECC consumes more time to consider the execution time of ECC as the total execution of the whole system. Because algorithms are running in parallel, the one that takes more time will be considered the overall system's execution time.

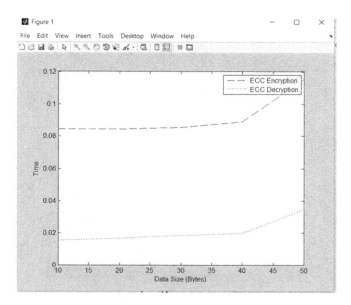

FIGURE 8.4
ECC Encryption and Decryption Time.

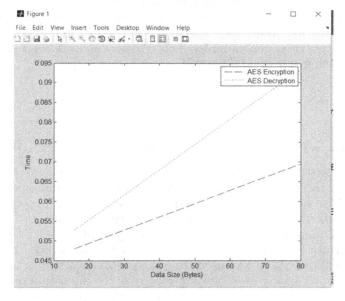

FIGURE 8.5
AES Encryption and Decryption Time.

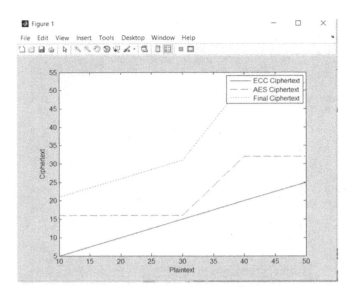

FIGURE 8.6
ECC and AES Ciphertext Size.

Figure 8.6 shows the size of ciphertext generated by the algorithms; indirectly, it shows the amount of memory that the algorithm needs for ciphertext generation. From the figure, it is clear that the ciphertext produced by the ECC algorithm is of less size as compared to the ciphertext generated by AES. When we check the final cipher text, it balances the increasing size of AES with ECC.

8.6 Comparison with Existing Algorithms

With cryptanalysis, the attacker may know about the type of encryption algorithm used by analyzing the pattern of transmitting bits to the destination. In our proposed system, we split the plain text into two equal parts, and then two different types of algorithms generate the varying type of bit pattern sequences of cipher text. This varying pattern sequence traps the intruder during cryptanalysis. The various parameters that determine the strength of any algorithm also include the two most important that is complexity and key used. In our proposed system, we use the AES-128 bit with ECC-128 bit. This increases the complexity of the algorithm numerically, so far cryptanalysis too. The keys used in our system are of different types: secret key, public key, and private key. This enhances the strength of the proposed hybrid algorithm. The dividing of data into two equal-sized parts and applying the encryption/decryption algorithm on these parts simultaneously in parallel reduces execution time and makes the algorithm swift. The hashing MD5 algorithm used for integrity checks is fast and resilient.

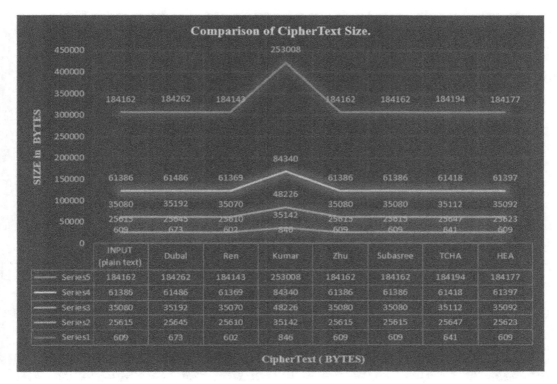

FIGURE 8.7
Comparison of Ciphertext Size.

Figure 8.7 shows the different sizes of the ciphertexts produced by the various algorithms from the different inputs of the plain text. Indirectly it shows the amount of memory that we require for the ciphertext generation. In the table, the largest size of ciphertext is produced by the "Kumar," while the smallest size is produced by the "Zhu" and is very close to our proposed system. However, when we look at the algorithm proposed by the "Zhu," it encrypts the message in the single phase that makes the message less secure, while our proposed system is more secure than the "Zhu" algorithm. Our proposed algorithm "HEA" ciphertext is very close to the ciphertext size generated by the "Zhu" algorithm.

Figure 8.8 shows the encryption time (in milliseconds) taken by the existing algorithms and our newly proposed HEA algorithm. In our system, we consider two separate processing units where these two algorithms are executed in parallel. Another thing is that the data collected by IoT devices like sensors are encrypted simultaneously and are sent after fixed intervals of time.

Figure 8.9 shows the decryption time (in milliseconds) taken by the existing systems and our newly proposed system. In our system, we are considering that there are two separate processing units where these two algorithms are executed in parallel.

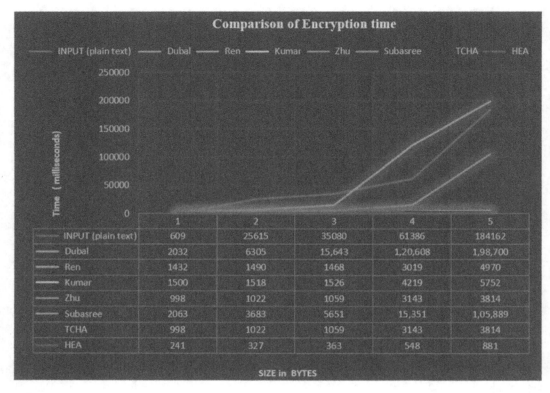

FIGURE 8.8
Comparison of Encryption Time.

The complexity of our proposed HEA algorithm for encryption will be the sum of AES and ECC encryption complexity. The complexity of the AES and ECC algorithm is $O(\log 2(n + 1) + \sqrt{n} + 4n)O(\log 2(n + 1) + \sqrt{n} + 4n)$. Similarly, the complexity for decryption will be the sum of ECC and AES decryption complexity. The complexity of the proposed system for decryption is $O(\log 2(n + 1) + \sqrt{n} + 5n)O(\log 2(n + 1) + \sqrt{n} + 5n)$.
Table 8.1 Shows the encryption and decryption complexities of various algorithms.

8.7 Conclusion

The hybrid encryption algorithm is proposed to solve the shortcomings in the existing cryptographic algorithms. The complexity, encryption-decryption time, ciphertext size, and battery consumption are the main issues in existing algorithms. The cloud-IoT network that mainly consists of low-powered devices like sensors has limited resources using the traditional algorithms is not a better choice. Using the proposed algorithm will

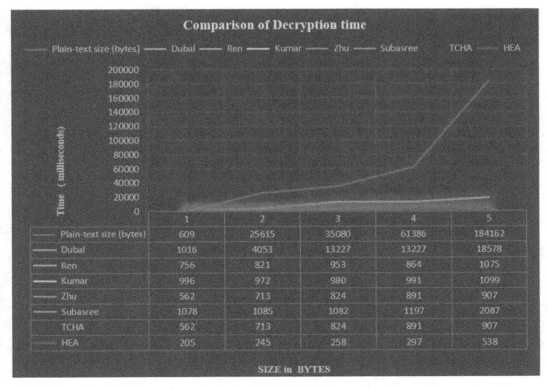

Comparison of Decryption time

	1	2	3	4	5
Plain-text size (bytes)	609	25615	35080	61386	184162
Dubal	1016	4053	13227	13227	18578
Ren	756	821	953	864	1075
Kumar	996	972	980	991	1099
Zhu	562	713	824	891	907
Subasree	1078	1085	1082	1197	2087
TCHA	562	713	824	891	907
HEA	205	245	258	297	538

SIZE in BYTES

FIGURE 8.9
Comparison of Decryption Time.

TABLE 8.1

Comparison of Algorithm Complexity

Algorithm	Encryption Complexity	Decryption Complexity
Dubal et al. [6]	$O(\log(n^2) + \log 2(n) + \sqrt{n} + 4n)$	$O(\log(2n^3) + \log 2(n) + \sqrt{n} + 4n)$
Ren et al. [3]	$O(\log(n^2) + \sqrt{n} + 4n)$	$O(\log(n^3) + \sqrt{n} + 4n)$
Kumar et al. [7]	$O(\log 2(n + 1) + \sqrt{n} + 4n)$	$O(\log 2(n + 1) + \sqrt{n} + 5n)$
Zhu et al. [5]	$O(\log 2(2n + 1) + \sqrt{n} + 4n)$	$O(\log 2(2n + 1) + \sqrt{n} + 4n)$
Subasree et al. [4]	$O(\log(n^2) + 4n)$	$O(\log(2n^3) + 4n)$
TCHA et al.	$O(\log(n^2) + \log(n) + 3n)$	$O(\log(n) + \log(2n^3) + 2n)$
HEA	$O(\log 2(n + 1) + \sqrt{n} + 4n)$	$O(\log 2(n + 1) + \sqrt{n} + 5n)$

save resource consumption and provide a good level of security. The proposed algorithm splits the plain text into two parts and then applies two different types of algorithms. This adds the pros of both symmetric algorithms and asymmetric algorithms like saving time for encryption and decryption, saving battery consumption, balancing the complexity of the overall system, etc.

References

[1] Hossain, Md.A., Islam, Md.K., Das, S.K. and Nashiry, Md.A., (2012) Cryptanalyzing of message digest algorithms MD4 and MD5. *Int. J. Cryptogr. Inf.Secure. (IJCIS) 2* (1), 1–13.

[2] Faye, S. and Myoupo, J.F., (2013) Secure and energy-efficient geocast protocols for wireless sensor networks based on a hierarchical clustered structure. *Int. J. Netw. Secure 15* (1), 121–130.

[3] Ren, W. and Miao, Z., (2010) A hybrid encryption algorithm based on DES and RSA in Bluetooth communication. In: Proceedings of the 2nd InternationalConference on Modeling, Simulation and Visualization Methods, China, pp. 221–225.

[4] Subasree, S. and Sakthivel, N.K., (2010) Design of a new security protocol using hybrid cryptography algorithms. *IJRRAS 2* (2), 95–103.

[5] Zhu, S., (2011) Research of hybrid cipher algorithm application to hydraulic information transmission. In: Proceedings of International Conference on Electronics, Communications, and Control (ICECC), China.

[6] Dubal, M.J., Mahesh, T.R. and Ghosh, P.A., (2011) Design of a new security protocol using hybrid cryptography architecture. In: Proceedings of 3rdInternational Conference on Electronics Computer Technology (ICECT), *vol. 5*, India.

[7] Kumar, N., (2012) A Secure Communication Wireless Sensor Networks Through Hybrid (AES+ECC) Algorithm, *386*, von LAP LAMBERTAcademic Publishing.

[8] R. Rizk and Y. Alkady, (2015) Two-phase hybrid cryptography algorithm for wireless sensor networks," *J. Electr. Syst. Inf. Technol.*, 2, 3, 296–313, 2015.

[9] Adnan, N.A.N. and Ariffin, S., (2018) Big data security in the web-based cloud storage system using 3D-AES block cipher cryptography algorithm. In International Conference on Soft Computing in Data Science (pp. 309–321). Springer, Singapore.

[10] Javaid, A.(2013),Top Threats to Cloud Computing published in USA: Cloud Security Alliance. Available at SSRN 2325234.

[11] Maghrabi, L.A., (2013) The Threats of Data Security Over the Cloud as Perceived by Experts and University Students. University of the West of England, Bristol, United Kingdom.

[12] Singh, A. and Shrivastava, M., (2012). Overview of attacks on cloud computing. *Int. J. Eng. Innovative Technol.* 1(4), 321–323.

[13] Yu, H.S., Gelogo, Y.E. and Kim, K.J., (2012) Securing data storage in cloud computing. *J. Secur. Eng.* 251–260.

[14] Nandakumar, K., Jain, A.K. and Pankanti, S., (2007) Fingerprint-based fuzzy vault: implementation and performance. In: *IEEE Transactions on Information Forensics and Security*, 2, 4.

[15] Li, X., Yu, L. and Wei, L., (2013) The application of hybrid encryption algorithm in software security. 978-1-4799-2860-6, IEEE.

[16] Tweney, A. and Crane, S., (2007) Trust guide: An exploration of privacy preferences in an online world. In: Expanding the Knowledge Economy Applications Case Studies. IOS Press, Amsterdam.

[17] Tang, Z., Wang, X., Jia, L., Zhang, X. and Man, W., (2012) Study on data security of cloud computing. IEEE Xplore: 978-1-4577-1964-6 © 2012 IEEE, pp. 1–3.

[18] Rong, C. and Nguyen, S.T., (2012) JaatUN, M.G.: Beyond lightning: A Survey on security challenges in cloud computing. In: Elsevier Computers and Electrical Engineering. pp. 47–54.

[19] Grobauer, B., Walloschek, T. and Stöcker Siemens, E., (2011) Understanding cloud computing vulnerabilities. *IEEE J. Comput. Reliab. Socities 9*(2), 50–57.

[20] Waleed, Al.W. and Li, C., Naji, H.A.H., (2014) The faults of data security and privacy in the cloud computing. *J. Netw. 9*(12), pp. 3313–3320.

[21] Lin, G., (2012) Research on electronic Data security strategy based on cloud computing. In: IEEE Xplore: 978-1-4577-1415-3 ©2012 IEEE, pp. 1228–1231.

[22] Divya, S.V. and Dr. Shaji R.S., (2014) Security in data forwarding through elliptic curve cryptography in cloud. In: 2014 International Conference on Control, Instrumentation, Communication and Computational Technologies (ICCICCT), 978-1-4799-4190-2 ©2014 IEEE, pp. 1083–1088.

[23] Kumar, A., Lee, B.G., Lee, H.J. and Kumari, A., (2012) Secure storage and access of data in cloud computing. ICTC 2012, IEEE Xplore: 978-1-4673-4828-7 ©2012 IEEE, pp. 336–339.

[24] Fu, Z., Cao, X., Wang, J. and Sun, X. (2014) Secure storage of data in cloud computing. In: 2014 Tenth International Conference on Intelligent Information Hiding and Multimedia Signal Processing, IEEE Xplore: 978-1-4799-5390-5 © 2014 IEEE, pp. 783–786.

[25] Tan, Y. and Wang, X., (2012) Research of cloud computing data security technology. In: IEEE Xplore: 978-1-4577-1415-3 © 2012 IEEE, pp. 2781–2783.

[26] Sinha, R., Srivastava, H.K. and Gupta, S., (2013) Performance based comparison study of rsa and elliptic curve cryptography. *Int. J. Sci. Eng. Res.* ISSN 2229–5518, 4(5), 720–725.

[27] Abdul, D.S.H., Abdul Kader, M. and Hadhoud, M.M., (2009) Performance evaluation of symmetric encryption algorithms. *J. Commun. IBIMA*, ISSN: 1943–7765, 8, 58–64.

[28] Pavithra, S. and Ramadevi, E., (2012) Performance evaluation of symmetric algorithms. *J. Global Res. Comput. Sci.* ISSN 2229-371X, 3(8), 43–45.

[29] Mahalle, V.S. and Shahade, A.K., (2014) Enhancing the data security in cloud by implementing hybrid (RSA & AES) Encryption Algorithm. IEEE 978-1-4799-7169-5 ©.

[30] Tripathi, A. and Yadav, P., (2012) Enhancing security of cloud computing using elliptic curve cryptography. *Int. J. Comput. Appl.* ISSN: 0975–8887, 57(1), pp. 26–30.

[31] Mohamed, E.M., Abdelkader, H.S. and EI-Etriby, S., (2012) Enhanced data security model for cloud computing. In: 8th International Conference on informatics and Systems (INFOS2012), pp. 12–17.

[32] Dinadayalan, P., Jegadeeswari, S. and Gnanambigai, D., (2013) Data security issues in cloud environment and solutions. In: 2014 World Congress on Computing and Communication Technologies, IEEE Xplore: 978-1-4799-2876-7 © 2013 IEEE, pp. 88–91.

[33] Kodali, R. and Sarma, N., (2013) Energy-efficient ECC encryption using ECDH. In: Emerging Research in Electronics, Computer Science and Technology, Lecture Notes in Electrical Engineering, *248*. Springer, pp. 471–478.

[34] Lenstra, A., (2001) Unbelievable security matching AES security using public-key systems. *Adv.Cryptol. ASIACRYPT 2248*, 67–86.

[35] Tillich, S. and Großschädl, J., (2005) Accelerating AES using instruction set extensions for Elliptic Curve cryptography. *Computational Science and Its Applications – ICCSA, 3481*, 665–675.

9

Security Issues and Challenges for Cyber-Physical Systems

Tanya Garg

Assistant Professor, Department of Computer Science & Engineering, Thapar Institute of Engineering & Technology, Patiala, Punjab, India

Surbhi Khullar

Department of Computer Science & Engineering, Thapar Institute of Engineering & Technology, Patiala, Punjab, India

Dr. Gurjinder Kaur

Associate Professor, Department of Computer Science & Engineering, Sant Longowal Institute of Engineering & Technology, Longowal, Punjab, India

9.1 Introduction

Cyber-physical systems are combinations of computation, physical processes, and networking. A CPS is a field of engineering which is focused on the technology related to a solid establishment in numerical abstractions [1,2]. The physical objects and the process that are controlled by the information management systems are called cyber–physical. The term cyber-physical was initially introduced in 2006 to describe the systems that unites the physical objects and the processes that exists among them [3]. The financial and cultural capability of such frameworks is immensely more prominent than what has been acknowledged, and significant speculations are being made worldwide to build up the innovation. The innovation expands on the more seasoned (yet extremely youthful) order of installed frameworks, PCs, and programming implanted in communication devices whose rule mission isn't calculation, like vehicles, toys, clinical gadgets, and logical instruments. CPS coordinates the physical process elements with the administration of product and systems giving reflections and demonstrating, plan, and identifies strategies for the incorporated entirely [1].

9.1.1 Characteristics of Cyber-Physical Systems

According to [3,4] there are various characteristics of CPSs that are mentioned below:

DOI: 10.1201/9781003202752-9

- **Advanced Correspondence and a Typical Information Climate:** Objects of CPSs play out their capacities with a serious level of reliance on one another through dynamic correspondence and trade of information and control activities.
- **Autonomy:** In spite of the way that numerous CPSs (for instance, SCADA frameworks) stay reliant upon human control, the self-rule of current arrangements and their individual parts is expanding.
- **Intellectualization:** Frameworks and their segments have an expanding level of insight due to the utilization of prescient and versatile advancements.
- **Distributed Control Place:** Mechanical modules and specialized articles in CPSs are controlled utilizing data innovation–based committed control circles.
- **Embedded Systems:** One of the most broad qualities of CPSs is that, in light of the fact that few of the PCs interfacing straightforwardly with the actual world (sensors, regulators, or actuators) perform a couple of explicit activities, they needn't bother with the overall registering force of traditional PCs—or indeed, even versatile frameworks—and in this manner they will in general have restricted assets.
- **Real-Time Systems:** To provide safety to the systems, it's very important to focus on the actual computations that take place in a particular time to ensure the integrity of the system. Cyber-physical systems provide this feature.

Cyber-physical systems (CPSs) will bring progress in the field of modern health care, traffic management, power generation, and conveyance like number of regions currently visualized. The cyber-physical systems involve connection of new, simple, physical, and human parts planned to do work by incorporated logic and physics. As demonstrated in Figure 9.1, the CPS innovations include :

- Smart technology
- Internet of Things (IoT)
- Medicines
- Transportation systems
- Manufacturing industries
- Smart appliances

Cyber-physical systems are an emerging area in research that attracted the consideration of the scholarly world, industry, and the public authority due to the wide effect CPS has on society, the economy, and the climate [5]. Despite the fact that actually deficient with regards to a proper definition, digital actual frameworks are to a great extent alluded to as the up-and-coming age of frameworks that coordinate correspondence, calculation, and control to accomplish steadiness, superior, strength, and efficiency as it identifies with actual frameworks [5]. While continuous exploration centers on accomplishing these objectives, security inside CPS is generally overlooked. Digital actual frameworks are currently being generally coordinated into different basic foundations, given the absence of countermeasures, security penetrates could have calamitous outcomes. For instance, if correspondence channels inside a force lattice are undermined, the entire force network may get flimsy, potentially causing a huge scope fell power outage. Indeed, the development of keen frameworks may additionally confuse the issue on the off chance that security isn't considered during the brilliant network development measure. Notwithstanding security

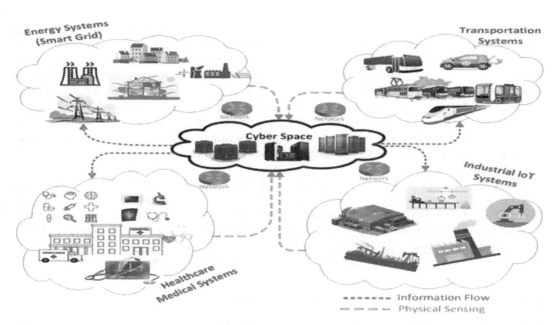

FIGURE 9.1
Applications of Cyber Physical System [2].

concerns, CPS protection is another difficult issue. Digital actual frameworks are regularly conveyed across wide geographic regions and ordinarily gather tremendous measures of data utilized for information examination and dynamic. Information assortment helps the framework settle on choices through complex AI calculations. Breaks in the information assortment cycle could prompt wide-scale information spillage, quite a bit of which is private or delicate data identified with public safety. Penetrates can happen in various stages of the system's operation, including data collection, data transmission, information activity, and information stockpiling. Most current CPS plan procedures don't think about information assurance. In this paper, we investigate digital actual frameworks from a cross-layer point of view with security in various layers being thought of. All the more critically, we will have a point-by-point conversation about the security contemplations made in current CPS structures. Through this conversation we will actually want to portray a full guide of safety needs for each layer. Unique in relation to past work that regards CPS as one substance and attempts to create security techniques for the whole framework, we distinguish the diverse security challenges present in each layer and sum up counter-measures. Risks associated with cybersecurity are pervasive in the present world, and news related to cyberattacks show up consistently in the news.

9.1.2 Cyber-Physical System Security and Privacy

The cyber-physical systems are actually the unification of two systems: embedded systems and technologies that help in communication; due to their dual nature, these systems are more vulnerable to threats. These systems require safety in terms of cybersecurity and reliability in their operations. So, it is very important to resolve the security-related issues and challenges to make the CPS reliable and secure [6].

The most crucial issue in the cyber-physical system security is the variation of the structure blocks. These systems comprise of different parts of various perspectives. There are numerous equipment parts like sensors, actuators, and inserted frameworks. Accordingly, every segment, too as their mix, can be a contributing component to a CPS attack. To understand the current security weaknesses of CPS, attacks and assurance mechanisms will give us a superior comprehension of the security stance of CPS. Thus, we ought to be capable point out the limits of CPS that make them subject to various assaults and devise ways to deal with safeguard against such attacks [7]. The intricacy of CPSs and the heterogeneity nature of CPS segments have acquainted significant difficulties with security and security assurance of the CPS. Specifically, with the complex digital actual cooperation, dangers and weaknesses become difficult to survey, and new security issues emerge. It is likewise difficult to recognize, follow, and analyze the threats, which may begin from, move between, and focus on different CPS parts. The detailed structured analysis of the weaknesses, hazards, and attacks is basic for the advancement of protection components. The review of available security and protection controls for CPS can help us to recognize incomplete pieces, weal connections, and upcoming considerations (Figure 9.2).

9.1.3 Security Overview for CPS (Cyber-Physical Systems)

Risks in the area of cybersecurity are very common these days. A number of people are being influenced by the cyberattacks. These attacks usually happens when users enter

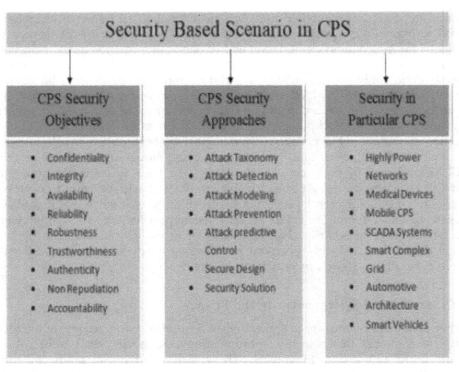

FIGURE 9.2
Security in Cyber-Physical System [4].

their information into some system for the purchase of products or online shopping, etc. by stealing their confidential information in the form of usernames and passwords. There has been very large increase in the attack of cyber-physical systems as reported by people. These types of attacks proved very harmful for the country as well as the world. Nowadays everything is actually dependent on information technology due to which people are suffering from high security threats.

Depending on the types of CPSs, the securities for the different systems have been discussed below [7]:

1. **Security in Smart Frameworks:** Satisfactory security in smart networks represents the danger of remote attacks that could bring about enormous scope power outages. Power outages could bring about security suggestions, for example, clinical hardware's breakdowns, loss of information in server farms, and surprisingly an increment in crime percentage [8].

2. **Security in ICS:** Need or shortcoming of safety in CPS could be disastrous relying upon the application. For instance, if the security of CPS utilized in an atomic plant has been undermined, an overall danger is the conceivable outcome. Besides, security infringement in smart frameworks could prompt the deficiency of administrations to the buyer and financial misfortunes to the service organization. Due to the CPS's inescapability and its wide use in the CI, CPS security is of a basic significance. Indeed, it is even recommended that ICS isn't yet fit to be associated with the Internet [9].

3. **Medical Devices Security:** Security in wearables and IMDs makes them invulnerable to attacks that may compromise patients' well-being and protection. In light of the various conditions encompassing clinical gadgets, the requirement for defining suitable security objectives emerges. Security objectives that incorporate the approved elements ought to have the option to get to precise information, recognize and configure gadgets, update programming, and keep up the gadget's accessibility; though protection objectives incorporate the assurance of private data about a gadget's presence, type, interesting ID, and patient's identification.

4. **Security for Cars:** Vehicle manufacturers seek to think of a variety of imaginative innovations that meet the requirements of their clients, providing them enhanced functionalities. Mostly, vehicles are protected through the use of a plan. Security ensures the vehicle's capability to work when there is non-suspicious occurrence. Security, then again, has not been a plan issue, but instead an extra component.

Likewise, security and well-being co-designing methodologies expect to distinguish, survey, and oversee hazards identified with reliability and protection in the structure that are influenced by both the digital and exact world. These methodologies are classified into three following categories as:

- **Security-Informed Safety Method**: These techniques work by expanding the extent of safety designing through adaptation of cybersecurity-related strategies.
- **Safety-Informed Safety Method**: These techniques involves expansion of the extent of safety designing through the adjustment of security-related strategies.
- **Combined Method (Safety & Security)**: Combined methodologies for security and network safety co-designing.

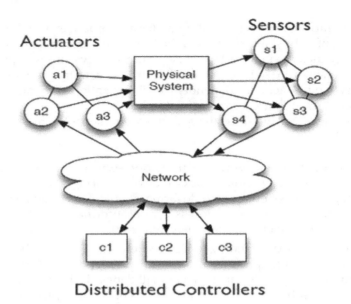

FIGURE 9.3
Architecture of Cyber-Physical System [10].

Now, let's discuss the architecture of the cyber-physical system and how it is vulnerable to various threats [10]: The term cyber-physical system (CPS) arose a little more than 10 years prior as an endeavor to bring together the basic exploration issues identified with the utilization of installed PC and correspondence innovations for the robotization of actual frameworks, including aviation, car, compound creation, common foundation, energy, medical care, producing, new materials, and transportation. CPSs are typically made out of a bunch of organized specialists communicating with the actual world; these specialists incorporate sensors, actuators, control processing units, and communication devices, as delineated in Figure 9.3.

The collapse of the apparatus that controls the physical system can lead to the destruction of environment, can affect the people around it and can harm other physical systems. So, there is need to develop and design the safety mechanisms that can help in detection of faults and can provide the tolerance that could help to protect against these above said incidents.

CPSs are at the heart of medical services gadgets, energy frameworks, weapons frameworks, and transportation management. Mechanical control systems frameworks, specifically, perform fundamental capacities in basic public foundations, like electric power dissemination, oil and gaseous petrol circulation, water and waste treatment. The interruption of these CPS could essentially affect health of people, security, and lead to enormous financial loss [10].

9.2 Types of Attacks on Cyber-Physical Systems

The CPS has an actual cycle under its influence, a bunch of sensors that report the condition of the interaction to a regulator, which thusly conveys control messages to

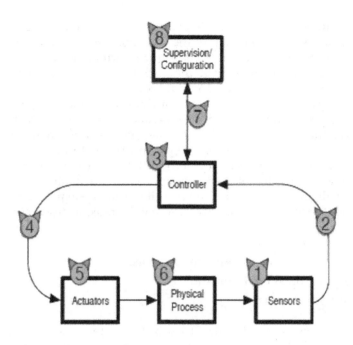

FIGURE 9.4
Attacks [11].

actuators (e.g., a valve) to keep up the framework in an ideal state. The regulator frequently speaks with an administrative and additionally setup gadget (e.g., a SCADA framework in the force matrix, or a clinical gadget developer), which can screen the framework or change the settings of the regulator. CPS attacks can occur anytime. This overall design where attacks at every point are described in Figure 9.4.

9.3 Security Issues and Challenges

A cyber-physical system is an integrated system of cyber and physical elements. It is primarily made of communication, computation, and control. The physical process is monitored and controlled by a computer over a network and in return a feedback from the physical process affects the computation. The most important aspect of the CPS is its ability to function accurately and efficiently in real time. Now a CPS can be defined as an interconnected network of embedded systems and physical input and output where the real-time data and information is exchanged and monitored.

A CPS is a systematic combination of physical process, software, and network, it has the ability to enhance scalability and usability in various areas of interest. The aerospace industry has benefitted from and revolutionised this design system in various ways. Today, power transmission units or even communication has seen major involvement of the CPS into the system. The CPS has the ability to enhance the manufacturing efficiencies by regulating the entire process and make decentralised decisions in manufacturing industries. Health care is another sector where the CPS can provide robustness and resiliency. With the help of the CPS installed at homes, it can detect illness or even study symptoms and provide the right information at the right time. Due to its security and accuracy in real time, the CPS has been used in the defence sector (like drones) to gain critical information and knowledge.

Cyber-physical systems are complex and include dynamics of control, design (both hardware and software), autonomy, networks, and Internet of Things (IoT) to enhance privacy, security, and verification. The CPS has evolved and changed the way people interact with and develop the engineering systems. But with this advancement comes a major threat to the security and privacy both in the physical and cyber dimension.

One can say when either one of the following i.e., confidentiality, integrity, availability, accountability, or all are compromised the security of the system is compromised [12]. As compared to other types of systems, CPS is more vulnerable to any security threat because

- It is heterogeneous in nature.
- It depends on a number of different elements.
- It operates in an open environment.
- It can be accessed wirelessly.

Cyber-physical systems are built with a trust in the system, its workings, and effectiveness. The purpose behind compromising the workings or the effectiveness of a system can be criminal intent or terrorism, can be political or even economical, but the loss and the after-effects can be unimaginable.

As the authors in [12] have discussed, a cyber-secure system provides

- resilience
- privacy
- protection against malicious attacks
- intrusion detection

When a system provides satisfactory results even in an unexpected or beyond a normal situation it is said to be resilient. An out-of-the-ordinary situation can be any, ranging from subsystem failure, an unanticipated input, or even the environment failure. Fault tolerance, fault detection, and adaption are ways by which a system can overcome such situations.

Privacy is simply to protect the information. As CPS works in a real-time environment, it works with real-time data and information. It is crucial for the system to protect this information from any kind of threat. Another aspect is to secure data flow during the transmission phase, the storage phase, as well as during the storage phase.

Any activity that is a deviation from the normal behaviour of a system is termed an intrusion into the system. The aim is to detect the intrusion at the right time and trigger an alert in the system in order to protect vital information. Intrusion detection also provides protection against malicious activities or attacks like back doors, denial of service attacks, and viruses.

9.3.1 Cyber-Physical System Security Issues

The CPS suffers from vulnerabilities at both the physical level and cyber level. Vulnerability is an exposed state which the attacker can easily exploit to tamper or gain unauthorized access to the information system. A CPS suffers from vulnerabilities majorly because it is heterogeneous in nature. It relies on a third party for its various components but cannot be sure of how secure these components are. When these components are integrated into the system, the security and reliability of these components is a problem. Also, at the software or the code level sometimes the code is easy to manipulate and modify or sometimes a small unhandled event results in a continuous loop [13].

Another problem is the homogeneity of various CPSs. When one of the similar CPSs is under attack, it becomes easy to exploit similar vulnerabilities in other CPSs. The communication channel might be wired or wireless and may be non-secure. Ethernet is prone to attacks like sniffing and eavesdropping, where important information might be at risk. Also, wireless channels are prone to botnet and remote access Trojan attacks.

Another vulnerable area where an attacker can take advantage is the server database. SQL injection is such an attack where it can access any server database without any authorization through injecting malicious code into it. The Stuxnet worm attack at the Iranian Nuclear Power Plant exploited such vulnerabilities [14].

As discussed earlier, a CPS consists of physical elements that are exposed easily without any security. Any unsecure physical element can be tampered or altered. One can easily modify such instruments or even install malwares to disrupt their actual functionality.

Now the vulnerabilities in a CPS can be seen in three different categories [15]:

- Network level
- Management level
- Platform level

The main aim while assessing such vulnerabilities should be to identify and then eliminate them at the right time to prevent any security attack or system failure in the near future.

9.3.2 Cyber-Physical System Threats and Attacks [16,17]

9.3.2.1 Smart Device Security

A smart device undergoes different types of security threats like:

- Boot process vulnerability
- Hardware exploitation
- Encryption and hash function
- Chip-level exploitation
- Software exploitation
- Backdoors in remote access

9.3.2.1.1 Boot Process Vulnerability

The boot process is the point from where any device starts operating; therefore, if an attacker is able to take control of this area he/she can easily control the following stages of execution. During the boot process, the different protection techniques do not execute and therefore the system can be targeted easily by an attacker. The attackers want to interrupt the execution of the normal starting process through the different susceptibility within the chain-of-trust and try to install kernel modules. Then malicious code can be inserted into the kernel modules easily [18].

9.3.2.1.2 *Hardware Exploitation*

Hardware is an easy gateway to any attack as all the security checks and protection are at the software level. Attackers look for ports left open by manufacturers or any such vulnerability that can result in timing attacks. When an attacker analyses the time taken to execute a cryptographic algorithm, they use it to compromise the cryptosystem; this is called a timing attack. An attacker studies thoroughly the time taken by the cryptographic algorithm to execute as per the input. This can lead to leakage of crucial information to the attackers.

9.3.2.1.3 *Encryption and Hash Functions*

Encryption and hash functions help to secure passwords and sensitive information. Instead of storing the passwords directly, hash functions store hash values of the password, hence providing security. Also, the hash functions help to check data integrity at the receiver end. It also helps to verify and authenticate the user for more security. These functions are difficult to exploit, but with right information-based cryptanalysis, the security of devices is threatened. One such technique is forging or producing identical values for a given message. One of the best practices to avoid encryption exploitation is to use randomness. Algorithms with a strong random number generator for secret keys are more secure than weak encryption algorithms.

9.3.2.1.4 *Software Exploitation*

Vulnerabilities at the software level in a smart device are very similar to any software vulnerability in a computing system. If any attacker knows about the existence of vulnerability in a system and is able to access it, it is very easy for him/her to exploit it. Buffer overflow is a common vulnerability at the software level. This happens when a program tries to add more data than the storage capacity of the buffer and it results in crashing the program or execution of malicious code. Integer overflow is another common example of software vulnerability that can result in huge errors if the device's decision-making ability is dependent on the calculation results.

9.3.2.2 **Hardware Security in Cyber-Physical Systems**

According to [19] the hardware level of a CPS is basically the hardware components like integrated circuits, sensors, actuators, and printed circuit boards. These form the core of the physical system of a cyber-physical system. The hardware security deals with the vulnerabilities at this level of the system. Some common attacks and vulnerabilities are

- Stealing a cryptographic key
- Stealing an identity
- Physical tampering of system elements
- Counterfeit elements with low/no security

9.3.2.2.1 *Stealing a Cryptographic Key*

As a cyber-physical system communicates over a network, it is essential to secure this communication layer. This is done with the help of encryption/decryption and a cryptographic key. It is essential to secure this key because if an attacker gains access to the key, it gives them access to the system. And one can never anticipate the destruction such an event can cause.

It is even more important to secure this key because one can never know if a key is compromised or not until it is exploited by the attacker. Therefore, it is essential to prevent theft of the key. Simple practices like not storing the key on the server or encrypting the key wherever it is stored should be kept in mind. It is also vital to protect the keys using tamper-resistant HSM (hardware security model) and also know how to respond spontaneously to any detected key compromise.

9.3.2.2.2 *Stealing an Identity*

Theft of identity is a situation when an attacker steals the ID of a device of a cyber-physical system. The attacker can easily introduce fraudulent devices into the system and launch attacks, resulting in an unsecure system.

9.3.2.2.3 *Physical Tampering of System Elements*

Sometimes a device or an element of a system can be easily modified or altered because of its vulnerability. If the attacker modifies it, it can disrupt its proper working and can result in loss and disrupt efficient functionality.

9.3.3 Security Challenges

A system as large as a cyber-physical system is required to be secure. If the guard is let down at any level i.e., cyber or physical or both, it can result in astonishing consequences. Some such challenges that are usually faced are [20]:

- Reduced performance
- Higher power consumption
- Transmission delays
- Operational security delays

The different types of vulnerabilities and threats are tabulated in Table 9.1 given below:

TABLE 9.1

Types of Vulnerabilities and Threats

Level	Exploitation Area
Perception Vulnerabilities	Malicious Data Injection
(includes vulnerabilities in sensors, smart meters)	Wormhole
	Spoofing
Transmission Vulnerabilities	DoS
(Wi-Fi, actuators)	DDoS (Smurf/Ping-of-Death)
	Eavesdropping
Application Vulnerabilities	Lack of Update patch
(Cloud computing, middleware)	Malicious Software/Malware
	Third-Party Applications

9.3.4 Strategies to Overcome Security Issues and Challenges

While designing a system, at the software or hardware level, the main aim of any designer is efficient functionality. Also, he/she tries to make it more secure so that in the future any practice does not compromise its security. There are certain ways to achieve a reliable and dependable system. The security at different levels can be achieved by different means, as shown in Table 9.2.

The security challenges in a CPS are dealt with and overcome at different levels in the system. With the combination of cyber and physical aspects of a system, it has led to certain attacks that would not occur otherwise. There are almost 90 billion attacks annually. Therefore, it is crucial as well as essential to overcome these security challenges. As suggested by authors in [20] a novel approach to overcome the issue is by combining the formal methods and the machine learning methods to overcome their individual limitations. The authors discuss how a security monitor at run-time and a security analyser during the offline process can help to provide a more secure system. It analyses the interaction history and any abnormal or anomalous behaviour to detect a threat at the right time.

Cryptographic solutions can provide reliability over the communication channel. It is necessary to protect the data or information as well as any exchange of keys. Lightweight authentication protocols, exchanging small cryptographic keys in asymmetric encryption between nodes, strong randomness in keys, and layered protection based on hash chains [21] are few advanced ways to overcome the novel attacks.

It is also important to fix any bugs at the software level. As soon as vulnerability is encountered, a patch update is essential. The Stuxnet attack on the Iranian Nuclear Power plant was fixed by a Windows patch update to avoid any such situation in the future. Intrusion detection systems and intrusion prevention systems must be designed and trained in a way that they can detect any malicious packet or even any anomaly accurately. Still, a problem with IDS is that it cannot detect zero-day attacks and the false alarm rate is relatively high.

9.3.5 Privacy Issues and Challenges

As described by NIST, privacy is "assurance that the confidentiality of and access to certain information about an entity is protected." The information can be an entity such as

TABLE 9.2

Types of Vulnerabilities and Security Solutions

Level	Security Solutions
Perception Vulnerabilities	Time stamps
(includes vulnerabilities in sensors, smart meters)	End-to-end encryption
	Advanced cryptography
Transmission Vulnerabilities	Timed packets
(Wi-Fi, actuators)	Well-trained IDS/IPS
	Next-gen firewalls
Application Vulnerabilities	Privacy preserving
(Cloud computing, middleware)	Data masking/Camouflage

As the technology evolves, it is necessary to reduce the gap between the design-time and run-time verifications [15]. It is expected of a CPS to perform efficiently under strict environments as to be available continuously without a failure.

a product, person, or machine. There is no or controlled release of information to unauthorised parties and this is how confidentiality is maintained.

The CIA triad defines the core principles of information security. CIA stands for

- Confidentiality
- Integrity
- Availability

Confidentiality is achieved by using encryption and hash functions to ensure only authorized parties can gain access to the information. In order to allow any modifications to data by only authorized personnel, it is necessary to use passwords, digital certificates, and digital signatures. Availability is when the information or assets are available at the appropriate time to the authorized parties [22].

With the advancement of digital era, it has become necessary that the information is available in a controlled manner; e.g., smart appliances, connected homes, and other smart devices collect user information, sometimes sensitive too, and without the user realizing it. Samsung Smart TV's voice activation feature collects user information even when it is not activated. Similar mishandling of data has happened and the surprising fact is that the users do not realise that their information is being collected or analysed. Sometimes this same data is leaked, which is a direct violation of user privacy. This information must be encrypted and then stored so that any such mishandling does not occur.

The most significant factor is the pace and volume at which this data is being generated. Smart appliances at home, connected homes are becoming common as the day passes. The data that is generated is collected, stored and then analysed. The problem is that this data can be correlated with other available processed data and it can trace down to an individual. This is clear violation of identity of an individual.

It is important to make this process of collecting information as transparent as possible, but due to the complex nature of a CPS, a user might not understand how the collected data will be used. The regulatory officials try to notify the public about the policies but it is not easy in the case of a system as large and interconnected as a CPS.

As the techniques evolve, it is important to pioneer new ways to enable processing the information about the parties but does not involve the individuals or their assets. The CPS privacy norms must be standardised so that the system can function efficiently without risking the privacy of an individual [23,24].

A person, system, or a component is authorized because it has a certain identity. This identity is maintained by correct credentials. These credentials are authorised by a central authority usually. But one needs to ponder how to maintain and authorise identities accurately if the CPS system is distributed. Therefore, it is vital to maintain a secure authorization process, communication channel, and identity management system over a distributed cyber physical system.

9.4 CPS Deployment Challenges

The various security and privacy issues, along with the challenges, have been discussed in this chapter; now, the overall challenges for the deployment of cyber-physical systems will be discussed below [25]:

1. **Availability:** Availability is related to the services provided by a system when it fails in its operations and continues with normal execution. If cyber-physical systems have to be used for emergency situations like in an area of medical services or in security-related systems, then it needs to be available all the time to handle exceptions if they occur. No delay should be there; the attacks that have been discussed so far can threaten the security of the CPS, which could lead to loss of privacy of the systems using them.

2. **Maintainability:** Cyber-physical systems are very complex so they need to be maintained. Maintainability is related to the servicing of a system in the situation of failure. The system is said to be highly maintainable if it has the capability to handle every kind of failure that exists in a short time duration at minimal expense without affecting the performance of other components. Some components need to be replaced during the maintenance task.

3. **Resilience:** It is the capability of the system to adapt themselves to the changes that occur during any kind of error that takes place during the normal operation of system. A system with the capability of being resilient should detect the errors and failures as early as possible so that later on the system will not be affected anymore. In cyber-physical systems, due to the use of sensors, there are many chances for node failures, which are very difficult to analyse at the beginning.

4. **Safety:** The system is considered to be safe if it does not have any threats or vulnerabilities. Moreover, it should be capable of tackling every threat to be safe while in operation. The system should ensure the safety so that no one can face any issues of data or privacy loss. In the CPS, the system is vulnerable to the number of threats due to a wireless infrastructure that endangers its safety.

5. **Sustainability:** It is the capability of a system to provide the services as long as it can and that means it is related to the life of the system during which it seamlessly provides services to the users. The system that is said to have sustainability should have durability, safety, and resiliency. It is the most challenging issue for the implementation of a CPS, as the systems can lead to early failure due to higher security threats.

9.5 Conclusions and Future Scope

A cyber-physical system is a very popular research area these days, with a variety of applications. It is actually the integration of the two systems: cyber systems and physical systems. Many challenges need to be faced for the deployment of a CPS. The main components of a CPS are sensors, actuators, computing, and processing devices. We have discussed the various aspects related to the privacy and security of a CPS in this chapter and the solutions to overcome these issues have also been elaborated. The issues that are faced while deploying the CPS have also been addressed. There are various future research areas in which work needs to be carried out as a CPS is new and the latest technology. The work to protect a CPS from various threats using cryptographic techniques is open for researchers. The deployment can become easy and failure-free by proposing solutions to different challenges that are faced by current CPSs. More work needs to be carried out in the field of security of CPSs to protect them from cyberattacks.

References

[1] An article on CPS. Available at https://ptolemy.berkeley.edu/projects/cps.

[2] Rehmani, M. H., and Chen, J., (2018) "Differential Privacy Techniques for Cyber Physical Systems: A Survey", IEEE Communications Surveys & Tutorials, 22(1), 746–789.

[3] Zegzhda, D.P., Vasil'ev, Y.S. and Poltavtseva, M.A., (2018) "Approaches to Modeling the Security of Cyberphysical Systems,". *Autom. Control Comput. Sci.*, *52*, 8, 1000–1009, doi: 10.3103/S014641161808031X.

[4] Yang, L.T., Wang, W., Perez, G.M. and Susilo, W., (2019) "Security, privacy, and trust for cyberphysical-social systems". *Secur. Commun. Networks*, *2019* 10.1155/2019/2964673.

[5] Wurm, J., *et al.*, (2017) "Introduction to cyber-physical system security: A cross-layer perspective". *IEEE Trans. Multi-Scale Comput. Syst.*, *3*, 3, 215–227, doi: 10.1109/TMSCS.2016.25 69446.

[6] Kavallieratos, G., Katsikas, S. and Gkioulos, V., (2020) "Cybersecurity and safety co-engineering of cyberphysical systems – A comprehensive survey,". *Futur. Internet*, *12*, 4, 1–17, doi: 10.3390/FI12040065.

[7] Humayed, A., Lin, J., Li, F. and Luo, B., (2017) "Cyber-physical systems security – A survey". *arXiv*, *4*, 6, 1802–1831.

[8] Powering Business Worldwide Eaton. (2014) Power Outage Annual Report: Blackout Tracker. [Online]. Available: http://www.eaton.com/blackouttracker.

[9] Chen, D., Kalra, S., Irwin, D., Shenoy, P. and Albrecht, J., (Sep. 2015) "Preventing occupancy detection from smart meters,". *IEEE Trans. Smart Grid*, *6*, 5, 2426–2434.

[10] Amin S., Cárdenas A.A. and Sastry S.S., (2009) "Safe and secure networked control systems underdenial-of-service attacks,". In *International Workshop on Hybrid Systems: Computation and Control*, Springer, 31–45.

[11] Krotofil, M., Cardenas, A., Larsen, J. and Gollmann, D., (2014) "Vulnerabilities of cyberphysical systems to stale data?determining the optimal time to launch attacks,". *Int. J. Crit. Infrastruct. Protection*, *7*, 4, 213–232.

[12] Wang, E.K., Ye, Y., Xu, X., Yiu, S.M., Hui, L.C.K. and Chow, K.P. (2010) "Security issues and challenges for cyber physical system,". *Proc. – 2010 IEEE/ACM Int. Conf. Green Comput. Commun. GreenCom 2010, 2010 IEEE/ACM Int. Conf. Cyber, Phys. Soc. Comput. CPSCom 2010*, 733–738, doi: 10.1109/GreenCom-CPSCom.2010.36.

[13] Rasim Alguliyev, L.S. and Imamverdiyev, Y. (2018) "Robust, secure, and cost-effective design for cyber-physical systems". *Sci. Direct*, 0–3.

[14] Khaitan, S.K. and McCalley, J.D., (2015) "Design techniques and applications of cyberphysical systems: A survey,". *IEEE Syst. J.*, *9*, 2, 350–365, doi: 10.1109/JSYST.2014.2322503.

[15] Rubio-Hernan, J., Rodolfo-Mejias, J. and Garcia-Alfaro, J., (2017) "Security of cyber-physical systems from theory to testbeds and validation,". *Lect. Notes Comput. Sci. (including Subser. Lect. Notes Artif. Intell. Lect. Notes Bioinformatics)*, *10166*, LNCS, 3–18, doi: 10.1007/978-3-319-61437-3_1.

[16] Fernandez, E.B., (2016) "Preventing and unifying threats in cyberphysical systems,". *Proc. IEEE Int. Symp. High Assur. Syst. Eng.*, *2016-March*, 292–293, doi: 10.1109/HASE.2016.50.

[17] Rasim Alguliyev, L.S. and Imamverdiyev, Y., (2018) "Cyber-physical systems security,". *Sci. Direct*, *1*, 1–47.

[18] Fouda, R.M., (2018) "Feature article: Security vulnerabilities of cyberphysical unmanned aircraft systems,". *IEEE Aerosp. Electron. Syst. Mag.*, *33*, 9, 4–17, doi: 10.1109/MAES.2018.1 70021.

[19] Ahmed, C.M. and Zhou, J., (2020) "Challenges and opportunities in cyberphysical systems security: A physics-based perspective". *IEEE Secur. Priv.*, *18*, 6, 14–22, doi: 10.1109/MSEC.2 020.3002851.

[20] Aigner, A. and Khelil, A., (2020) "An effective semantic security metric for industrial cyber-physical systems". *Proc. – 2020 IEEE Conf. Ind. Cyberphysical Syst. ICPS 2020, 100*, 87–92, doi: 10.1109/ICPS48405.2020.9274710.

[21] Albrekht, Y. and Pysarenko, A. (2020) "Multimodular cyberphysical systems: Challenges and existing solutions". *ATIT 2020 – Proc. 2020 2nd IEEE Int. Conf. Adv. Trends Inf. Theory*, 376–379, doi: 10.1109/ATIT50783.2020.9349291.

[22] Singh S., Yadav N. and Chuarasia P.K. (2020) "A review on cyber physical system attacks: Issues and challenges". *Proc. 2020 IEEE Int. Conf. Commun. Signal Process. ICCSP 2020, 2*, 1133–1138. doi: 10.1109/ICCSP48568.2020.9182452.

[23] Fink, G.A., Edgar, T.W., Rice, T.R., MacDonald, D.G. and Crawford, C.E. (2017) "Overview of security and privacy in cyber-physical systems". *Secur. Priv. Cyber-Physi. Syst.*, 1–23, doi: 10.1002/9781119226079.ch1.

[24] Ashibani, Y. and Mahmoud, Q.H. (2017) "Cyber physical systems security: Analysis, challenges and solutions". *Comput. Secur.*, *68*, 81–97, doi: 10.1016/j.cose.2017.04.005.

[25] Lokesh, M.R., Kumaraswamy, Y.S. and Tejaswini, K.N., (2016) "Challenges and current solutions of cyber physical systems". *IOSR J. Comput. Eng.*, *18*, 2, 104–110, doi: 10.9790/0661-1821104110.

10

Security Vulnerabilities of Cyber-physical Systems: Autonomous Vehicles Perspective

Faisal Rasheed Lone
Baba Ghulam Shah Badshah University, Rajouri, J&K;
National Institute of Technology, Jalandhar, Punjab

Harsh Kumar Verma and Krishna Pal Sharma
National Institute of Technology, Jalandhar, Punjab

10.1 Introduction

Cyber-physical-integrated systems (CPS) refer to complex, multi-disciplined embedded computing devices integrated with the physical world [1]. It is embedded computers and networks that track the physical processes, almost always using feedback loops to affect the computations [2]. CPS unifies previously disparate fields such as embedded systems, control theory, and mechatronics. Cyber-physical systems are the product of the convergence of computational and physical processes; a CPS employs computer hardware, software and communication networks, and communicates with the physical process being performed to enhance its capabilities significantly.

Computing is used to strengthen and improve the effectiveness of typical physical systems in the CPS. The technology is interdisciplinary, encompassing embedded systems, computers, and communications. The code is embedded in devices whose primary objective is not computing alone, such as automobiles, medical devices, research tools, and intelligent transportation systems [3]. There are plenty of examples of CPSs in our daily life. We have cleaning robots; smart lighting systems; and intelligent heating, ventilation, and air conditioning (or HVAC) systems. Automobiles, planes, motorized scooters, Segways, and electric bicycles are examples of cyber-physical systems from the transportation perspective. CPSs are diverse entities that include physical devices and software, sensors and actuation, and devices for the cyber realm. As demonstrated in Figure 10.1, Computation, communication, and control can help the CPS perform its tasks in the real world. Because the CPS comprises both cyber and physical components, it is referred to as a cyber-physical system. The CPS is based on an embedded information processing computer system in a product such as a car, plane, or other devices to achieve a specified goal [4] .

The CPS and IoT are usually confused with being the same, whereas both have distinct origins. The CPS has its roots in the systems engineering and control domain. IoT stems

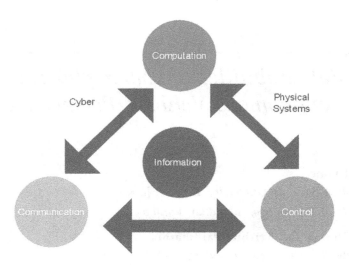

FIGURE 10.1
3Cs of Cyber-physical Systems.

from the networking and information technology paradigm to extend the digital environment to the physical entities. The CPS comprises mainly three parts, a cyber part for computations, a physical that can be controlled, and the network part to facilitate communication [5].

A cyber-physical system is a collection of computational elements that work cooperatively to control physical entities. It occurs when mechanical and electrical systems are connected via software components. They manage logistics and production systems independently by leveraging shared knowledge and information from processes [6].

The term Internet of Things *encompasses various aspects related to the idea of the extension of the Internet and the Web into the physical world, such as the ubiquitous distribution of devices embedded with sensors and/actuators* [7]. The general architecture of CPS is demonstrated in Figure 10.2.

CPS expands the perspective to include the many benefits of a more informed and intelligent planet, which allows for multidimensional optimization and cooperation. This chapter highlights the application domains of the CPS in Section II, characteristics of the CPS in Section III, challenges of the CPS in Section IV, security requirements, and possible attacks and their countermeasures in autonomous vehicles in Section V and Section VI finally concludes the chapter.

10.2 CPS Application Domains

With the evolutions of the CPS, the application domains of the CPS have grown considerably, ranging from manufacturing, health care, intelligent transportation, agriculture, and smart grids, to name a few. This section provides an overview of the application of the CPS. The core application domains of CPS are demonstrated in Figure 10.3.

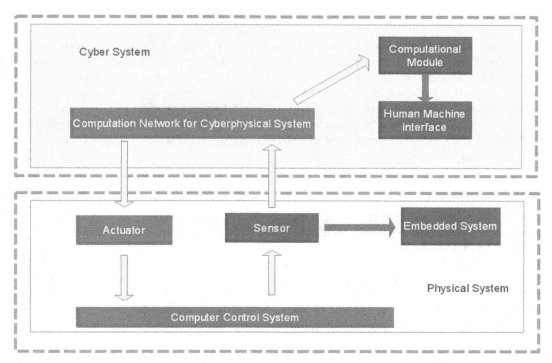

FIGURE 10.2
General Architecture of a Cyber-physical System.

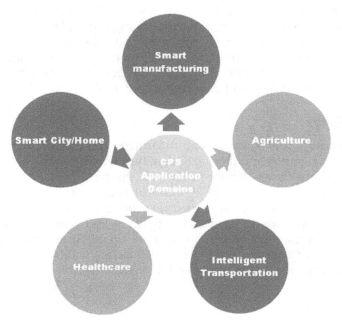

FIGURE 10.3
CPS Applications Domains.

10.2.1 Smart Manufacturing

The term *smart manufacturing* means using embedded software and hardware technologies to maximize efficiency in producing products and services [1]. The CPS is a critical technology for smart manufacturing to be realized. The CPS is used in the manufacturing setting for self-measuring and controlling the manufacturing process. The CPS can enhance manufacturing processes by communicating the information between machines, the network, supply chain, businesses, systems, and customers. Due to mass production, domestic and foreign marketing, and economic development, smart manufacturing is one of the leading CPS technology domains.

10.2.2 Agriculture

The CPS plays a significant role in helping with overall food production and efficiency by applying new techniques like precision agriculture, smart water management, and expanded food availability. The system is based on an adaptive method that considers various parameters, including temperature, humidity, irrigation, and light. The CPS's required response depends upon the values of the received parameters to ensure optimal conditions. The CPS can provide pest control in agricultural fields, reducing the cost of such purposes [8]. The deployment of the CPS in agriculture has the potential to bridge the increasing food supply-demand gap.

10.2.3 Intelligent Transportation

Through advanced sensing, communication, computation, and control technologies, intelligent transportation can significantly improve safety, throughput, coordination, and services in traffic management. Essential advancements in electronics and communication technology are encompassed in an intelligent transportation system (ITS). It offers numerous technological advances such as incorporating a high level of electronic devices, operation, improved traffic efficiency, and a lower fatality rate by avoiding accidents. With the inclusion of CPS infrastructures, travel time can be shortened without any reductions in the possibility of traffic flow and V2V communication to conserve energy, emissions, collision avoidance, and countless safety applications [1].

10.2.4 Health Care

The CPS plays a critical role in the healthcare industry. This research category focuses on intelligent sensor systems for monitoring patient health in real-time, telemedicine systems that enable virtual healthcare services to benefit the health industry. Integrating computing and control mechanisms with the critical health data communicated is a prerequisite for designing high-confidence medical cyber-physical systems resulting in more effective treatments for elderly or disabled patients and reduces hospitalization. The future Cyber-physical medical systems should be capable of extensive data integration and access, exhaustive data acquisition and evaluation, real-time visual analytics, and plug-and-play functionality with interoperable medical devices.

10.2.5 Smart City/Home

The term *smart city* encompasses innovative transportation, environmental regulation, medical care, commerce, business, and industry [9]. The purpose of a smart home, a smart building, and a smart city are to enable comfortable living spaces. Not only do intelligent cities improve public safety in particular, but they also implement smart transportation to alleviate congestion.

The greenhouse effect is a significant issue in today's world. We can achieve the zero net energy goal by integrating wireless sensor networks, cognition managers, and control systems.

10.3 CPS Characteristics

The primary objective of the CPS is to integrate the physical and the cyber world. The CPS is an amalgamation of the physical processes/elements and cyber components. CPSs are vastly different from traditional control systems due to the cyber aspect for control and flexibility.

10.3.1 Complexity/Heterogeneity/Interoperability

CPSs are complex, owing to the unique nature of their constituents. CPSs are equipped with embedded systems capable of generating, communicating, and analyzing massive amounts of data about ongoing activities CPSs are by nature heterogeneous because of the complexity of their constituent technologies and their underlying computational elements, command, and controls.

Interoperability issues in the CPS arise due to data management from I/O devices, sensors, and actuators. Standardization is critical for interoperability, as components must communicate with one another [10]. The heterogeneity of the multitude of devices involved in a CPS gives rise to the inherent complexity. The system's complexity and heterogeneity necessitate the proper encapsulation of devices [11,12].

10.3.2 Flexibility and Modularity

Flexibility is the capability of a CPS to be modified and reconfigured to accommodate different customer demands and changes. Modularity allows a CPS to be flexible and adapt to ever-changing customer requirements. Modularity is considered to be one of the key enablers of a CPS. As per [13], CPS components should be plug and play to achieve modularity and flexibility to be adaptable.

10.3.3 Realtime

The ability of a CPS to analyze and detect any change in the environment determines its real-time capability. It is a crucial characteristic as it enables a CPS to ascertain any change in the operating environment and react immediately to ensure safety and failure; e.g., in vehicles with ADAS (advanced driver assistance system), sensors such as radars and cameras are used to obtain information about the environment for the driver to take action or for automated action.

10.3.4 Intelligent

CPSs impart intelligence to the physical systems by empowering them with communication and computation capability. The ability to sense events and make decisions accordingly determine the intelligence of a CPS [14]. CPSs should be intelligent enough to gather information using sensors to analyze the information collected, enabling them to make smart decisions in real time and adapt to changing conditions by controlling the physical components.

10.4 Challenges in a CPS

CPSs have brought about a revolution in how we interact with the physical world, but it does come with its fair share of challenges. To make CPS fully reliable and trustable, we need to focus our attention on these next-generation systems. CPSs have tremendous market potential, but various difficulties facing CPSs must be resolved to realize such potential. The challenges faced by a CPS range from social to technical. Social challenges involve the fear of security, loss of privacy, lack of trust, among a few. Technical challenges concern issues such as interoperability, heterogeneity, dependability, maintainability, and more. The challenges are broadly visualized in Figure 10.4.

10.4.1 Security

Security refers to the protection of resources against unauthorized access and illegal tampering or disclosure of information. A mechanism of protecting the system against illicit actions should be in place. With the increase in penetration of a CPS, they are

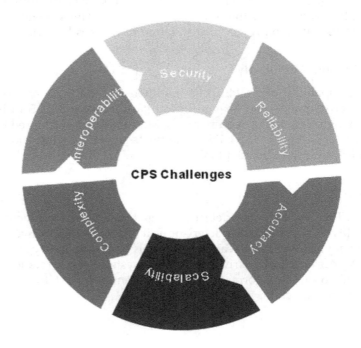

FIGURE 10.4
CPS Challenges.

becoming more and more vulnerable to security threats relating to integrity, confidentiality, availability, and authenticity. Offering system protection and resolving security threats is one of the prime research issues in a CPS. Integration of large-scale networks (Internet) and insecure communication protocols alleviate the security threats to the CPS.

10.4.2 Complexity

CPSs are composed of heterogeneous elements communicating with each other and generating enormous amounts of data. The physical dynamics, computational elements, control logic, and deployment of diverse communication technologies render CPSs inherently heterogeneous. Future CPSs are expected to provide component autonomy, joint coordination, real-time guarantee, and highly customized configurations far more capable and complex than today's. Managing the complexity of these competent and heterogeneous systems should be incorporated as a design consideration [5].

10.4.3 Scalability

The ability of a system to behave and function appropriately in case of a change in size and magnitude is known as scalability. In general, CPSs may comprise thousands of embedded computers, sensors, and mechanisms that must be calibrated and connected to work well together. Entities of a highly scalable system should be able to join or leave the network dynamically. For achieving maximum performance, a highly scalable system should incorporate load balancing mechanisms and efficient communication protocols .

10.4.4 Interoperability

Interoperability is defined as the capability of the system to connect for information exchange and service provision. Interoperability issues in the CPS arise due to data management from I/O devices, sensors, and actuators. Standardization is critical for interoperability, as components must communicate effectively and efficiently [10]. The heterogeneity arising due to the multitude of devices involved in a CPS gives rise to the inherent complexity. A system deficient in interoperability leads to inaccurate output, which can be fatal in safety-critical applications.

10.4.5 Reliability

Reliability determines the degree of dependability of a system to perform the required operations without any intervention. A reliable and dependable system should perform necessary functions and deliver essential services without performance deterioration. Ensuring reliability is an extremely tough challenge considering the scale of heterogeneous elements comprising a system.

10.4.6 Accuracy

The correlation of the observed output of a system with the actual output determines the accuracy of a system. A system with high accuracy should generate output as close to expected as possible. High accuracy of a system is of vital importance in time and safety-critical applications such as ADAS (advanced driver assistance systems), where an untimely and inaccurate output may lead to disastrous consequences.

10.5 Autonomous Vehicles as Cyber-physical Systems

Vehicular adhoc networks (VANETs) have, over the years, transformed into the Internet of vehicles (IoV) which in turn are evolving into the Internet of autonomous vehicles (IoAV) [15]. IoAV aspires to enable self-driving vehicles and intelligent infrastructure without human intervention. However, as the number of connected vehicles grows, the demand for autonomous decision making increases proportionately [16].

Modern vehicles are equipped with a variety of driver assistance features. To categorize such automobiles with varying degrees of autonomy in a consistent manner, SAE (the Society of Automotive Engineers) suggested creating six levels of autonomy for the J3016 specification [2]. The higher degree of automation brings with it increased security risks. An autonomous vehicle can be viewed as a subset of a CPS and a variant of the Internet of Things (IoT) system, as it's implemented using a highly interconnected array of embedded subsystems. CPSs, such as autonomous vehicles, make lives much more manageable by reducing human involvement. That being said, the major hurdles to widespread autonomic vehicle use in our daily lives is public acceptance and trust in autonomous machines/vehicles [17]. The Figure 10.5 demonstrates the intra-vechicle and V2X communication scenario.

Satellite navigation, adaptive cruise control, and anti-lock braking systems (ABS), and park assist systems are well-known examples of automation technology integrated into modern automobiles. Autonomous vehicles are becoming more and more mainstream due to advancements in fields such as robotics and AI. Data is collected from many sensors, including but not limited to image sensors, LIDAR, GPS, proximity sensors, etc. The data so collected is processed and analyzed to enhance the travelling experience by improving safety and providing real-time traffic information and entertainment services. Autonomous vehicles are posed to replace human drivers with enhanced decision making and driving finesse [18]. AVs have the potential to change the transportation paradigm completely. AVs, once deployed, are expected to improve safety, traffic management, and reduce fatalities due to human drive errors .

Machine learning and other related technologies are at the forefront of deployment to detect and interpret sensor data at the local level for decision making. These technologies are progressing to make vehicles fully autonomous, making us increasingly dependent on such technologies.

AVs have their share of safety and security challenges. A failure or an attack on certain components may lead to disastrous consequences [19]. For example, an attack on adaptive cruise control may lead to increased vehicle speed leading to fatal accidents. A connected vehicle consists of various sensors, data from which is collected and analyzed for further action. The Onboard Unit (OBU) processes information from these sensors and provides connectivity to the outside world for V2X communication. As a result, the vehicle is susceptible to intra-vehicle and inter-vehicle attacks. For example, an attack or failure of the GPS module may lead to wrong location information among nearby vehicles, causing unnecessary traffic congestion and crashes [20]. Safety and security are critical aspects of an AV, as any safety or security issue may lead to fatal consequences [21]. This section will focus on the security requirements and attacks on autonomous vehicles.

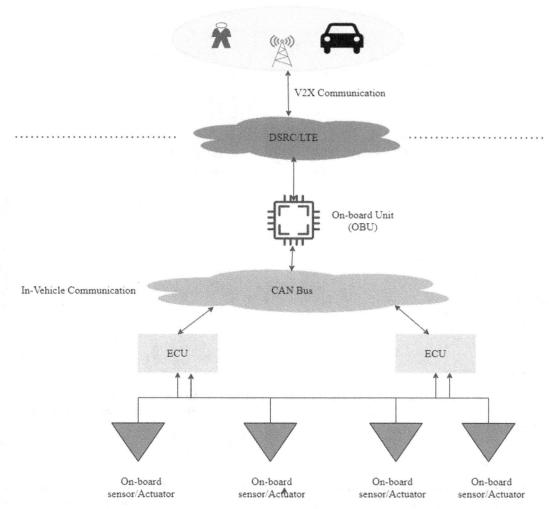

FIGURE 10.5
Intra-vehicle and V2X Communication Scenario.

10.5.1 Security Requirements, Possible Attacks, and Counter Measures

The importance of security requirements depends on inherent network characteristics. The security requirements of AVs have been highlighted as [22–24] and demonstrated in Figure 10.6:

10.5.1.1 Confidentiality

Confidentiality protocols are in place to guard against unauthorized access to sensitive information. Unauthorized users should not have access to the exchanged data.

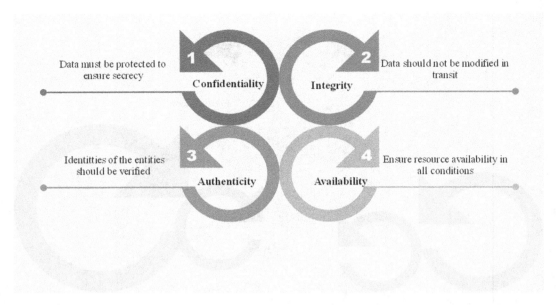

Data must be protected to ensure secrecy
1 Confidentiality

2 Integrity
Data should not be modified in transit

Identitties of the entities should be verified
3 Authenticity

4 Availability
Ensure resource availability in all conditions

FIGURE 10.6
Security Requirements.

10.5.1.2 Integrity

The data exchanged between communicating parties should not be tampered with or modified. The data should maintain its integrity, consistency, and reliability over the entire cycle.

10.5.1.3 Authenticity

Authenticity involves authenticating the source and location of the data transmitted to prevent communication with fake identities. A malicious user posing as a legitimate one can lead to undesired consequences.

10.5.1.4 Availability

Availability implies that the information must be available consistently in real time to the authorized users of the network.

Ongoing research mainly focuses on security issues in traditional connected vehicles, whereas researchers need to focus their attention on AVs for effective deployment of such technologies. Security countermeasures available for connected vehicles apply to AVs, but there has been less attention to evaluating their effectiveness in AVs. Secure intra-vehicle and V2X communication are critical for ensuring effective functionality and deployment of AVs.

Intra-vehicle attacks target on-board components such as sensors used to measure parameters such as location, speed, proximity, etc. The attackers can penetrate and compromise on-board components to gain control of the vehicle. Intra-vehicle attacks include attacks on ADAS (advanced driver-assistance systems) like adaptive cruise control, electronic steering, and ABS and GPS sensor to provide wrong location coordinates. The connections between the controller network (CAN Bus) and ECU (electronic control unit), ECU, and the actuators can also be compromised. A V2X communication network is also susceptible to attacks wherein adversaries can compromise information exchange between every entity a vehicle can communicate with due to an open wireless channel.

The malicious users may be internal or external, active or passive, or independent and cooperative. Internal attackers are authenticated members of the network, whereas external attackers are non-authenticated members. Active attackers disturb the network in real time, whereas passive attackers continuously eavesdrop on network communication to launch an attack later after gaining valuable information from the captured data.

The security threats affecting AVs involve attacks on different security requirements. Due to the severity of the challenges involved, this section discusses various attacks and their countermeasures on various security requirements.

10.5.2 Attacks on Confidentiality

Confidentiality is a vital component in ensuring the privacy of the users in the network. AVs exchange confidential information such as location, route information, etc. The pervasive Internet connectivity, autonomy, and massive information exchange among AVs and the network render them highly susceptible to such attacks [25]. Various examples of attacks on confidentiality and respective countermeasures are as follows.

10.5.2.1 Passive Eavesdropping

Eavesdropping or passive eavesdropping falls in the passive category of attacks. It is a covert attack that involves sniffing network information to gather as much information about the network as possible [26]. The information collected is used to carry out other attacks by analyzing patterns in network data.

Secure credential management systems [27] and implementing secure information exchange can be used to prevent such attacks [28].

10.5.3 Attacks on Authenticity

Authenticity enables network entities to protect themselves from communicating with unauthorized intruders. This security requirement makes sure that the communicating network entities are genuine by using authentication mechanisms. A weak authentication protocol can render the network susceptible to unauthorized users leading to devastating consequences. Cryptographic mechanisms are deployed to authenticate members of a network. Various attacks on authenticity and their countermeasures are discussed as follows.

10.5.3.1 Sybil Attack

A Sybil attacker fakes multiple identities [29] to transmit fake messages within the network. The network is flooded with counterfeit messages making the receivers believe in the information received from multiple identities. A robust authentication mechanism [30] can be used to prevent such attacks. A radar-based scheme [31] for the physical detection of a vehicle for validating information was proposed. An event-based reputation scheme [32] for the detection of Sybil attacks was proposed. Counterfeit Sybil messages and identities are detected by analyzing trust and reputation values. In a consensus-based scheme [33], the receiver determines the validity of the received beacons based on the distance and transmission range of the sending neighbours to generate a trust score.

10.5.3.2 GPS Spoofing Attack

Malicious vehicles can generate and inject false location information by spoofing GPS using GPS simulators that produce a stronger signal than the actual GPS module. This attack can be used to deceive a vehicle and neighbours about its location. A plausibility check-based solution [34] proposed help mitigate such attacks by adapting to changing traffic and road conditions. Dead reckoning based solution [35] estimates the current position using the previous position, speed, and direction to mitigate GPS spoofing attacks.

10.5.3.3 Masquerading Attack

In a masquerading attack, the attacker uses a forged identity by exploiting a legitimate one to access the network. A malicious vehicle may disguise itself as a legitimate vehicle for propagating false messages within the network. A genetic framework [36] is proposed to prevent a masquerading attack. A genetic feeder acts between vehicles and RSU to transmit parameters such as packet information and vehicle information for calculating the fitness function. The packet drop ratio is reduced considerably.

10.5.3.4 Timing Attacks

Timing of the transmitted messages is of utmost importance in time-critical applications. A delayed message does not serve any purpose and may lead to undesired consequences [37]. The attacker doesn't modify the data but delays message delivery.

10.5.4 Attacks on Integrity/Trust

Integrity implies that the message content must not be altered in any way since its generation. A malicious node can tamper with in-transit data or even on-board data by manipulating the in-vehicle sensors. These attacks can be detrimental in an AV environment, so a network should be resilient against such attacks.

10.5.4.1 Replay Attack

In a replay attack, a malicious node stores already broadcasted messages for transmission at a different time slot to deceive other vehicles. For example, a malevolent node may capture a message at a location L, and retransmit the same message at a location M, or it may capture a message at time T and transmit the same message at a time slot S where they are no longer valid and assume no importance [15]. Such attacks can also lead to bandwidth consumption due to repeated transmission within the network.

A timestamp-based mechanism has been employed to detect replay attacks. The mechanism compares the timestamp of the received message with the current timestamp [38], and if the difference is greater than the threshold, the message is dropped. Security solutions employing sequence numbers [39] also help in mitigating such attacks.

10.5.4.2 False Information Attack

A bogus information attack aims to spread false or erroneous information throughout the network to divert a vehicle from its current intent. A malicious/compromised vehicle performs this attack by fabricating and broadcasting fake messages within the network. For example, it may broadcast fake information regarding accidents or traffic conditions to fool other vehicles into taking different routes. A message filtering scheme [40] that uses a threshold curve and certainty of event (COE) to detect bogus information has been proposed . The mapping of various attacks, violated security requirements and proposed solutions are tabulated in Table 10.1.

10.5.4.3 Message Alteration Attack

A message alteration attack modifies or changes the contents of a source message to disturb communication between communicating vehicles. Authentication mechanisms for AVs can be used to mitigate such attacks [37].

10.5.5 Attacks on Availability

Availability ensures the presence of data whenever needed by a legitimate node. Data availability assumes critical importance in delay intolerant networks such as those utilized by AVs as non-availability of data at any point may lead to lack of decision making leading to untoward incidents. An attacker can perform attacks on availability in various ways denying access to network resources to a legitimate node.

10.5.5.1 Distributed Denial of Service Attack

The motive behind the distributed denial of service (DDoS) attack is to render network resources unusable for legitimate vehicles. A DDoS attack paralyzes communication between vehicles, barring them from receiving critical information about road safety, traffic, and other environmental parameters, leading to undesired results. A Bloom-filter

TABLE 10.1

Mapping of Various Attacks, Security Requirements Violated, and Proposed Solutions

Attack	Security Requirement Violated	Proposed Solutions
Eavesdropping	Confidentiality	[27,28]
Sybil Attack	Authenticity	[30–33]
GPS Spoofing Attack	Authenticity, Integrity	[34,35]
Masquerading Attack	Authenticity	[36]
Replay Attack	Integrity	[38,39]
False Information Attack	Integrity	[40]
Message Alteration Attack	Integrity, Confidentiality	[37]
DDoS Attack	Availability	[41,42]
Jamming Attack	Availability	[43]
Flooding Attack	Availability	[44–46]
Blackhole/Greyhole Attack	Availability	[47,48]

[41] based mechanism to monitor incoming and outgoing IP addresses is proposed to mitigate DDoS attacks. An algorithm based on comparing communication time [42] between interacting vehicles is presented to detect DDoS attacks. If the communication time crosses a certain threshold, a DDoS attack is detected.

10.5.5.2 Communication Channel Jamming Attack

A jamming attack is usually performed at the physical layer by generating a high-frequency signal to disturb the communication channel. These attacks can lead to increased latency and packet dropping, proving fatal in time-critical safety applications. The solutions include frequency hopping and using multiple radio transceivers [43].

10.5.4.3 Flooding Attack

A malicious node sends too many packets to a victim node exhausting its resources and rendering it unavailable for services to other nodes in the network. The attackers generate a huge amount of bogus messages to overwhelm the network or a particular victim. Solutions observing channel access patterns [44] may be used to detect flooding-based attacks. A trust-based mechanism [45,46] can detect flooding attacks by calculating the trust values of neighbouring vehicles and limiting the number of received messages from the neighbours.

10.5.4.4 Blackhole and Greyhole Attacks

Blackhole and greyhole attacks are similar, where attackers either completely or partially drop packets destined for a legitimate vehicle. A blackhole attacker completely drops the packets routed through it, whereas a greyhole attacker drops packets partially. The consequences of these attacks are serious in an AV environment due to safety-critical applications that could lead to life-threatening accidents. These attacks may lead to denial of service, hampering availability. Quality control mechanism based on statistical process control (SPC) [47] represents abnormal behaviours using a p-chart to determine packet loss. A watchdog-based mechanism [48] is where a sender monitors packet forwarding of the receiver by overhearing its transmission covertly.

10.6 Conclusion

In the past few years, CPSs have evolved considerably and attracted a lot of attention that will continue to grow further. Autonomous vehicles have emerged as one of the most promising applications of a CPS. Most automakers are investing a considerable amount of money in developing fully autonomous vehicles to improve traffic flow, safety, reduce travel time, and several other promising applications. Despite rapid progress in CPSs, especially autonomous vehicles face considerable challenges. In this chapter, we presented one of the most critical challenges facing autonomous vehicles, i.e., security. Several proposed solutions for mitigating various attacks have been discussed, but security in a CPS, especially autonomous vehicles, needs further research before they are fully deployed.

List of Acronyms

Acronym	Full Form
CPS	Cyber-Physical System
AV	Autonomous Vehicle
ECU	Electronic Control Unit
OBU	Onboard Unit

References

[1] Gunes, V., Peter, S., Givargis, T. and Vahid, F. (2014) "A survey on concepts, applications, and challenges in cyber-physical systems". *KSII Trans. Internet Inf. Syst*, 8, 12, 4242–4268, doi: 10.3837/tiis.2014.12.001.

[2] Seshia, S.A., Hu, S., Li, W. and Zhu, Q. (2017) "Design automation of cyber-physical systems: Challenges, advances, and opportunities". *IEEE Trans. Comput. Des. Integr. Circuits Syst*, 36, 9, 1421–1434, doi: 10.1109/TCAD.2016.2633961.

[3] Shi, J., Wan, J. Yan, H., & Sou, H. (2011), A survey of cyber-physical systems. In 2011 international conference on wireless communications and signal processing (WCSP), IEEE, 1–6.

[4] Amrutur, B. (2013) "Cyber physical systems". *J. Indian Inst. Sci.*, 93, 3, doi: 10.4018/978-1-7998-2466-4.ch008.

[5] Jirkovsky, V., Obitko, M. and Marik, V. (2017) "Understanding data heterogeneity in the context of cyber-physical systems integration". *IEEE Trans. Ind. Informatics*, 13, 2, 660–667, doi: 10.1109/TII.2016.2596101.

[6] Oriwoh, E. and Conrad, M. (2015) "'Things' in the Internet of Things: Towards a definition". *Int. J. Internet Things*, 4, 1, 1–5.

[7] Miorandi, D., Sicari, S., De Pellegrini, F. and Chlamtac, I. (2012) "Internet of things: Vision, applications and research challenges". *Ad Hoc Networks*, 10, 7, 1497–1516, doi: 10.1016/j.adhoc.2012.02.016.

[8] Mehdipour, F., Nunna, K.C. and Murakami, K.J. (2013) "A smart cyber-physical systems-based solution for pest control (work in progress)". *Proc. – 2013 IEEE Int. Conf. Green Comput. Commun. IEEE Internet Things IEEE Cyber, Phys. Soc. Comput. GreenCom-iThings-CPSCom 2013*, 1248–1253, doi: 10.1109/GreenCom-iThings-CPSCom.2013.217.

[9] Cassandras, C.G. (2016) "Smart cities as cyber-physical social systems". *Engineering*, 2, 2, 156–158, doi: 10.1016/J.ENG.2016.02.012.

[10] Ruppert, T., Jaskó, S., Holczinger, T. and Abonyi, J. (2018) "Enabling technologies for operator 4.0: A survey". *Appl. Sci*, 8, 9, 1–19, doi: 10.3390/app8091650.

[11] Morgan, J. and O'Donnell, G.E. (2017) "Enabling a ubiquitous and cloud manufacturing foundation with field-level service-oriented architecture". *Int. J. Comput. Integr. Manuf.*, 30, 4–5, 442–458, doi: 10.1080/0951192X.2015.1032355.

[12] Engel, G., Greiner, T. and Seifert, S. (2018) "Ontology-Assisted Engineering of Cyber-Physical Production Systems in the Field of Process. Technology," *IEEE Trans. Ind. Informatics*, 14, 6, 2792–2802, doi: 10.1109/TII.2018.2805320.

[13] Lins, R.G., de Araujo, P.R.M. and Corazzim, M. (2020) "In-process machine vision monitoring of tool wear for Cyber-Physical Production Systems". *Robot. Comput. Integr. Manuf.*, 61, September 2019, 101859, doi: 10.1016/j.rcim.2019.101859.

[14] Lin, C.Y., Zeadally, S., Chen, T.S. and Chang, C.Y. (2012) "Enabling cyber physical systems with wireless sensor networking technologies". *Int. J. Distrib. Sens. Networks*, 2012, doi: 10.1155/2012/489794.

[15] Sakiz, F. and Sen, S. (2017) "A survey of attacks and detection mechanisms on intelligent transportation systems: VANETs and IoV". *Ad Hoc Networks*, 61, 33–50, doi: 10.1016/j.adhoc.2017.03.006.

[16] Nanda, A., Puthal, D., Rodrigues, J.J.P.C. and Kozlov, S.A. (2019) "Internet of autonomous vehicles communications security: Overview, issues, and directions". *IEEE Wirel. Commun.*, 26, 4, 60–65, doi: 10.1109/MWC.2019.1800503.

[17] Yağdereli, E., Gemci, C. and Aktaş, A.Z. (2015) "A study on cyber-security of autonomous and unmanned vehicles". *J. Def. Model. Simul.*, 12, 4, 369–381, doi: 10.1177/1548512915575803.

[18] Fagnant, D.J., Kockelman, K. (2015) "Preparing a nation for autonomous vehicles: Opportunities, barriers and policy recommendations". *Transp. Res. Part A Policy Pract*, 77, 167–181, doi: 10.1016/j.tra.2015.04.003.

[19] Cui, J. and Sabaliauskaite, G. (2019) *US 2: An unified safety and security analysis method for autonomous vehicles*. 886. Springer International Publishing.

[20] Cui, J. and Sabaliauskaite, G. (Nov. 2017) "On the alignment of safety and security for autonomous vehicles", 59–64, 2018.

[21] Eiza, M.H. and Ni, Q. (2017) "Driving with sharks". *IEEE Veh. Technol. Mag.*, 12, June 2017, 45-51. [Online]. Available: http://ieeexplore.ieee.org/stamp/stamp.jsp?tp=&arnumber=7908939&isnumber=7932615.

[22] Malla, A.M. (Nov. 2015) "Security attacks with an effective solution for DOS attacks in VANET security attacks with an effective solution for DOS attacks in VANET". doi: 10.512 0/11252-6467.

[23] "What is the CIA Triad? Definition, Explanation and Examples". https://whatis.techtarget.com/definition/Confidentiality-integrity-and-availability-CIA (Accessed May 07, 2021).

[24] Engoulou, R.G., Bellaïche, M., Pierre, S. and Quintero, A. (May 2014) "VANET security surveys". *Comput. Commun.*, 44, 1–13, doi: 10.1016/j.comcom.2014.02.020.

[25] Aloqaily, M., Balasubramanian, V., Zaman, F., Al Ridhawi, I. and Jararweh, Y. (Oct. 2018) "Congestion mitigation in densely crowded environments for augmenting QoS in vehicular clouds". *DIVANet 2018 – Proceedings of the 8th ACM Symposium on Design and Analysis of Intelligent Vehicular Networks and Applications*, 49–56, doi: 10.1145/3272036.3272038.

[26] Mokhtar, B. and Azab, M. (Dec. 01, 2015) "Survey on security issues in vehicular ad hoc networks". *Alexandria Eng. J.*, 54, 4, 1115–1126, doi: 10.1016/j.aej.2015.07.011.

[27] Whyte, W., Weimerskirch, A., Kumar, V. and Hehn, T. (2013) "A security credential management system for V2V communications". In *IEEE Vehicular Networking Conference, VNC*, 1–8, doi: 10.1109/VNC.2013.6737583.

[28] Abuelela, M., Olariu, S. and Ibrahim, K. (2009) "A secure and privacy aware data dissemination for the notification of traffic incidents", In VTC Spring 2009-IEEE 69th Vehicular Technology Conference , IEEE, 1-5, doi: 10.1109/VETECS.2009.5073340.

[29] Shrivastava, D. and Pandey, A. (2014) "A study of Sybil and temporal attacks in vehicular ad hoc networks: Types, challenges, and impacts". *Int. J. Comput. Appl. Technol. Res.*, 3, 5, 284–291, doi: 10.7753/ijcatr0305.1002.

[30] Lo, N.W. and Tsai, J.L. (May 2016) "An efficient conditional privacy-preserving authentication scheme for vehicular sensor networks without pairings". *IEEE Trans. Intell. Transp. Syst.*, 17, 5, 1319–1328, doi: 10.1109/TITS.2015.2502322.

[31] Yan, G., Olariu, S. and Weigle, M.C. (Jul. 2008) "Providing VANET security through active position detection". *Comput. Commun.*, 31, 12, 2883–2897, doi: 10.1016/j.comcom.2008.01.009.

[32] Feng, X., yan Li, C., Xin Chen, D. and Tang, J. (2017) "A method for defensing against multi-source Sybil attacks in VANET". *Peer-to-Peer Netw. Appl.*, 10, 2, 305–314, doi: 10.1007/s12083-016-0431-x.

[33] Sowattana, C., Viriyasitavat, W. and Khurat, A. (Sep. 2017) "Distributed consensus-based Sybil nodes detection in VANETs", 1–6, doi: 10.1109/JCSSE.2017.8025908.

[34] Alsharif, N., Wasef, A., Shen, X. (2011) "Mitigating the effects of position-based routing attacks in vehicular ad hoc networks", In 2011 IEEE International Conference on Communications (ICC),1–5,doi: 10.1109/icc.2011.5962855.

[35] Studer A., Luk M. and Perrig A. (2007) "Efficient mechanisms to provide convoy member and vehicle sequence authentication in VANETs". In *Proceedings of the 3rd International Conference on Security and Privacy in Communication Networks, SecureComm*, 422–431, doi: 10.1109/SECCOM.2007.4550363.

[36] Malhi, A.K. and Batra, S. (Oct. 2016) "Genetic-based framework for prevention of masquerade and DDoS attacks in vehicular ad-hoc networks". *Secur. Commun. Networks*, 9, 15, 2612–2626, doi: 10.1002/sec.1506.

[37] Samara, G. and Al-Raba'nah, Y. (Dec. 2017) "Security issues in Vehicular Ad Hoc Networks (VANET): A survey". *arXiv*, 2, 4, 50–55, Accessed: May 08, 2021. [Online]. Available: http://arxiv.org/abs/1712.04263.

[38] Raffo, D., Adjih, C. and Mühlethaler, P. (May 09, 2021) "Attacks against OLSR: Distributed key management for security". Accessed: [Online]. Available: https://www.researchgate.net/publication/242417041.

[39] Lonc, B. and Cincilla, P. (Jul. 2016) "Cooperative ITS security framework: Standards and implementations progress in Europe". doi: 10.1109/WoWMoM.2016.7523576.

[40] Kim, T.H.J. *et al.* (2010) "VANET alert endorsement using multi-source filters". In *Proceedings of the Annual International Conference on Mobile Computing and Networking, MOBICOM*, 51–60, doi: 10.1145/1860058.1860067.

[41] Verma, K., Hasbullah, H. and Kumar, A. (Nov. 2013) "Prevention of DoS attacks in VANET". *Wirel. Pers. Commun.*, 73, 1, 95–126, doi: 10.1007/s11277-013-1161-5.

[42] Shabbir, M., Khan, M.A., Khan, U.S. and Saqib, N.A. (Mar. 2017) "Detection and prevention of distributed denial of service attacks in VANETs". In *Proceedings – 2016 International Conference on Computational Science and Computational Intelligence, CSCI 2016*, 970–974, doi: 10.1109/CSCI.2016.0186.

[43] Engoulou, R. (2013) "Sécurisation des VANETS par la méthode de réputation des noeuds".

[44] Soryal, J. and Saadawi, T. (2013) "DoS attack detection in Internet-connected vehicles". In *2013 International Conference on Connected Vehicles and Expo, ICCVE 2013 – Proceedings*, 7–13, doi: 10.1109/ICCVE.2013.6799761.

[45] Kerrache, C.A., Lagraa, N., Calafate, C.T. and Lakas, A. (Jul. 2017) "TFDD: A trust-based framework for reliable data delivery and DoS defense in VANETs". *Veh. Commun.*, 9, 254–267, doi: 10.1016/j.vehcom.2016.11.010.

[46] Hasrouny, H., Bassil, C., Samhat, A.E. and Laouiti, A. (2017) "Security risk analysis of a trust model for secure group leader-based communication in VANET". *Adv. Intell. Syst. Comput.*, 548, 71–83, doi: 10.1007/978-981-10-3503-6_6.

[47] Cherkaoui, B., Beni-Hssane, A. and Erritali, M. (Jan. 2017) "Quality control chart for detecting the black hole attack in vehicular Ad-hoc networks". *Proc. Computer Sci.*, 113, 170–177, doi: 10.1016/j.procs.2017.08.337.

[48] Marti, S., Giuli, T.J., Lai, K., and Baker, M. (2000) "Mitigating routing misbehavior in mobile ad hoc networks". In *Proceedings of the Annual International Conference on Mobile Computing and Networking, MOBICOM*, 255–265, doi: 10.1145/345910.345955.

11

Employment of Cyber-Physical Systems Towards Smart Healthcare Assistance

Shubham Joshi and Radha Krishna Rambola
Computer Engineering, SVKM's NMIMS MPSTME Shirpur

Nonita Sharma
Computer Science Engineering, NIT Jalandhar

Monika Mangla
Department of Information Technology, Dwarkadas J. Sanghvi College of Engineering, Mumbai

11.1 Introduction

Cyber-physical systems (CPSs) may be viewed as integration of computation, communicating, and various physical cycles. This integration of various kinds of devices has greatly transformed the facets of various industries like agriculture, healthcare, transportation, etc. The generic architecture of CPS is demonstrated in Figure 11.1. The CPS has been undergoing innovative evolution since its inception and, as a result, has been employed for use in an an assortment of fields including auto, businesses, health care, aviation, etc. The CPS can also be considered an interlink among the web and its clients and has a multidisciplinary approach encouraging the requirements of physical input and output. A few vital characteristics of CPS are as follows:

- Firmly incorporated cyber ability in each physical part
- Organized at various scales
- Complex numerous fleeting and spatial scales
- Capability of progressive redesigning/reconfiguring
- Closed-loop control and high levels of computerization

The medical device industry is going through a transformation in order to accept the capability of embedding programming and network organization. Resultantly, rather than independent gadgets, now medical devices are planned and designed with a perspective to aid health care by treating patients. For the same, it needs to have dispersed frameworks for controlling numerous parts of the patient's physiology at the same time. Medical CPS can be considered the blend of installed programming that controls and

DOI: 10.1201/9781003202752-11

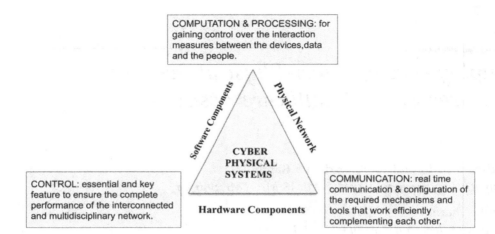

FIGURE 11.1
Structure of a Cyber-Physical System.

manges numerous gadgets that are otherwise muddled and clumsy. These organized gadgets are used to indicate the vital physical parameters of the patient so as to achieve an unambiguous and accurate diagnosis. Such frameworks can be utilized in emergency clinics to facilities customized and tweaked and quality medical administrations to the patients. It wholeheartedly accepts the capability of implanted programming and organization availability. A portion of the utilizations of the CPS in this field incorporate shrewd working rooms and devices, pictures and outwardly guided medical procedures, treatments and activities, computerized liquid stream controls to be utilized while infusing restorative medications, advancements in physical and neural prostheses, etc. The evolution of the protected and powerful medical cyber-physical systems needs a new plan, confirmation, and approval strategies because of expansion in size and intricacy. Model-based innovation should assume a bigger part in the MCPS plan. Models should cover devices and correspondences in between them, yet additionally, similarly and significantly, patients and parental figures. Moreover, MCPS also requires another administrative method to affirm their utilization for treating patients. The authors have attempted to present a brief outline of the utilization of the CPS in the healthcare domain.

This chapter has been organized into various sections. The authors discuss the emerging medical device systems (MDSs) using various technologies in Section 1. The related work is presented in section 2. The emergence of health care as a result of advancement in CPS is discussed in section III3. The role of MCPS with reference to social networks has been presented in section IV4. Various associated issues and challenges have been presented in section V5 and finally the conclusion and future work is presented in section VI6.

11.2 Background and Related Works

A rapid and unprecedented transformation has been recognized in the field of health care for the past few decades. This transformation has been particularly experienced in the software intensive medical devices, such as ventilators and infusion pumps. This progression in health care has some associated challenges also in terms of interoperability, availability, and heterogeneity, etc. [1].

The implementation of medical CPS in the field of implanting has given interesting and motivating results. The usefulness of medical CPS in implanting may be generally determined by the additional opportunities that it has contributed. In the domain of robotic surgery, a new feature is observed that requires continuous preparation of high-goal pictures and haptic input. Another model is proton treatment. Such kinds of treatments in implants is the result of medical CPS, and thus establishes its efficacy on a large scale. In such technology, exact doses of radiation are given to cancer patients. It also proves to be useful to give the exact amount of proton beam to a patient out of a cyclotron. According to the work in [2], the creators have dissected the safety of proton treatment machines where the examination focuses on a solitary framework, the crisis closure. According to the work in [2], MCPS is competent in efficient analysis of the disease, however proper approval is required for large and complex systems.

Currently, the systems administration abilities of most medical devices are restricted to usefulness and generally depends on the exclusive correspondence conventions offered by major vendors. In this direction, medical device plug-and-Ppay (MD PnP) interoperability activity [3] can be considered as a late exertion that plans to give an open norms structure to protected and adaptable interconnectivity of medical devices to improve the wellbeing and effectiveness of patients and medical staff, respectively.

The medical device industry has used the scenarios based on physiological closed loop control. Patient-controlled analgesia (PCA) is a clinical scenario that garners benefit from the closed-loop approach. During administrating opioids (class of drugs) for pain management, PCA infusion pumps are used. Inpatients give diverse responses to such drugs and need specialized and customized measurements and conveyance plans. For the same, the patient is provided with a button in such pumps and when he/she presses this button, a dose is given to them, unlike being given by a caregiver.

In [4], the authors contemplated a patient-controlled analgesia framework that contains a boss to screen the patient information for early indications of respiratory disappointment. The essential data flow and the devices used in such a control loop are shown in Figure 11.2. Physiological signals from the patient are received by the pulse oximeter. These signals are processed to produce heart rate and SpO2 outputs. The outputs are given to the supervisor to make a controlled decision by sending a stop signal to the PCA pump. The patient is then delivered a drug at its programmed rate by the PCA pump. The patient model calculates the level of drug in the patient's body as it gets the drug rate as an input. Because of that, the physiological output signals are influenced through a drug absorption function. Figure 11.2 also recognizes that the supervisor should be responsible for the source of delays in the control loop. One should be open-minded to issues that intrude the control loop, specifically correspondence disappointments between the devices.

11.3 Emerging Medical Device Systems

Wired/wireless interfaces are included in rising medical device architecture to enable networked device communication in order to record patient's data. A closed loop is

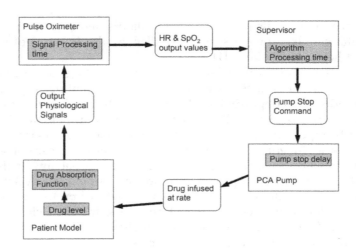

FIGURE 11.2
PCA Control Loop.

required in such devices so that medical devices are connected to the patients simultaneously. Another task of these devices is drug delivery and checking breathing regulation. Analysis and aggregation of the acquired health information from different medical devices is done in a coordinated manner. For this, IT-based social services are used, however it may face some issues regarding information overload or miscommunication. For an adverse patient outcome these aspects are combined. Some devices provide life support in the operation theatre using the information fetched through monitoring devices [5]. In order to fetch the information through monitoring devices, digital technology is used. The collected information is aggregated and further transferred to medical professionals so that they could initiate a trigger through a device. The requirement to provide medical assistance and care in a home, considering the distant and timely clinical practice, further underlines the requirement for dispersed system administration. Correspondence is the predominant part of such a home medical care system by electronically moving records of vital physical parameters using friendly administrations. In such a way, control instruments and processing of the genuine and accurate medical data conveyed through systems administration frames a fundamental pre-imperative of the CPS with a high assurance to help the execution of clinical frameworks. Further, in order to further enhance the quality of home care patients, numerous high assurance level medical CPSs should operate together, overcoming the issues of heterogeneity and communication issues.

11.4 MCPS, Social Network, and Big Data Platforms

It was mentioned earlier that medical CPS aims to fetch the data pertaining to physical parameters of patients in a continuous manner. This continuous collection of data has various associated issues like volume, variety, and velocity. In order to address these issues, medical CPS needs to efficiently handle this. For the same, it involves efficient handling approaches to engage improved understanding disclosure, measure stream-lining and dynamics that is referred to as big data. Big data may be referred to as an assortment of organized and unorganized data that is created by numerous physical and portable detecting devices. Further, it also includes data from remote sensor organizations, far off (ethereal) detecting, radio recurrence ID peruses, programming sensors, synthetic and natural sensors, and programming logs just like medical CPS frameworks. This is converged with information that is enveloped in culturally amassed open sources. The data collected from various sources may be in the form of sound, text, images, and video that are redirected for semantic fusion in order to infer meaningful diagnosis. In order to infer efficient diagnosis, big data design requires new ideas to model spatial and time constraints along with classical data structures.

Management and inference of data are the prime challenges associated with big data. Here, inference of meaning from big data requires subjective and quantitative analysis of crude data in assorted settings. Various CPS web search tools apply PC learning systems for this purpose. The created data by the MCPS dynamic segments needs to be processed using detailed understanding of the system in order to infer necessary objectives. The blended or separated data either stays inside the framework or outside for the clients, whereas the extracted data should be imparted among MCPS modules. Further, in order to implement the MCPS in real life, it requires finance, progressed data and structures for handling unrivaled dataand dynamism [6].

The transformation abilities require another class of devices for a wellbeing check framework. Nonetheless, the utilization explosion for sensors and a few correspondence media in wellbeing observation have initiated a central concern for the overarching stages. The CPS architecture model has been illustrated in Figure 11.3, which contains various components like users, storage platforms, computing systems, and WSN. In Figure 11.3, the framework uses a collection of devices that are controlled from cyber-space with a collection of order and control proclamations. Any modifications in the physical devices are influenced by cyberspace. In healthcare-related applications, MCPSs are widely utilized. A tiny implanted framework can be integrated in the human body in order to provide far-off medical services that fetch the different body parameters. The

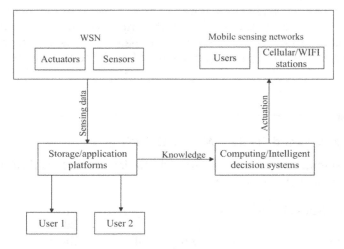

FIGURE 11.3
The CPS Architecture Model.

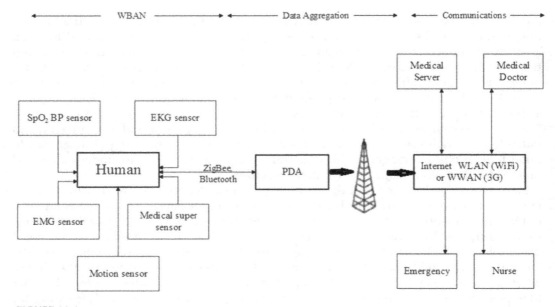

FIGURE 11.4
Architecture of Wireless Sensors for Monitoring Systems.

data collected through an implanted framework is handled locally and occasionally the data is transferred to cyberspace through the web or portable devices. This continuous remote sensing [7] for the social PCS medical services is portrayed in Figure 11.4.

The CPSs also have a basic job in long-range interpersonal communication, big data investigation, and medical care application examination. Medical networks are competent in addressing challenges like increasing medical expense and lack of medical workforce. Further, pervasive health monitoring systems (PHMSs) are used to ease the present circumstances by screening the individual's wellbeing in a consistent and progressive manner. PHMS collects the health information of patients and maintains data privacy. Body area networks (BANs), wireless networks that use ambient devices, are used to perform the monitoring process.

Although there is a widespread increase in the implementation of medical CPSs during the past few decades due to the technological transformations and advancements, some associated issues and challenges will be discussed in the following section.

11.5 Challenges Faced by the Medical CPS

The various challenges faced by widespread employment of medical CPSs have been divided into various aspects as follows.

- **Executable Clinical Workflows**

The increased interconnectivity and interoperability of medical devices opens the avenues for development and transfer of MCPS to realize the customized clinical care that proves to be best for the patient. In order to portray the clinical situations, a language is required for prerequisites for data streams among devices and the patient, operational methodology, and closed-loop control among devices. Clinical situation work processes ought to be given exact operational semantics. Investigation of such exact portrayals of a situation ensures that directions for parental figures are unambiguous and cover every conceivable circumstance, guarantees that devices can connect with one another as wanted, and investigates the impacts of issues and client blunders.

- **Model-Based Development**

With executable clinical work process details, MCPS presents a remarkable choice for a nearby model-based sequence of events. It can be implemented using a singular device or even a framework consisting of devices to the degree of clinical situations that would fill in as high-level framework prerequisites. As examined above, there is a pattern towards dynamic arrangement and sending of a medical device framework for a given clinical situation. Investigation of a situation model requires investigating the patient's health in a situation before a device framework is constructed, and then determines the devices that can be utilized for execution and interconnections between them. Such necessities would then be used during arrangement, guaranteeing wellbeing of the execution. The test, in any case, clearly indicates that it checks the interface among static and dynamic components.

- **Patient Modeling and Simulation**

A firmly related test is a patient demonstrating where a patient model is required to plan for closed-loop control for the secured investigation of situations. For instance, the closed-loop PCA situation it is required to show drug ingestion in the patient body through the connection between the medication portion and fixation, from one viewpoint, and patient fundamental signs, like heart and respiratory rates. Pharmacokinetic models of medication assimilation are known from the writing and there is measurable data that impacts the medication on essential signs [8]. Nonetheless, far-reaching models are too perplexing to a way utilized in the plan and examination, consequently advancement of new reflection methods is vital for tending to this test. Simultaneously, high-devotion models and effective test systems are required for testing and approval of MCPS.

- **User-Centered Design**

Parental figure mistakes in utilizing medical devices are a significant wellspring of antagonistic occasions [9,10]. Without a doubt, a portion of these mistakes are because of stress and over-burden that guardians experience every day. Be that as it may, countless mistakes can be ascribed to a helpless UI plan. On the off chance that a device is difficult to work, has an irrational interface, or reacts to client inputs in an unforeseen way, client blunders can happen. Plan and approval of medical devices needs to consider client assumptions. To utilize model-based plans for intelligent medical devices, we need to join models of parental figure conduct. Such client displaying is a famously difficult issue. Nonetheless, joining data of probability of specific activities into parental figure models opens the best approach to quantitative thinking about device security.

- **Infrastructure for Medical-Device Integration and Interoperation**

Right now, conveyed MCPSs are worked by a solitary producer utilizing exclusive correspondence convention. While this methodology may make administrative endorsement simpler, it restricts the advantages of between device correspondence and smothers the imagination of medical experts [11]. Open interconnectivity principles for MCPS, for example, the Integrated Clinical Environment (ICE) [12] standard proposed through the MD PnP activity, lays the foundation for medical device interoperability. However, for these guidelines to be compelling, improvement and arrangement stages ought to be created. A new advancement around is the open-source MCDF toolset [13]. MCDF has demonstrated to be helpful in the improvement of closed-loop MCDF. Nonetheless, it depends on the generally significant burden of the Java Messaging System. More agile sending stages, intended to be amiable to confirm, may ease administrative endorsement of MCPS.

- **Security and Privacy**

While organizing abilities let medical devices gain usefulness that was never conceivable beforehand, they additionally make the way for a large group of new expected issues. Security and protection concerns are a portion of those new issues [14]. Patients can be harmed or get killed as attackers reprogram the medical devices by entering into the MCPS network [15]. Nowadays, the only approach used by the device manufacturers is to restrict the functionality of the device. So in this case the medical device cannot accept the commands but can send out data. This approach is used to increase the security of the system. An important challenge faced by the MCPS is to find the correct harmony between adaptability and security. To ensure security to electronic health records, developers are using extensive solutions [16].

- **Verification, Validation, and Certification**

The design practice used currently assigns confirmation and certification at the design cycle exit. We require more validation and certification because nowadays devices are more complex and mutually joined. This should be possible: from one perspective, the "plan for check" approach [17] can help confirmation methods scale better and make the age of check proof simpler. Then again, model-based generative methods permit to perform confirmation right off the bat in the plan and afterward expand the assurances given by the check to the execution through code generation.

11.6 Conclusion

A huge set of new potentials in control are opened by the Internet and computing revolutions that impact the human life in many ways; for e.g., new services and energy management or provide new healthcare services. Cyber-physical systems (CPSs) are networked and hybrid complex systems that are a central aspect include human interactions. MCPSs are medical care basic integration of an organization of medical devices. MCPS frameworks are continuously utilized in emergency clinics/e-medical care applications to have quality and effectiveness (less expensive), i.e., excellent medical services administrations. The perpetuation and execution along with algorithmic design and encompassing modeling is applicable in this consideration. Analysing, modelling, and understanding are rigorously needed by the human element. The area of MCPS offers a remarkable arrangement of difficulties, particular from some other CPS space [18]. The region is going to go through a generous change, both as far as specialists' and parental figures' assumptions for how MCPS can help them, and regarding how these frameworks are created and affirmed. The difficulties confronting MCPS are imposing, yet they present immense freedoms for research with quick pragmatic effects.

Our primary point is to improve the proficiency and wellbeing in e-medical services applications. Through that, we can help specialists/experts of clinics/medical devices to settle numerous urgent issues (identified with medical machines/devices) or difficulties in the plan of the medical device's organization. In this chapter, the authors summed up the difficulties and laid out the most encouraging ideas. Displaying and model-driven designing, which progressively grab hold in numerous different spaces, should be the main jobs in MCPS advancement, too.

References

[1] Lee, I., Pappas, G.J., Cleaveland, R., Hatcliff, J., Krogh, B.H., Lee, P., Rubin, H. and Sha, L. (April 2006). High-confidence medical device software and systems. *Computer*, *39*, 4, 33–38.

[2] Ackerman, M.J., Burgess, L.P., Filart, R., Lee, I. and Poropatich, R.K. (Jan/Feb 2010). Developing next generation telehealth tools and technologies: Patients, systems, and data perspectives. *Telemed. e-Health*, *16*, 1, 93–95.

[3] Alexander, K. and Clarkson, P. (2000). Good design practice for medical devices and equipment, Part II: Design for verification. *J. Med. Eng. Technol.*, *24*, 2, 53–62.

[4] Sheeran, M., Singh, S. and Stalmarck, G. (2000). Checking safety properties using induction and a sat-solver. In FMCAD '00: Proceedings of the Third International Conference on Formal Methods in Computer-Aided Design, volume 1954 of LNCS, pages 108–125.

[5] Vicente, K.J., Kada-Bekhaled, K., Hillel, G., Cassano, A. and Orser, B.A. (2003). Programming errors contribute to death from patient-controlled analgesia: Case report and estimate of probability. *Can. J. Anesthesiol.*, *50*, 4, 328–332.

[6] Hotchkiss, J., Robbins, J. and Robkin, M. (July 2007). MD-Adapt: A proposed architecture for open-source medical device interoperability. In Joint Workshop on High Confidence Medical Devices, Software, and Systems and Medical Device Plug-and-Play Interoperability (HCMDSSMDPnP), pages 167–170.

[7] Halperin, D., Heydt-Benjamin, T., Fu, K., Kohno, T. and Maisel, W. (January-March 2008). Security and privacy for implantable medical devices. *Pervasive Comput.*, *7*, 1, 30–39.

[8] Voit, H. (2013). An Arbitrated Networked Control Systems Approach to Cyber-Physical Systems (PhD Thesis). Technische Universität München, Diss, München.

[9] Yi, M.Y., Fiedler, K.D. and Park, J.S. (2006). Understanding the role of individual innovativeness in the acceptance of it-based innovations: Comparative analyses of models and measures. *Decis. Sci.*, *37*, 3, 393–426.

[10] Haque, S.A., Aziz, S.M. and Rahman (2014). Review of cyber physical system in healthcare. *Int. J. Distrib Sensor Netw.*, *10*, 4, 217415.

[11] Baronchelli, A., Ferrer-i-Cancho, R., Pastor-Satorras, R., Chater, N. and Christiansen, M.H. (2013). Networks in cognitive science. *Trends Cogn. Sci.*, *17*, 7, 348–360.

[12] Qian, L., Luo, Z., Du, Y. and Guo, L. (2009). Cloud computing: An overview. *Cloud Comput.*, 626–631.

[13] Lee I. and Sokolsky O. (2010). Medical cyber physical systems. In Design Automation Conference (DAC), 2010 47th ACM/IEEE. IEEE, 743–748.

[14] Levin, E., Pieraccini, R. and Eckert, W. (2000). A stochastic model of human-machine interaction for learning dialog strategies. *IEEE Trans. Speech Audio Proc.*, 8, 1, 11–23.

[15] DeSmit, Z., Elhabashy, A.E., Wells, L.J. and Camelio, J.A. (2016). Elsevier, cyber physical vulnerability assessment in manufacturing systems, Procedia manufacturing, 5, 1060–1074.

[16] Raghupathi, W. and Raghupathi, V. (2014). Big data analytics in healthcare: Promise and potential. *Health Inf. Sci. Syst.*, 2, 3.

[17] Gu, L., Zeng, D., Guo, S., Barnawi, A. and Xiang, Y. (2017). Cost efficient resource management in fog computing supported medical cyber physical systems. *IEEE Trans. Emerg. Topics Comput.*, 5, 1, 108–119.

[18] Zhang, W., Qi, Q. and Deng, J. (2017). Building intelligent transportation cloud data center based on SOA. *J. Ambient Comput. Intel. (IJACI).*, 8, 2, 1–1.

12

A Road Map Towards Industrial Transformation Using the Cyber-Physical System

Shubham Joshi
Computer Engineering, SVKM's NMIMS MPSTME Shirpur

Kamal Mehta
SVKM's NMIMS MPSTME Shirpur

Nonita Sharma
Computer Science Engineering, NIT Jalandhar

Monika Mangla
Department of Information Technology, Dwarkadas J. Sanghvi College of Engineering, Mumbai

12.1 Introduction

The cyber-physical system (CPS) may be considered the system that integrates mechanized systems in order to control the tasks of physical reality with computing systems [1–3]. These installed systems additionally necessitate an interface that integrates the information with other implanted systems or the cloud. The information exchange among various components (comprising of physical and processing devices) is the main component of a CPS. A CPS can be considered a framework that sends and receives information over a network. A generic structure of a CPS is portrayed in Figure 12.1. The CPS has impacted and revolutionized various sectors affecting mankind. The various sectors that have been largely influenced by CPS are health care, agriculture, transportation, and industries. The integration of CPS and IoT in industries is referred to as Industry 4.0.

The CPS, an arising arrangement of Industry 4.0, is relied upon for giving recognized answers for changing and updating the activity and job of major existing mechanical methods; such as modern foundation plan, CPS-related key strategies, and cybersecurity systems [4]. These days, the generally acknowledged definition for the CPS is the implanted arrangement of incorporating the physical and computerized universes by building up worldwide organizations for business and giving real-time data access and processing services. By integrating the CPS with industries, we are able to create a smart world. The cyber-physical system is the key component addressing the new modern

DOI: 10.1201/9781003202752-12

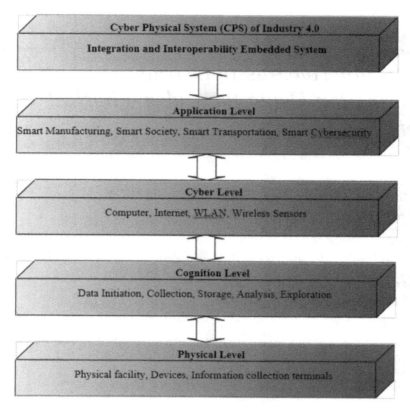

FIGURE 12.1
Framework of a CPS.

insurgency. Many cyber-physical system projects run in industries that include airplanes, programmed advanced mechanics, ecological observing, medical services, fabricating, security observation, and others.

In this paper we talk about the compatibility of the CPS with industries. Then we discuss the key features of the CPS with IoT. Further, we discuss the applications of the CPS in industries. Then we talk about technical challenges and standardization faced by CPS applications. Finally, we discuss some research trends based on CPS applications along with the Internet of Things.

12.2 Scope of the CPS in Industry 4.0

An embedded system needs to be extended by using an interface that is connected to the Internet and further connected to a cyber-physical system. To accomplish this, different methodologies are examined with regards to this turn of events and will be momentarily introduced.

- **Extending the system directly**

Communication interfaces are used to extend the embedded systems. For enabling the communication, we change the software accordingly using the Internet. At the end, the control unit transfers the sensor signals to the cloud, as shown in Figure 12.2. Actuators are controlled by the methods that are implemented through the Internet.

- **Using the microcontroller board**

Here we use a microcontroller board that contains many interfaces like ethernet, CAN, etc. We connect the board to the embedded system and communicate via the Internet. Each system has its own software. For transferring variants from one system to another, reworking of mapping is required accordingly. Figure 12.3 shows the arrangement.

- **Using sensors and actuators**

Actuators and sensors are integrated with a control unit using a field bus. Sensors employ this field bus for transferring its own data to the control unit ,whereas actuators can correctly check their status independently. In order to extend this framework to the CPS, it transfers information from the sensors and actuators through the field transport. This information is sent to the cloud for further processing there. In case there is a huge volume of information, the cost of savvy sensors and actuators should be thought of. Such an illustration has been demonstrated in Figure 12.4.

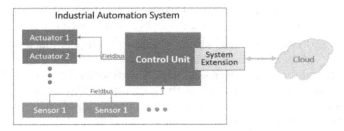

FIGURE 12.2
Direct System Extension.

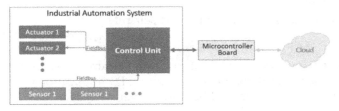

FIGURE 12.3
Extension of System Using a Microcontroller.

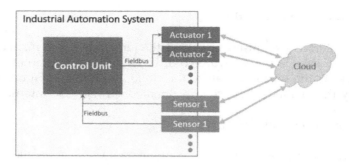

FIGURE 12.4
Implementation of Smart Sensors and Actuators.

12.3 Key Features of the CPS and IoT

In this section, the authors highlight the attributes of the CPS and IoT in order to introduce and explain the connected advances. This section initially discusses the key attributes of the CPS, followed by certain highlights that have been proposed by numerous researchers. It is agreed by various related industries that the CPS is undoubtedly considered as novel and unprecedented evolution. However, many also consider the CPS to be a modernized assembling system. Authors in Lee et al. [5] claimed that the CPS basically comprises two parts as follows:

1. High-level network that guarantees that ongoing information obtained from the physical world and data input from the cyber workspace
2. Examination and computational ability building the cyberspace

Any system with the above characteristics may be symbolized as a CPS. We come across various such examples of CPSs because of the expanding digitalization of installed systems. The expansion in the abilities of network computational systems leads to the advancement of new systems, which can be enlisted as follows [6]:

1. Sending of a CPS in mass-item applications, for example, advanced cell empowered administrations.
2. The odds in rise of new cross-space applications, for instance, the smart transportation systems;
3. Expanding transparency, versatility, and self-rule.

CPS applications
- Cross-space sensor sources and information streams: various kinds of sensors will be processed simultaneously in canny CPS applications. Also, this cross-space detecting information will be traded over heterogeneous organizations.
- Inserted and versatile detecting limit: efficient portability of sensors based on cell phones limiting the versatile detecting inclusion over the long haul.
- Client commitment and collaboration using models like through give-and-take where participatory detection would be the fundamental in the CPS.

- Versatile burdens necessitating processing capability and cloud-upheld capacity: With the development of distributed computing, the pay more only as costs arise idea is probably going to be embraced in the CPS to cater stockpiling, registering, and correspondence needs.

- Amassed insight and information through information mining and learning advancements: With high elements and vulnerability of information in the CPS, learning and information mining innovations can be utilized to recover helpful information. At that point, the input from clients and actuators may assist us with collecting or even finding obscure information.

Key IoT features in contrast to the current manufacturing systems are as follows:
- Acquaint a user-friendly and simple to-convey design and solution for executing shrewd assembly in the entire assembling systems utilizing the IoT.
- Plan the brilliant structure and models to improve the knowledge of base-level assembling assets; for example, keen vehicles and shrewd stations since they are vital to the insightful assembling framework.
- Build up another technique and strategy choice for ongoing data-based creation planning and inward coordination improvement that can be directly applied to the assembling framework, e.g., shop floor, to improve effectiveness.
- Present a basic occasion-based constant key creation exhibitions investigation model, in order to effectively recognize continuous creation exceptions [7].

12.4 CPS Applications in Industries

A. Cybersecurity

In networked systems, the latest changes have brought about different sorts of safety trade-offs. One of the significant disadvantages of the CPS is the weakness of the unavoidable cyberattacks that happen normally in the software and Internet-based systems. Truth be told, the development of physical systems powers cybersecurity consideration, an extraordinary treatment that goes without a doubt across scientists and professionals. Security issues in this space have become a worldwide issue, consequently, planning a powerful, secure, and proficient cyber-physical system is a functioning space of examination. A tale cross-space suggestion model is proposed, which not just learns the normal rating design across areas with the adaptability in controlling the ideal degree of sharing, however, learns the space explicit rating designs in every area including discriminative data auspicious to execution improvement. The CPS-based foundation is increasing and becoming more decentralized, subsequently the CPS is more powerless against assaults. As per security issues, new prerequisites as a modern strategy are needed. Security is one of the significant worries as gadgets speak with each other, utilizing various conventions that are defenseless to different kinds of attacks. Due to the wellbeing and protection chances, implanted savvy lattices are another CPS area that has obtained huge consideration in the writing. Security in assembling has been basic, yet as the assembling interaction turned out to be more modern, the dangers increased [8–11].

B. **Big data manipulation**

The CPS controls sensitive information by improving the safety measures and enhancing the level of checks. During a literature survey, it is noticed that researchers present another preemptive fixed-need booking calculation fusing a security limitation that is known as lowest security level first (LSF). The solid schedulable investigation of LSF diminishes the chances of data spillage, thus impacting the accurate widespread utilization of big data. It also helps towards how to recover helpful information from the enormous information—at that point, it is feasible to consistently incorporate the physical world and virtual world. An information-driven Bayesian model is driven by outer sources of info and under boisterous estimations. Spatial information distribution centers have demonstrated their effectiveness in completing CPS tasks. Researchers propose to perform the SETL undertakings in a conveyed, equal way through a network of registering assets to manage information volume and tedious issues. A plan of a work area web index, search implicit memories (SIM), is introduced and uses both express and verifiable recollections. Similarly, the authors [12–15] also outline that matching up with the novelty of information in dynamic CPS leads to a display of multi-modular behavior.

C. **Vehicles**

Vehicles can be considered the modernized framework that connects new physical sensors, synergistic detecting, self-governing vehicles, and collective data sharing. An epic learning automata (LA)-based crossover bunching plan for vehicles in vehicular CPS (VCPS) is built to manage high speed and steady topological changes. Some analysts created approaches in an auto-control systems plan that contemplate execution assets, intending to escalate the control exhibitions for a given set of assets in order to understand the necessary control exhibitions with less resources. Due to the enormous number of transmission transfer speed and requirements, group head becomes over burdened.

D. **Human-related interaction**

It is productive to oversee, control, screen, and inquire on gear, hardware, and faculty state. To plan the pacemaker regulator, a CPS can handle a pacemaker plan that exploits the fractal properties of human pulse and determines the fractal ideal control issue under six diverse expense functions. A biometrics, edge-based unique mark check for upgrading the security of finger impression confirmation is intended to improve security. A novel model of hybrid brain-computer interface (BCI) is fit for detecting mental assignment, closed eyes recognition, and steady-state visual evoked potential (SSVEP) with the help of two EEG channels. A re-creation approach is embraced to create reproduction to anticipate results of machine-intervened human associations, and exhibits the handiness of the design [16–18].

E. **Healthcare service**

The CPS is an amazing framework incorporated with remote sensor organizations, clinical sensors, and cloud computing that is applied to medical services serving patients physically and distantly. As a developing medical care pattern, MCPS empower consistent and shrewd cooperation between the computational components and the clinical gadgets. Although numerous CPS models have been given, the number of medical CPSs still takes a backseat. They depict the trade-off between security, wellbeing, and accessibility in a CPS and apply it to implantable clinical gadgets. The investigation features two significant parts: the safety efforts needed for impeding unapproved admittance to the gadget and the security of the patient in crisis circumstances. Furthermore, targeting decreasing expenses, task appropriation, base station affiliation, and virtual machine situation are the significant properties that must be considered toward cost effectiveness [19,20].

F. **Cell phones**

Cell phones are a CPS-based information control and correspondence gadget. Cell phones can be utilized for raising observations including a telephone gatherer, a regulator, and a worker. An epic versatile cyber-physical framework for swarm detecting applications empower portable clients to perform versatile crowd-sensing errands in an effective manner. Many analysts present another SfM system that is enhanced for portable in-creased reality and quickly creates a total 3D point haze of an objective scene [21].

G. **Robotics**

Advanced mechanics has been an interesting issue for some time and there are a few ex-aminations identified with CPSs. Some scientists claimed an improvement strategy for robots that use the deliberations of software and equipment segments in a multi-faceted design for cyber-physical robot systems. Numerous scientists portray and delineate a methodology to plan OKD-MES that is built over CPSs in order to control robot workstations [22].

H. **Other industries**

A co-enhancement conspiracy is portrayed to consider the trade-offs among costs related with the physical activation effort needed for computational exertion required to procure and handle approaching data. A little automated airplane framework observation mission, and examination of pipeline, is suggested in order to explore the features of a cyber-physical system. A multidisciplinary cost limits energy and augments mission productivity and effectiveness. Several researchers present a novel stream-based food recognition CPS to integrate with huge business designs. A versatile access control model for emergences (AC4E) for crucial CPSs is also proposed by some researchers. An altered molecule swarm advancement calculation of inclusion streamlining of CPS to recognize coal mine shaft fire is presented. Savvy cyber society is alluded to as a virtual and physical correspondence stage that consists of six useful correspondence layers to coordinate the CPS and WoT and executes a virtual stage named Xebra, discussing the requirement for acknowledging global-scale CPS organization. Further, a multi-quadcopter cyber-physical framework can be employed to assess the genuine confinement of air pollution [23–25].

12.5 Technical Challenges and Standardizations Faced by CPS Applications

Although a great deal of examination endeavors have been made on CPS advances, there are as yet specialized difficulties. It is basic how to develop a CPS as appropriate models or calculations that decide the cyber-physical system's level of characteristic hetero-geneity, simultaneousness, and affectability to timing.

- The plan of foundation for a CPS is a major test, wherein administration-based things may experience the ill effects of execution and cost limits. Based on this contention, countless articles talk about the CPS framework from various points. Many heterogeneity and trustworthiness issues often emerge as an ever-increasing number of physical articles associated with the CPS-related organizations. The most effective method to change the heterogeneity into a combination is tricky at various levels including information moves and systems administration, information handling and the executives, and administration provisioning [26].

- From the perspective of the organization, the CPS is an extremely muddled heterogeneous and inserted framework that incorporates the joining between different sorts of organizations through different specialized gadgets and ad-vances. Right now, there is an absence of a broadly acknowledged normalized CPS framework that defeats the heterogeneity of expanded organizations/cor-respondence innovations and offers an orchestrated support to different appli-cations. There actually exist numerous information control issues: information transmission, information stockpiling, information trading, information ex-posure, information security. It is a provoking assignment to create organizing calculations and guidelines that can permit information activity by different gadgets for various prerequisites to travel adequately inside CPS systems in Industry 4.0 [27,28].

To offer great types of assistance to end users, a CPS's specialized guidelines should be intended to characterize the determination for data trade, preparing, and corre-spondences between objects. The achievement of a CPS relies upon normalization, which gives interoperability, coordination, and powerful procedure for an expansive scope; for instance, enormous scope systems and arrangement of systems. The normalization of advancements in cyber-physical systems speeds up the utilization of this system's in-novations and its technology. What makes normalization difficult is its rapid growth. The development of cyber-physical systems is accelerated by using some CPS principles like security and communication standards and some ID norms.

12.6 Research Trends

CPS applications in the near future will be used in savvy clinical gadgets, keen urban areas, brilliant homes, transportation systems, keen energy, keen matrix, keen specialist, keen structure, etc. In coming years, one of the most talked-abou issues will be the use of remote healthcare monitoring system in medical CPS. It will also face some big challenges like integrating big data with cloud computing algorithms for securing patients' personal data. MCPS will be used for achieving accuracy in both software and hardware systems, undeniable degree of interoperability and robotization, and high insight of setting mindfulness. In energy regions, there will be systems for more productive, successful, free from any and all harm age, transmission, and conveyance of electric force. Energy resources can be delivered securely using a smart grid, improve effectiveness for generators and merchants, look at and assess the exhibition and security of MCPS, and give adaptable decisions to prosumers, related with observing, control, correspondence, sensor, and organization advancements. In transportation and mobility [29], smart transport systems will be developed that will contain monitoring of the driver's safety and warning methods and more powerful open transportation orchestrating and planning stream models. In manufacturing [30], there will be more brilliant, ideal, more versatile cycles for spry and effective gathering and creation; to embrace the sending of prescient prediction systems IoT and WoT are used as they enhance modern manufacturing; and lastly, features including safety and accuracy will be upgraded in robots.

- Social network integration: For enhancing the correspondence in many devices and technologies, we use social networking along with cyber-physical system solutions. Nowadays, the CPS is based on industrial methods that include interworking and integration.
- Creating CPS-based middleware solutions: We propose service-oriented frameworks to help reliable assistance synthesis with the diverse, unique physical substances inside a cyber-physical system. At present, most CPS middleware arrangements just offer restricted setting mindfulness benefits. In the near future, a global CPS network will be created that will be connected with diverse gadgets and offer different types of assistance, like transportation, clinical gear, cars, housing development, and so on.
- Joining CPS with cloud computing and human exercises: Clouds give a more extensive approach to objects to get associated and permit individuals to get to alternate points of view on the Internet. Future CPS-based help could offer expanded and customized types of assistance, like reconnaissance, climate observation, the executives of vehicular traffic, control of creation exercises, efficient computation, cost assessment, and so forth. This differentiated and customized administration requires a significant degree of distributed computing to satisfy. We also need a far-reaching algorithm to manage complex CPS-related issues coordinated with human practices.

12.7 Conclusion

Cyber-physical systems (CPS) give incredible Internetworking and integration between IoT, network correspondence methods, and the physical world. The cyber-physical system is an ongoing and inserted framework that needs explicit applications for profoundly exact planning, little memory impressions, adaptable sensors and actuator interfaces, and powerful wellbeing attributes. As an unpredictable and incorporated framework, the CPS coordinates different gadgets furnished with detecting, ID, preparing, correspondence, and systems administration capabilities. In this chapter, compatibility of the CPS with Industry 4.0 is discussed. Key highlights of the CPS and IoT are additionally discussed. This paper portrays a few well-known modern applications of CPSs. Afterwards, the specialized difficulties and future trends related with CPSs are introduced.

References

[1] Broy, M., (2010). Cyber Physical Systems – Wissenschaftliche Herausforderungen bei der Entwicklung. Springer Berlin Heidelberg, Verlag. Auflage: 1st Edition.

[2] German National Academy of Science and Engineering. (December 2011). Cyber Physical Systems – Driving force for innovation in mobility, health, energy and production. *Aca-tech Position Paper*.

[3] Lee, E. Cyber Physical Systems: Design Challenges. University of California, 2008, Berkeley. Technical Report No. UCB/EECS-2008-8.

[4] Xu, L. (2007). Editorial inaugural issue. *Enterprise Information Systems, 1*, 1, 1–2.

[5] Lee, J., Bagheri, B. and Kao, H.A. (2015). A Cyber-Physical Systems architecture for Industry 4.0-based manufacturing systems. *Manufacturing Letters, 3*, 18–23.

[6] Wu, F.-J., Kao, Y.-F. and Tseng, Y.-C. (2011). From wireless sensor networks towards cyber physical systems. *Pervasive and Mobile Computing, 7*, 4, 397–413.

[7] Zhang Y.F. and Tao F. (2016). Optimization of Manufacturing Systems Using the Internet of Things. Elsevier. (ISBN 978-0-12-809910-0).

[8] Banerjee, A., Venkata Subramanian, K.K., Mukherjee, T. and Gupta, S.K.S. (2012). Ensuring safety, security, and sustainability of mission-critical cyber-physical systems. *Proceedings of the IEEE, 100*, 1, 283–299.

[9] Gharavi, H., Chen, H.H. and Wietfeld, C. (2015). Special section on cyber-physical systems and security for smart grid. *IEEE Transactions on Smart Grid, 6*, 5, 2405–2408.

[10] Poovendran, R. (2010). Cyber-physical systems: Close encounters between two parallel worlds. *Proceedings of the IEEE, 98*, 8, 1363–1366.

[11] Poovendran, R., Sampigethaya, K., Gupta, S.K.S., Lee, I., Prasad, K.V., Corman, D. and Paunicka, J.L. (2012). Special issue on cyber-physical systems. *Proceedings of the IEEE, 100*, 1, 6–12.

[12] Woodard M., Sarvestani S.S. and Hurson A.R. (2015). A survey of research on data corruption in cyber-physical critical infrastructure systems. In Advances in Computers, A.R., Hurson (ed.), *Vol. 98*, pp. 59–87.

[13] Rodriguez-Molina, J., Martinez, B., Bilbao, S. and Martin-Wanton, T. (2017). Maritime data transfer protocol (MDTP): A proposal for a data transmission protocol in resource constrained underwater environments involving cyber-physical systems. *Sensors, 17*, 6, 1330.

[14] Kang, W., Kapitanova, K. and Son, S.H. (2012). RDDS: A real-time data distribution service for cyber-physical systems. *IEEE Transactions on Industrial Informatics, 8*, 2, 393–405.

[15] Liu, K., Lee, V.C.S., Ng, J.K.Y., Chen, J. and Son, S.H. (2014a). Temporal data dissemination in vehicular cyber-physical systems. *IEEE Transactions on Intelligent Transportation Systems, 15*, 6, 2419–2431.

[16] Mangharam, R. and Pajic, M. (2013). Distributed control for cyber-physical systems. *Journal of the Indian Institute of Science, 93*, 3, 353–387.

[17] Bogdan, P., Jain, S. and Marculescu, R. (2013). Pacemaker control of heart rate variability: A cyber physical system perspective. *ACM Transactions on Embedded Computing Systems, 12*, 1s, 50 (1–22).

[18] Pfeifer, D., Valvano, J. and Gerstlauer, A. (2013). SimConnect and SimTalk for distributed cyber-physical system simulation. *Simulation-Transactions of the Society for Modeling and Simulation International, 89*, 10, 1254–1271.

[19] Silva, L.C., Almeida, H.O., Perkusich, A. and Perkusich, M. (2015). A model-based approach to support validation of medical cyber-physical systems. *Sensors, 15*, 11, 27625–27670.

[20] Gu, L., Zeng, D.Z., Guo, S., Barnawi, A. and Xiang, Y. (2017). Cost e±cient resource management in fog computing supported medical cyber-physical system. *IEEE Transactions on Emerging Topics in Computing, 5*, 1, 108–119.

[21] Bae, K., Krisilo®, J., Meseguer, J. and Olveczky, P.C. (2015). Designing and verifying distributed cyber-physical systems using multirate PALS: An airplane turning control system case study. *Science of Computer Programming, 103*, 13–50.

[22] Choi, S.H., Jeong, I.B., Kim, J.H. and Lee, J.J. (2014). Context generator and behavior translator in a multilayer architecture for a modular development process of cyber-physical robot systems. *IEEE Transactions on Industrial Electronics, 61*, 2, 882–892.

[23] Bradley, J.M. and Atkins, E.M. (2014). Cyber-physical optimization for unmanned aircraft systems. *Journal of Aerospace Information Systems, 11*, 1, 48–59.

[24] Cassandras, C.G. (2016). Smart cities as cyber-physical social systems. *Engineering, 2*, 2, 156–158.

[25] Shen, B., Zhou, X.S. and Kim, M. (2016). Mixed scheduling with heterogeneous delay constraints in cyber-physical systems. Future generation computer systems. *The International Journal of Escience, 61*, 108–117.

[26] Lin, S.Y. and Wu, H. (2015). Bloom filter-based secure data forwarding in large-scale cyber physical systems, Mathematical Problems in Engineering.

[27] Shin, D., Park, J., Kim, Y., Seo, J. and Chang, N. (2012). Control-theoretic cyber-physical system modeling and synthesis: A case study of an active direct methanol fuel cell. *ACM Transactions on Embedded Computing Systems, 4*, 1–24.

[28] Srbljic, S., Skvorc, D. and Popovic, M. (2012). Programming languages for end-user personalization of cyber-physical systems. *Automatika, 53(3)*, 294-310.

[29] Zhang, X.L. and Liu, P. (2015). A new delay jitter smoothing algorithm based on Pareto distribution in cyber-physical systems. *Wireless Networks, 21*, 6, 1913–1923.

[30] Lanza, G., Haefner, B. and Kraemer, A. (2015). Optimization of selective assembly and adaptive manufacturing by means of cyber-physical system based matching. *CIRP Annals Manufacturing Technology, 64*, 1, 399–402.

13

UAV-Based Cyber-Physical Systems: Concepts, Applications, and Issues

Vikramjit Singh, Krishna Pal Sharma, and Harsh K. Verma
Dr. B.R. Ambedkar National Institute of Technology Jalandhar, Punjab, India

13.1 Introduction

The recent technological advancements in communication, sensing, and computational capabilities have resulted in the development of intelligent unmanned aerial vehicles (UAVs), which are capable of performing tasks without the intervention of human personnel. The unique characteristics of UAVs, such as deployment ease, ability to fly, and low installation and maintenance cost make them suitable for a wide range of military as well as civil applications [1,2]. Some of the common applications in which UAVs provide a feasible solution are search and rescue operations [3], surveillance [4], precision agriculture [5], environmental monitoring [6], forest fire monitoring [7], target detection and tracking [8], construction [9], traffic monitoring [10], and many more. Even though single UAV systems have been used for a variety of applications, the use of multiple UAVs improves the capabilities of existing systems in numerous ways [11]. As in search and rescue operations, UAVs need to scan the whole area of interest and detect the target in a time-efficient manner. Therefore, multiple UAVs can work together on the scanning task and complete the operation in less time. Moreover, when a UAV fails due to any unforeseen reason while performing its tasks, the performance of a multi-UAV system degrades only to some extent instead of total failure as in a single UAV system. Therefore, it is always preferable to use multiple UAVs, which can further cooperate and interconnect to form a UAV network.

The deployment of multiple UAVs to accomplish a task in an autonomous manner requires tight coupling between sensing, communication, computation, and control unit. UAVs sense data from the environment and then process it with an on-board computing unit before sharing that with other UAVs. The shared information is then exploited by UAVs for collaborative decision making that affects future control actions. The context in which UAVs perform tasks is similar to the cyber-physical systems (CPSs). A CPS is an integration of the cyber systems with the physical world in which communication, control, and computation units perform in a closed loop [12]. Thus, in this chapter, we highlight the possibilities of UAVs to be viewed as CPSs, along with the basic concepts of UAV networks and the CPS. The rest of the chapter is structured as follows: Section 2 describes the basic concepts of UAV systems. Section 3 discusses the cyber-physical

DOI: 10.1201/9781003202752-13

system and section 4 describes the UAV-enabled CPS and issues involved in sensing, communication, computation, and control unit of UAVs. Section 5 describes the potential usage of UAVs in CPS applications and section 6 concludes the chapter.

13.2 Basic Concepts Related to UAV Networks

It is necessary to discuss the basics of UAV networks before exploring their use and incorporation into the CPS. In this section, classification of UAVs, the architecture of UAV networks, and communication in UAV networks are discussed.

13.2.1 UAVs Classification

The UAVs can be broadly classified into various categories based on the type of landing, operational altitude, size, range, and endurance, as shown in Figure 13.1. Firstly, UAVs are categorized according to their takeoff and landing [2]. The horizontal takeoff and landing (HTOL) mainly consists of fixed-wing UAVs predominantly used for long-range missions due to their high cruise speed and ability to fly for long time periods. On the other hand, rotary-winged UAVs come under the category of vertical takeoff and landing (VTOL). Rotary-winged UAVs do not require a specific field and device for takeoff and landing. Moreover, their ability to hover makes them suitable for a wide range of applications, including indoor missions. However, rotary-winged UAVs have limited speed and flight time compared to fixed-winged aircraft. Secondly, UAVs are classified based on their operational altitude, ranging from low-altitude UAVs used for data collection to high-altitude UAVs mainly used for a wide range of applications [13]. According to the size, UAVs are categorized into four classes: very small (30–50 cm), small (50 cm–2m), medium (5–10 m),

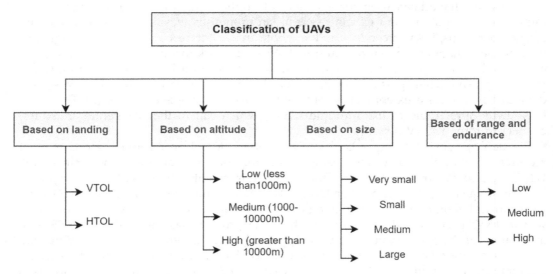

FIGURE 13.1
Classification of UAVs.

and large (>10 m) UAVs. Lastly, based on the range and endurance, UAVs are classified into three categories. Low-range UAVs have a flying range of less than 100 km and endurance time of less than 5 hours. The mid-range UAVs can work in an area ranging from 100 km to 400 km, with a flight time from 5 hours to 24 hours. The long-range UAVs have a range of greater than 400 km with a flight time greater than 24 hours.

13.2.2 Architecture of UAV Networks

There are UAV nodes and ground stations connected directly or indirectly via relay nodes in the UAV network. The flow of information between these nodes depends upon the organization of the network. In most cases, the organization of UAV nodes and ground stations is dependent on the type and nature of the application. There are application requirements where a central device does all the decision making and task assignments. In such a case, UAVs need to be directly connected to the ground station to receive instructions in real time. On the other side, the application scenarios where UAVs need to perform operations autonomously and the decision making is performed by an individual UAV or on a consensus basis. In such scenarios, peer-to-peer links between UAVs are required. In addition, when UAVs are deployed for large-scale applications, the direct connection between all UAVs and the central node is not possible due to limited communication range. Thus, instead of a direct link, the multi-hop communication link is established between the sender UAV and the ground station while other nodes act as relay nodes. There are different architectures of UAV networks that are shown in Figure 13.2: infrastructure-based, ad hoc, multi-group, and multi-layer UAV networks.

i. *Infrastructure-based UAV network:* In this architecture, all UAVs are connected to one or more ground stations and inter-UAV communication is established only through the ground station. It is one of the simplest architectures, but there are certain flaws associated with this organization. First, in this architecture, the presence of a central entity constitutes a single point of failure, which can disrupt the entire network in the case of failure or a security attack. Second, it is difficult to scale the network due to limited bandwidth since each UAV requires a dedicated link for communication. Moreover, the presence of the ground station between the inter-UAV communications introduces extra latency for the transmission of data packets.

ii. *Ad hoc UAV network:* Under this, UAVs are connected directly with each other, and some UAVs are connected to the ground station. It supports UAV-to-UAV and UAV-to-ground-station communication, making this architecture more reliable and flexible. If the direct link between source and destination is not present, intermediate nodes act as a relay and forward the data packets towards the destination.

iii. *Multi-group UAV network:* When a large number of UAVs are required to complete a mission successfully, it is not feasible to organize them all in a single group. Thus, multiple groups or clusters are formed, and each group contains one gateway responsible for communication with other groups and the ground station. The communication inside the group can take place without the intervention of the gateway.

iv. *Multi-layer UAV network:* In heterogeneous UAV networks, there are nodes with different capabilities in terms of speed, operational altitude, and endurance. It

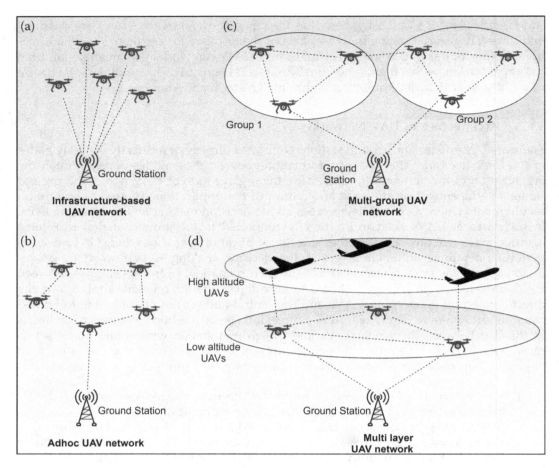

FIGURE 13.2
Architecture of UAV Networks.

is preferable to organize them into multiple layers according to their characteristics. Generally, fixed-winged UAVs are deployed at a higher altitude than rotary-winged due to their endurance and robustness. For instance, in [14] fixed-winged UAVs are deployed at the higher layer to assist the lower-layer UAVs in communication to provide efficient coverage and reduce transmission delay.

13.2.3 Communication in UAV Networks

Basically, wireless communication in UAV networks consists of two types of links, i.e., the control and non-payload communications (CNPC) link, and the data link. In addition to the standard data communication links, UAV systems require additional links for control and non-payload communications to support critical functions like collision avoidance, coordination, and real-time control. CNPC links are used for low latency, highly reliable, and low data requirement communication between UAV-to-UAV (U2U) and UAV-to-ground (U2G). This information includes commands from GS to UAV, aircraft status information from UAV to GS and coordination information among UAVs. Currently, two bands, i.e., the L-band (960–977 MHz) and the C-band (5030–5091 MHz), have been allotted to CNPC links to support critical information exchange [15]. On the other hand, data links are required to transfer mission-related information among UAVs and between GS and UAVs. The capacity requirements of data links vary according to the traffic requirements of the application. Like in search and rescue operations, the sensed information in the form of images and videos requires throughput up to 2 Mbps with delay bound between 50 and 100 ms [16]. Thus, wireless technologies like Wi-Fi, WiMAX, WAVE, and LTE can be considered according to the size of the mission and density of nodes.

13.3 Cyber-Physical Systems

A cyber-physical system is the integration of the physical and cyber world with a closed loop in which processes in the physical world affect the cyber world and vice versa. In 2006, Helen Gill coined the term CPS at the National Science Foundation (NSF) in the United States [17]. Until then, it was described from different perspectives by the research community and there are multiple definitions available for a CPS. For instance, in [18] a CPS is described as "physical and engineered systems, whose operations are monitored, coordinated, controlled, and integrated by a computing and communicating core." In [19], a CPS is considered as engineered systems that require a tight integration of control, communication, and computational technologies to deal with physical systems. The ability of a CPS to integrate multiple technologies not only innovates the existing industry but also unfolds new dimensions in a wide range of applications such as precision agriculture, surveillance, health care, home automation, and air traffic management. Like in precision agriculture, a CPS is used to monitor the vegetation status of potato crop [20], which enables farmers to make decisions so as to improve productivity. Moreover, in [21], a CPS-based pest control system is proposed to monitor the rodents in agricultural fields. Similarly, the utilization of a CPS in the healthcare sector triggers various innovations like monitoring patients in real time, tele-medication systems, and robot-assisted surgeries. The key components of CPSs are cyber space, physical world, sensed data, actuation commands, and communication network, as shown in Figure 13.3. The cyberspace includes processing units, communication modules, middleware, software, and algorithms that are responsible for decision making. The physical world consists of any physical process that is required to be monitored. The sensor data includes any type of data (such as temperature reading, image, video, audio, position information, and many more) that is accumulated by sensors. The actuation commands contain the actions that are required to be performed by actuators to control the processes of the physical world. The communication network contains the networking devices to connect the cyberspace with the physical world.

13.4 UAV-Enabled CPS

The CPS integrates the physical and cyber world with the help of interfaces. The physical world refers to the real-world process that are required to be monitored or controlled. The cyber world consists of embedded systems that are responsible for data processing and

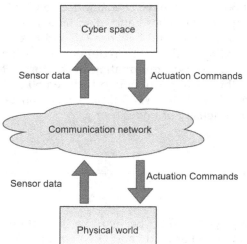

FIGURE 13.3
Components of Cyber-Physical Systems.

communication with other systems. Interfaces include communication networks, sensors, and actuators, which are responsible for perceiving data from the real world and input it into the cyber world and then control the physical world according to the instructions provided by the cyber system [22]. Thus, a CPS can be considered a synergistic integration of physical and cyber domains with the help of communication networks. This type of integration can also be seen in UAV networks where multiple UAVs cooperate to accomplish a common goal [23–26]. Typically, a UAV consists of an onboard computational device to process data, sensors, or cameras to perceive data from the physical world; a communication module to communicate with other systems; and a control block to alter the processes of the physical world and its state. When UAVs equipped with such capabilities are deployed in an area of interest, they gather data (sensor readings, images, audio, or video) from the environment and process that data with onboard processors. After processing, UAVs share information for collaborative decision making and then perform actions accordingly. Further, actions performed in the current cycle can be evaluated and influence the next cycle's decision-making process. Thus, UAV networks can be seen as CPSs, and their architecture is shown in Figure 13.4.

In the following, the functionalities and issues faced by primary high-level building blocks (i.e., sensing, communication, computation, and control) of UAV-based CPSs are described in detail. The issues related to each building block are illustrated in Figure 13.5.

13.4.1 Sensing

For the successful completion of missions by UAV networks, accurate and reliable sensor data is required. UAVs sense data from the physical world and transfer that to the computational block for further processing, which could be shared with other UAV devices or ground stations for distributed decision making. UAVs could be equipped with various types of sensors as per the application requirements to measure the physical quantities. For instance, in search and rescue operations, UAVs may be equipped with visual or thermal sensors to search the target in a given area [27–29]. Moreover, to detect the source of a chemical plume [30] UAVs are equipped with a chemical analyzer,

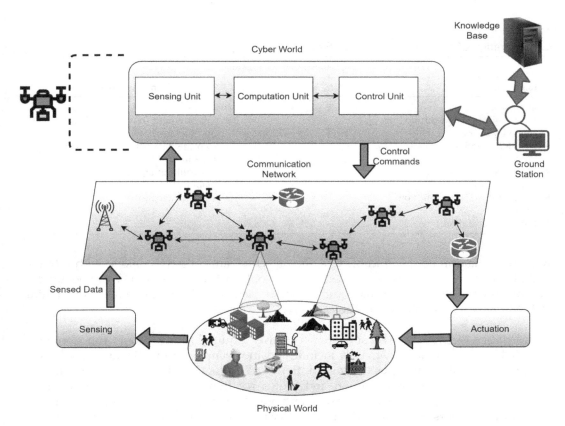

FIGURE 13.4
Architecture of UAV-Based CPS.

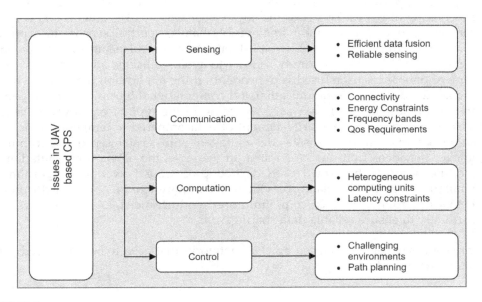

FIGURE 13.5
Issues Related to UAV-Based CPS.

TABLE 13.1

Categorization of Sensors Used in UAV Systems

Classification of Sensors	
Primary Sensors	**Secondary Sensors**
Position sensors	Visual sensors
• For localization and positioning	• Capture light from visible bands
Motion sensors	Spectral sensors
• Deal with motion	• Capture data from non-visible bands
Environment sensors	Proximity sensors
• Sense physical quantities	• For collision avoidance
Power sensors	Stabilization
• Monitor power consumption	• For balancing load
Radios	
• For communication	

whereas to determine the volcanic CO_2 flux, electrochemical sensors along with infrared and ultraviolet spectrometers are used [31]. The onboard sensors of UAVs can be divided into two broad categories: primary and secondary sensors [32], based on their functioning in UAV networks, as shown in Table 13.1.

a. *Primary sensors*: These sensors are necessarily required for the proper functioning of UAVs. This category mainly includes position sensors like GPS and gyroscopes for localization and positioning, motion sensors like accelerometers and rotary encoders to deal with motion and motor rotations respectively, environment sensors to report the overheating and wind disturbance to a controller, and power sensors to monitor the power consumption and radio to ensure communication between a UAV and the ground controller.

b. *Secondary sensors*: UAVs are equipped with secondary sensors only to satisfy the targeted application requirements and are not directly associated with the functioning of UAVs. This class includes visual sensors like cameras and colour sensors used to capture light from visible bands, spectral sensors to capture image data from non-visible bands, stabilization for balancing the equipment carried by UAVs, and proximity sensors to avoid collisions and obstacles. The type of onboard sensors used is dependent on the application demands, which impact the design of communication and computational block. The amount and frequency of data generation vary according to the type of employed sensors. Visual sensors generate a large amount of datacompared to temperature or position sensors. Suppose UAVs are equipped with visual sensors to capture images or videos from the target area. In that case, the onboard computational module needs to be armed with desired processing power and algorithms. Similarly, if gathered images or videos are required to be shared with other UAVs or ground stations, communication modules need to be designed accordingly to ensure reliable data sharing.

There are some sensing issues faced by UAV networks that need to be considered before designing UAV-based CPSs.

i. *Efficient data fusion*: Generally, UAVs are equipped with various sensors like position sensors, visual sensors, proximity sensors, and so on. So, there is a requirement for efficient data fusion techniques to combine data from diverse sensors and reduce the amount of data transmission in the network.

ii. *Reliable sensing*: The reliability of sensing information affects the quality of decisions made by UAVs and ground stations. The sensed data is directly linked to the effectiveness of collision avoidance, mission planning, and coordination between UAVs. The tilting of UAVs due to flight dynamics, wind, and other environmental disturbances affects the accuracy of a sensor reading, which needs to be rectified by mounting sensors on active suspensions [33].

13.4.2 Communication

Communication is one of the essential components of a CPS, which provides connectivity between different components and is responsible for data flow from sensors to a commutation block and then from commutation to actuators. Similarly, in a UAV network, the data is shared among UAVs and the ground station to ensure efficient decision making, coordination, and control. The exchanged data can be divided into three categories: sensed data, coordination data, and control data [16]. The data sensed by UAV devices is shared with ground stations and other UAVs for better coordination and efficient decision making. Generally, UAVs have limited computational power, so data is transferred to the ground station for advanced analysis. There are different types of sensor data, as described previously, and each data has different quality of service (QOS) requirements that need to be satisfied with relevant communication technologies. Coordination traffic varies according to mission requirements and nature of decision making: centralized or distributed. The coordination data mainly includes telemetry data, sensor data, and commands related to decision making and task allocation. In centralized decision making, the coordination data is primarily exchanged between UAV devices and the decision-making unit (ground station in most cases due to a higher power). On the other hand, in distributed decision making, data is exchanged between UAV devices to decide the future action plan through consensus among different network entities. The control data is considered mandatory for all applications, including telemetry data from UAVs to ground stations and control commands from ground stations to UAVs. With the help of telemetry data, a ground station continuously tracks the flight of the UAV and, whenever required, interferes (in case of emergency or mission updates) by sending control instructions to the UAV. In CPS, coupling between various components demands reliable and efficient communication. Before designing a UAV-based CPS, subsequent issues related to communication need to be considered.

i. *Connectivity*: UAVs are generally deployed in a three-dimensional space, and their movement is highly dynamic, ranging from being static to flying at high speed. As a result, there is intermittent connectivity between nodes, leading to frequent path failures during data transmission. Besides this, large-scale missions and limited communication range of UAVs result in limited connectivity between nodes. Therefore, in addition to deploying sufficient relay nodes to ensure connectivity, there is a requirement for communication protocols that are resistant to high mobility and fluid topology.

ii. *Energy constraints:* UAVs have limited battery power due to size and payload constraints. Most of the energy is consumed by motor operations and the remaining is left for other tasks like sensing, communication, coordination, and computation, which should be utilized consciously. Therefore, lightweight communication protocols are desired to increase the network lifetime and keep UAVs away from unexpected failures.

iii. *Frequency bands:* UAV systems utilize unlicensed bands such as S-Band, L-Band, and ISM (industrial, scientific, and medical) bands, which can suffer from scarcity and interference due to the workings of other communication systems in the same band.

iv. *QOS requirements:* In UAV networks, nodes gather different types of data from the environment, such as images, videos, temperatures, and other physical quantities. Each data type has different QOS requirements according to the requirements of an application. Thus, it is desirable to have a communication module that can cater to varying QOS demands of the application.

13.4.3 Computation

It is a critical component in the closed loop since everything from simple data analysis to complex decision making relies on the computation ability of UAV networks. The decisions, information, and response from the physical world are stored in the knowledge base that influences the next cycle's decisions. The data collected from the environment by a UAV device needs to be processed before using it for decision making. The data processing in computationally intensive tasks like image and video processing require high computational power. UAVs can compute these tasks either by using an onboard processor or by offloading them to ground stations. For offloading, this component relies on the communication block of a CPS to transfer the tasks to other nodes and then get back the results. The decision to select online or offline computation can be based on the type of processing required by the application. In UAV networks, data processing can be divided into real-time and non-real-time processing. In real-time processing, data needs to be processed quickly for time-critical decision making. So, data may be processed locally or offloaded to the local server and neighboring UAVs to meet the delay constraints. On the other hand, non-real-time processing is used in delay-tolerant applications in which processed data is not immediately required. So, collected data can be processed and stored at a remote cloud or server, and whenever data is needed, UAVs can send a request for it.

With recent advancements in embedded systems and miniaturization technology, it has become possible to develop small and low-weight hardware platforms for UAVs. Some of the available lightweight and powerful platforms are Jetson, Odroid U3, mini-ITX I7, and Snapdragon Flight. Although platforms can execute complex algorithms like image processing, pattern recognition, and path planning, there is a possibility of further improving the system's performance by offloading the computationally heavy tasks. In UAV networks, offloading can be done by migrating the tasks to resourceful devices, either ground stations or counterpart UAVs. There are various approaches proposed in the literature for computation offloading to improve the performance of UAV networks. In [34], cloud-based architecture is proposed for the Internet of drones in which UAVs offload heavy tasks to the cloud. In [35], an opportunistic computation offloading scheme is proposed in which, drone cluster with heavy load seeks resources from other clusters. The cluster head takes the decision of task offloading after communicating with neighboring cluster heads. Although several computational optimization and offloading techniques are available, there are some challenges faced by UAV-based CPS that need to be considered.

i. *Heterogeneous computing units:* In UAV networks, multiple computing units with different capabilities are involved. When a UAV has a heavy computational task, it is not always possible to transfer tasks to any available resourceful unit due to heterogeneity. Thus, efficient task allocation algorithms are required to assign tasks in dynamic scenarios based on the available information about tasks and neighboring units.

ii. *Latency constraints:* In real-time applications, UAVs require results of computational tasks in a time-critical manner. The transfer of computationally heavy tasks for offline processing leads to additional delay, which varies according to available network resources. Moreover, it is difficult to set a reliable path due to the dynamic nature of UAVs, which could further delay the results of offline computed tasks.

13.4.4 Control Unit

The control unit generates the control actions according to the commands, which affect the state of the UAV and the physical world. The control system guarantees that the UAV behaves consistently and reliably, such as following a desired trajectory with adequate accuracy in the face of external disruptions. A typical block diagram of a UAV control system is shown in Figure 13.6. A control system tries to reduce the tracking error between the desired and estimated states.

The navigation system generates the estimation of states by combining information from various available sensors. In UAVs, control systems can be divided into two categories: low-level control and high-level control. Low-level control is responsible for controlling low-level tasks such as altitude, speed, or actuator control. In contrast, the high-level control layer runs on an onboard processor and can handle computationally complex operations, including path planning, formation control, and target tracking missions, as depicted in Table 13.2.

Higher-level control performs complicated calculations to build a task plan that includes a certain set of actions. Each action specifies a command sequence that is provided

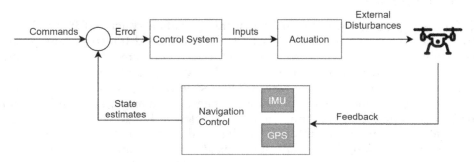

FIGURE 13.6
Architecture of UAV Control System.

TABLE 13.2

Categories of UAV Control Systems

UAV Control System	
Low-level control layer	High-level control layer
• Altitude control	• Target detection
• Speed control	• Formation control
• Actuator control	• Target tracking

to the low-level control, as shown in Figure 13.6, to perform desired actions. In the following, certain issues faced by the control system of UAVs are described.

   i. *Challenging environments:* UAVs are required to have high control bandwidth to successfully navigate challenging environments such as interior building and urban areas. Small-sized UAVs, on the other hand, are always constrained in terms of computing and mechanical payloads. Thus, intelligent, robust, and lightweight control algorithms are required to perform effectively in uncertain and highly dynamic environments.

   ii. *Path planning:* Path planning aims to find a flight path of UAVs from the starting point to the finishing point. The optimal path is not only required to have the shortest distance from source to destination, but it should also provide collision-free flight. There are several path planning strategies available for 2-D environments. However, energy-efficient, connectivity-aware, and collision-free 3-D path planning algorithms for multi-UAV systems are required.

13.5 Potential Usage of UAVs in CPS Applications

In this section, we describe the use of a CPS in various application domains. Besides that, it is also discussed how the use of UAVs provides additional benefits for the completion of tasks in CPS applications.

13.5.1 Transportation

The CPS plays a pivotal role in the intelligent transportation system (ITS), which is one of the primary requirements of future smart cities. CPS-enabled transportation systems integrate various technologies like sensing, communication, computation, and control to ensure safety, coordination, and other services. It covers ground, sea, and air transportation, which are connected with the help of wireless technologies. ITS can achieve safety, driver assistance, collision avoidance, limiting congestion, smart parking, and autonomous driving by integrating CPS into infrastructures, vehicles, and highways. In ITS, reliable and real-time data is required to be captured, which is further processed and analyzed to ensure intelligent decision making. The installation of fixed cameras is one of the popular solutions that is helpful in inspecting and monitoring of vehicles [36]. However, there are several drawbacks: high cost, limited coverage, and hidden views associated with it. These issues can be easily resolved with the help of a multi-UAV system that can provide on-demand, wide and efficient coverage in a cost-efficient manner. Moreover, it is challenging to provide reliable communication from vehicle-to-vehicle and vehicle-to-infrastructure due to buildings and other obstacles in urban areas. As a result, UAVs can be deployed to provide better connectivity and line of sight links [37].

13.5.2 Disaster Management

Natural disasters are unpredictable phenomena and cannot be avoided, but their consequences can be mitigated with adequate warnings and recovery processes. CPSs can also provide rapid response in which various nodes and sensors need to access the situation and quickly inform the desired authority. In [38], a CPS is used for the monitoring and mapping of areas affected by a disaster to get situational awareness. This task is accomplished by using a set of autonomous ground and aerial nodes equipped with sensors to capture the data. These nodes share collected information with each other and with the central node to make effective decisions. In addition to mapping and monitoring, aerial nodes can also be used to provide communication services to first responders and victims in post-disaster scenarios.

13.5.3 Surveillance

The use of a CPS for surveillance is a cost-effective solution that reduces the risk to human life and increases efficiency. In surveillance, the visual observations of the environment need to be collected with the help of sensors. For the accomplishment of such tasks, multi-UAV systems can act as a potential solution due to their easy deployment and large coverage [39]. For example, in [40], UAVs are used in collaboration with other devices to monitor wildfire, wildlife, and climate change.

13.5.4 Construction

A CPS can be considered as a promising technology to assist the construction activities by providing real-time monitoring, inspection, and coordination between supervisors and field workers. CPS gathers information from various sensors, such as human behaviour sensors, gas sensors, radio frequency identification, and global positioning systems, to detect the dangerous situation at a site and inform field workers and supervisors to mitigate the adverse impact of accidents [41]. UAVs' use in construction can further improve the performance of CPSs by providing on-demand, cost-effective, and reliable aerial inspection and monitoring of the site.

13.5.5 Smart Grid

The smart grid is a new concept that aims to create a next-generation energy network that exploits communication and control technologies to establish an automated and bidirectional flow of electricity and information between producers and consumers. The use of a CPS in a smart grid helps to provide integration between various heterogeneous units to ensure real-time information exchange and efficient decision making [42]. Moreover, a CPS can be used as a power system monitoring and diagnostic tool that can significantly reduce the number of system failures, catastrophes, and natural disasters that result in unreliable and defective power services. In such cases, UAVs can be utilized in smart grid CPS applications that include damage assessment, power line inspection, and work-in-progress monitoring [43,44].

13.5.6 Precision Agriculture

CPS plays a prominent role in the field of precision agriculture to improve the crop yield, lower labor cost, and ensure the optimal usage of fertilizers, pesticides, and water. With the help of a CPS, it has become possible to continuously monitor the agriculture fields and perform desired action whenever required. In [20], a CPS is used to monitor the vegetation status of a potato crop, which allows farmers to make suitable decisions on the development of certain conditions. In this system, data collection is done with the help of aerial and terrestrial nodes. There are other numerous ways in which UAVs can collaborate and integrate with such systems to perform operations like crop monitoring, pesticide spraying, and field and soil analysis.

13.6 Conclusion

The recent advancement in networking, computing, and sensing technologies has stimulated UAVs' integration with a CPS to provide services in a wide range of applications. However, several challenges need to be addressed before designing a UAV-based CPS. This chapter described the basic concepts of UAVs and CPSs along with highlighting the issues related to sensing, communication, computation, and control unit of UAV-enabled CPSs. Besides that, the architecture of UAV-enabled CPS and the use of UAVs in different CPS applications are also discussed.

References

[1] Shakhatreh, H., et al. (2019). Unmanned Aerial Vehicles (UAVs): A survey on civil applications and key research challenges. *IEEE Access, 7*, 48572–48634.
[2] Singhal, G., Bansod, B. and Mathew, L. (2018). Unmanned Aerial Vehicle classification, applications and challenges: A review. *Preprint*, no. November, 1–19.
[3] Waharte, S. and Trigoni, N. (2010). Supporting search and rescue operations with UAVs. *Proc. – EST 2010 – 2010 Int. Conf. Emerg. Secur. Technol. ROBOSEC 2010 – Robot. Secur. LAB-RS 2010 – Learn. Adapt. Behav. Robot. Syst.*, pp. 142–147.
[4] de Moraes, R. S. and de Freitas, E. P. (2018). Distributed control for groups of unmanned aerial vehicles performing surveillance missions and providing. *J. Intell. Robotic Syst., 92*, 645–656.
[5] Tsouros, D. C., Bibi, S. and Sarigiannidis, P. G. (2019). A review on UAV-based applications for precision agriculture. *Information, 10*, no. 11, 349–354.
[6] Lu, Y., Macias, D., Dean, Z. S., Kreger, N. R. and Wong, P. K. (2015). A UAV-mounted whole cell biosensor system for environmental monitoring applications. *IEEE Trans. Nanobiosci., 14*, 8, 811–817.
[7] Ghamry, K. A., Kamel, M. A. and Zhang, Y. (2017). Multiple UAVs in forest fire fighting mission using particle swarm optimization. *2017 Int. Conf. Unmanned Aircr. Syst. ICUAS 2017*, pp. 1404–1409.
[8] Yanmaz, E. and Guclu, H. (2010). Stationary and mobile target detection using mobile wireless sensor networks. *Proc. – IEEE INFOCOM*, pp. 1–5.

[9] Ahmed, F., Amir, M. and Anwar, N. (2018). Construction monitoring and reporting using drones and unmanned aerial vehicles (UAVs). *Tenth Int. Conf. Constr. 21st Century*, no. July, pp. 1–8.

[10] Ro, K., Oh, J. S. and Dong, L. (2007). Lessons learned: Application of small UAV for urban highway traffic monitoring. *Collect. Tech. Pap. – 45th AIAA Aerosp. Sci. Meet.*, *10*, no. January, 7160–7178.

[11] Skorobogatov, G., Barrado, C. and Salamí, E. (2020). Multiple UAV systems: A survey. *Unmanned Syst.*, *8*, 2, 149–169.

[12] Haque, S. A., Aziz, S. M. and Rahman, M. (2014). Review of cyber-physical system in healthcare. *Int. J. Distrib. Sens. Networks*, *2014*, 217415–217424

[13] Arjomandi, M., Agostino, S., Mammone, M., Nelson, M. and Zhou, T. (2006). Classification of unmanned aerial vehicles. *Rep. Mech. Eng. Class, Univ. Adelaide, Adelaide, Aust.*, 1–48.

[14] Zhang, Q., Jiang, M., Feng, Z., Li, W., Zhang, W. and Pan, M. (2019). IoT Enabled UAV: Network architecture and routing algorithm. *IEEE Internet Things J*, *6*, 2, 3727–3742.

[15] Zeng, Y., Zhang, R. and Lim, T. J. (2016). Wireless communications with unmanned aerial vehicles: Opportunities and challenges. *IEEE Commun. Mag.*, *54*, 5, 36–42.

[16] Hayat, S., Yanmaz, E. and Muzaffar, R. (2016). Survey on unmanned aerial vehicle networks for civil applications: A communications viewpoint. *IEEE Commun. Surv. Tutorials*, *18*, 4, 2624–2661.

[17] Lee, E. A. (2015). The past, present and future of cyber-physical systems: A focus on models. *Sensors (Switzerland)*, *15*, 3, 4837–4869.

[18] Ragunathan, R., Lee, I., Lui, S. and Stankovic, J. (2010). Cyber-Physical systems: The next computing revolution. *Des. Autom. Conf.*, 731–736.

[19] Kim, K. D. and Kumar, P. R. (2013). An overview and some challenges in cyber-physical systems. *J. Indian Inst. Sci.*, *93*, 3, 341–352.

[20] Rad, C.-R., Hancu, O., Takacs, I.-A. and Olteanu, G. (2015). Smart monitoring of potato crop: A cyber-physical system architecture model in the field of precision agriculture. *Agric. Agric. Sci. Procedia*, *6*, 73–79.

[21] Mehdipour, F., Nunna, K. C. and Murakami, K. J. (2013). A smart cyber-physical systems-based solution for pest control (work in progress). *Proc. – 2013 IEEE Int. Conf. Green Comput. Commun. IEEE Internet Things IEEE Cyber, Phys. Soc. Comput. GreenCom-iThings-CPSCom 2013*, pp. 1248–1253.

[22] Gunes, V., Peter, S., Givargis, T. and Vahid, F. (2014). A survey on concepts, applications, and challenges in cyber-physical systems. *KSII Trans. Internet Inf. Syst.*, *8*, 12, 4242–4268.

[23] Wang, H., Zhao, H., Zhang, J., Ma, D., Li, J. and Wei, J. (2020). Survey on unmanned aerial vehicle networks: A cyber physical system perspective. *IEEE Commun. Surv. Tutorials*, *22*, 2, 1027–1070.

[24] Shakeri, R., et al. (2018). Design challenges of multi-uav systems in cyber-physical applications: A comprehensive survey, and future directions. *arXiv*, *21*, 4, 3340–3385.

[25] Namuduri, K., Wan, Y., Gomathisankaran, M. and Pendse, R. (2012). Airborne network: A cyber-physical system perspective. *Proc. Int. Symp. Mob. Ad Hoc Netw. Comput.*, pp. 55–59.

[26] Guo, R. X., Tian, J. W., Wang, B. H. and Te Shang, F. (2020). Cyber–physical attack threats analysis for UAVs from CPS perspective. *Proc. – 2020 Int. Conf. Comput. Eng. Appl. ICCEA 2020*, pp. 259–263.

[27] Cooper, J. and Goodrich, M. A. (2008). Towards combining UAV and sensor operator roles in UAV-enabled visual search. *HRI 2008 – Proc. 3rd ACM/IEEE Int. Conf. Human-Robot Interact. Living with Robot.*, pp. 351–358.

[28] Israel, M. (2012). A UAV-based ROE deer fawn detection system. *Int. Arch. Photogramm. Remote Sens. Spat. Inf. Sci.*, *XXXVIII-1/*, no. September, 51–55.

[29] Molina, P., et al. (2012). Searching lost people with Uavs: The System and Results of the Close-Search Project. *ISPRS – Int. Arch. Photogramm. Remote Sens. Spat. Inf. Sci.*, *XXXIX-B1*, no. September 2012, 441–446.

[30] Porter, M. J. and Vasquez, J. R. (2006). Bio-inspired navigation of chemical plumes. *2006 9th Int. Conf. Inf. Fusion, FUSION*.

[31] McGonigle, A. J. S., Aiuppa, A., Giudice, G., Tamburello, G., Hodson, A. J. and Gurrieri, S. (2008). Unmanned aerial vehicle measurements of volcanic carbon dioxide fluxes. *Geophys. Res. Lett.*, *35*, 6, 3–6.

[32] Mukherjee, A., Misra, S. and Raghuwanshi, N. S. (2019). A survey of unmanned aerial sensing solutions in precision agriculture. *J. Netw. Comput. Appl.*, *148*, 102461.

[33] Yanmaz, E., Yahyanejad, S., Rinner, B., Hellwagner, H. and Bettstetter, C. (2018). Drone networks: Communications, coordination, and sensing. *Ad Hoc Networks*, *68*, 1–15.

[34] Qureshi, B., Koubâa, A., Sriti, M.-F., Javed, Y. and Alajlan, M. (2016). Dronemap – A cloud-based architecture for the internet-of-drones. *Int. Conf. Embed. Wirel. Syst. Networks*.

[35] Valentino R., Jung W. S. and Ko Y. B. (2018). Opportunistic computational offloading system for clusters of drones. *Int. Conf. Adv. Commun. Technol. ICACT*, *2018-February*, 303–306.

[36] Barmpounakis, E. N., Vlahogianni, E. I. and Golias, J. C. (2016). Unmanned Aerial Aircraft Systems for transportation engineering: Current practice and future challenges. *Int. J. Transp. Sci. Technol.*, *5*, 3, 111–122.

[37] Menouar, H., Guvenc, I., Akkaya, K., Uluagac, A. S., Kadri, A. and Tuncer, A. (2017). UAV-enabled intelligent transportation systems for the smart city: Applications and challenges. *IEEE Commun. Mag.*, *55*, 3, 22–28.

[38] Cortez, R. (2009). A cyber-physical system for situation awareness following a diaster situation. *IEEE*, no. 5 , 1–2.

[39] Thakur, N., Nagrath, P., Jain, R., Saini, D., Sharma, N. and Hemanth, D. J. (2021). Artificial intelligence techniques in smart cities surveillance using UAVs: A survey, Machine Intelligence and Data Analytics for Sustainable Future Smart Cities, 1(1), 329–353.

[40] Wang, H., Liu, J. and Han, J. (2015). RS-CPS: A distributed architecture of robotic surveillance cyber-physical system in the nature environment. *2015 IEEE Int. Conf. Cyber Technol. Autom. Control Intell. Syst. IEEE-CYBER 2015*, pp. 1287–1292.

[41] Jin, W., Liu, Y., Jin, Y., Jia, M. and Xue, L. (2020). The construction of builder safety supervision system based on CPS. *Wirel. Commun. Mob. Comput.*, *1*, 1–11.

[42] Karnouskos, S. (2011). Cyber-physical systems in the SmartGrid. *IEEE Int. Conf. Ind. Informatics*, pp. 20–23.

[43] Zhou, Z., Zhang, C., Xu, C., Xiong, F., Zhang, Y. and Umer, T. (2018). Energy-efficient industrial internet of UAVs for power line inspection in smart grid. *IEEE Trans. Ind. Informatics*, *14*, 6, 2705–2714.

[44] Toth, J. and Gilpin-Jackson, A. (2010). Smart view for a smart grid – unmanned aerial vehicles for transmission lines. *2010 1st Int. Conf. Appl. Robot. Power Ind. CARPI 2010*, pp. 1–6.

14

An AI-Based Cyber-Physical System for 21st-Century-Based Intelligent Health Care

Tawseef Ayoub Shaikh

Department of Computer Science & Engineering, Pandit Deendayal Energy University, Gandhinagar, Gujrat, India

Tabasum Rasool

Research Associate, Interdisciplinary Centre for Water Research (ICWaR), Indian Institute of Science, Bangalore

Younis Ahmed Malla

Department of Computer Engineering, Aligarh Muslim University, Uttar Pradesh, India

Shabir Sofi

Department of Information Technology, National Institute of Technology, Srinagar, Jammu & Kashmir, India

14.1 Introduction

The Internet of Things (IoT) is one of the most popular modern inventions. Cyber-physical systems (CPSs) are created when these connected devices link up. Used extensively in various sectors, like health care, automation, communication, energy, robotics, smart buildings, transportation, and physical security, cyber-physical systems are referred to as feedback systems [1]. In many cases, one can look at a CPS in the context of engineering and see quite a bit of abstraction. Innovative subjects such as computer science and mathematics have driven advancements in the core subject areas over the years. Usually it focuses on dynamic systems and data-algorithm transformation processes. It additionally supports communication and storage features with monitoring and controls, as well as being capable of handling entities with enhanced capabilities in the physical world [2].

A wide range of defence, manufacturing, and e-healthcare industries use these smart devices to automate workflows, often without the intervention of a human. Figure 14.1 depicts the integration of a CPS with computation, networking, and numerous physical processes at the core of the design. A CPS is increasingly being used in numerous fields, including the automotive industry, the defence sector, health care, and aerospace. It is essentially an interlink between the Internet and its users, which incorporates multiple

DOI: 10.1201/9781003202752-14

233

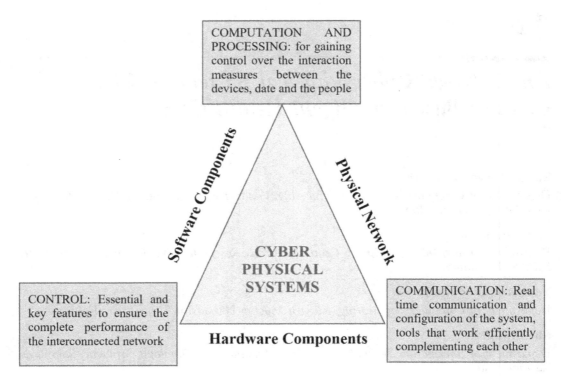

FIGURE 14.1
Structure of Cyber-Physical System.

approaches to meet both the functional and emotional needs of users [3]. Nonetheless, in this current period (smart era), the medical field has attained a great deal of importance, and innovations and developments in this field are being made gradually. An everyday human life example was included in [4], where authors described ordinary human activities, such as having a normal life with intelligent connected devices. However, the application in question is also under attack due to an Internet of Things (IoT)–based infrastructure [5]. The primary disadvantage of an attack on these systems is that it can cause financial issues or has to do with privacy. Real-time and virtual world issues, such as dependability, safety, security, and efficiency, are helping to address some of the challenges in a CPS. The first step in combating attacks of this nature would be to identify the physical systems in which safety is critical and integrate the rapidly evolving technologies.

In an effort to enable technology to assist automation of health care, a CPS incorporates a digital and physical world approach [6]. A CPS extracts information from the physical world through sensors and processes that information in order to fulfil the system's requirements. In order to verify the listed metrics known as S3, viz "safe," "security," and "sustainability," their operation must meet the requirements. Control is exercised through feedback loops in embedded systems, with computational results obtained. Currently, a large number of researchers are devoting their time to the CPS, and it's rapidly becoming a technology breakthrough. Just as the Internet changed the way we communicated with one another, with maybe unintended implications on privacy, individual freedom, and ethics, a CPS will radically alter how we intercommunicate with

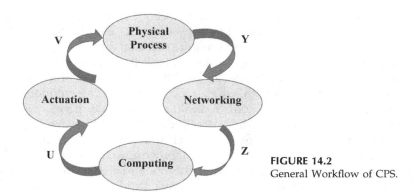

FIGURE 14.2
General Workflow of CPS.

the physical world [7]. As an NSF director put it, "you should care about CPS because your life depends on them."

Based on the findings of the National Science Foundation, a CPS has the potential to revolutionise our world by making systems more responsive (for example, allowing them to avoid collisions without any user input), more precise (for example, surgical robots or nanosized manufacturing), able to function in hazardous or unapproachable settings (for example, self-directed search and rescue systems), which provides extensive disseminated organization (for example, automated traffic control), and which increases human capabilities. A CPS is influenced by societal and industrial demands as well. As seen in Figure 14.2, a general workflow of a CPS can be defined.

Let y stand for "data acquisition" from sensors, z for "in-network physical data accumulation," u for the "physical system state's legal calculated result" that might help the controller choose effective directions, and v for the "control commands" issued to the actuators.

The transportation system infrastructure is having difficulties coping with the increase in both ground and air traffic over the last few decades. The fuels that are currently the main source of energy for the world are being depleted, and with a rising concentration of carbon dioxide gas emissions, drastic changes have occurred in the global climate. More people means greater demand for such technologies, like power, transportation, water, and health care. A CPS has been designated as a top federal research priority by the USA with an invensement of almost USD $150 million since 2009. Additionally, the EU adapted a few programmes striving to improve expertise for entrenched intelligence and systems [8].

Also, CPS Week since 2008 has also brought about a plethora of conferences and workshops about CPS [9]. Co-sponsored by the ACM and the IEEE, ICCPS is a novel conference recognized in 2010. As can be seen in the transportation, defense, finance, and large-scale infrastructure sectors, the CPS may reveal a discrepancy based on where it was applied. "Vehicular cyber-physical system" (VCPS) is a term that is used to describe the new intelligent technology that consists of mobile devices, smartphones, and tablets communicating with drivers and offering assistance with driving.

14.1.1 Medical Cyber-Physical Systems (MCPSs)

The use of interconnected healthcare devices and smart systems help patients in their medical handling and to ensure availability during emergency situations. The MCPS is an embedded system for patients who have been electronically monitored. In the medical domain, monitoring has now become an important service [10]. Providing better patient comfort while treating patients in critical situations will help. With this telemonitoring, patients no longer have to visit the hospital every time they are sick. Elderly people, pregnant women, and patients with critical illnesses that require constant monitoring will find it more useful. The MCPS has taken advantage of technological advancements in order to raise the standard of care for patients. However, the MCPS still faces some design matters that can critically impact patient health, which requires human intervention. Whenever something starts running, there is no control and, as a result, dangerous situations arise for the patients. This was previously discussed in the 2015 PDES workshop, where attendees were presented with various scenarios in real time [11]. Major technological advances are being made in control systems to replace many human activities. The footprints were laid on nearly all of the fields, including the ones related to the "industry," "automobiles," "security," "health care," and "consumer products." The component that enables cyber-physical systems to sense, compute, and communicate with the physical world is key. An MCPS combines various medical devices to monitor and treat a patient [12]. When patients encounter life-threatening situations, they require continued monitoring and treatment.

When hospitals and clinics use MCPSs, these machines and devices are automated and personalised, and high-quality care is provided to patients. It believes in the capability of the intrinsic decision making smartness and network connectivity with every fibre of its being. As these ideas become a reality, we'll be able to have an intelligent operating room and devices that aid in the image and visually guided surgeries, as well as treatments and operations that utilise automated fluid flow controls while administering therapeutic medicines [13]. Heterogeneous data generated through clinical examinations, surveys, treatments, and other devices include structured, semi-structured, and non-structural data. In general, assisted and controlled CPSs are used in applications like healthcare units. The health care's architecture and design framework must draw on both server-based and cloud-based perspectives. Currently, MCPS organisations are confronted by numerous significant issues with regards to privacy and security, and there are inoperable systems, along with strict design standards for system software, in order to thwart MCPS attacks and destructions. Figure 14.3 depicts the MCPS' overall general architecture.

With this system, effective, independent, and efficient results can be obtained. The main objective of MCPS is to provide high patient safety through continuous monitoring and patient support that is individualised. However, the MCPS has many issues with regards to design. Verification and validation techniques should be employed to overcome these design challenges. Effective goals have been established for researchers to focus on solving these problems. Patient safety is the most important component of the MCPS. Prior to using the new MCPS, its risk factors must be evaluated to determine if they are appropriate. Whenever a new requirement is presented, the system is expected to address it. The old way to gain FDA approval for medical devices is time-consuming and expensive. The safety measures of those devices must be taken into consideration, but the process must be made as simple as possible [14]. Information from all of the equipment should be kept out of the patient's reach so the caretaker can utilise it properly, i.e., to ensure patient data privacy, that is. It's also crucial that the device utilised in the process is safeguarded against denial of service attacks.

14.1.1.1 Crucial Medical Devices Behaviour

This is just a brief section describing the most important aspect of medical devices, such as how they behave. Consider the following scenario: A cancer patient has just completed

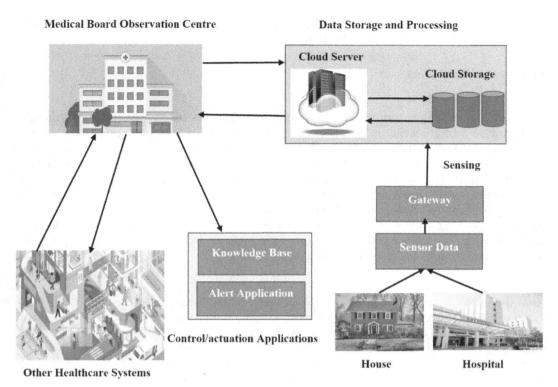

FIGURE 14.3
Overall CPS Setup for Self-Adjustable Health Care.

radiation therapy treatment [15]. Significant healthcare device systems are needed to administer precise doses of radiation with modern medical technology. At the same time, the Cyclotron emits precisely the right amount of protons in such a way that it reacts with even the slightest variations in the patient's posture. A higher level of treatment exactness results in higher total radiation doses. To this end, patient safety requirements have been placed higher. Tight timing constraints are put on the ability to control proton beams with considerably less tolerance [16]. Multiple areas on the patient's body get the same beam, with minimal or no interference, and then the locations are switched to provide more knowledge. Catching the exact position of the patient and sense any patient movement is a critical feature of today's real-time image processing softwares. Due to proton therapy machine safety analyses, thre is a greater emphasis on a solitary organization: the emergency shutdown. There are numerous challenges that face the medical device industry when analysing and validating system leftovers.

14.1.1.2 MCPS Architecture

Since the late 20th century, there have been improvements in the ability to adopt new classes of health monitoring devices. As long as the embedded network system consists of healthcare strategies to dispense doses to patients and sensors that acquire data for monitoring, MCPSs (medical cyber-physical systems) can be referred to as embedded network structures [17]. An electronic health record (EHR) generates patient treatment records over time. In this case, the caregiver is able to take notice of that information and is able to start treatment so that the patient can be cured.

14.1.1.3 MCPS Applications

14.1.1.3.1 Infusion Pump

The PCA is primarily explored for supply pain medications and, when the need arises, it is capable of administering a low-dose bolus of medication. This postoperative pump is used mainly on patients who have undergone surgery. Furthermore, there is no control over the system in this system, which means that the infusion pump could break down, and if something has overdosed on the patient, it may result in death. In order to ensure a high level of safety, prior to using these medical devices, basic standards must be met. More than 56,000 adverse events have been documented as a result of faulty infusion pumps, according to the FDA [18]. These devices clearly show that high availability testing must be completed before using them for patients. In this scenario, a goal has been set for researchers to further carry out investigations.

14.1.1.3.2 DOA Monitoring

Assuring accurate dosage of drugs to the patients while maintaining the depth of anaesthesia in clinical surgery is of critical importance. The "done for you" analysis is grounded on the examination of the "EEG" or the "auditory-evoked potentials" of the mid-latency range [19]. This examination serves to provide highly accurate prescription drugs to patients. Anaesthesia is achieved when the dosage of the anaesthetic is perfectly balanced with the patient's level of consciousness. Because the level of surgical stimulation varies, and because the effects of anaesthetic drugs can decrease the quantity of anaesthetic drugs that can be administered safely, there will almost always be a critical imbalance between the requirement for anaesthetic and the amount of anaesthetic drugs administered.

14.1.1.3.3 Ambient-Intelligence Compliant Objects (AICOs)

Ordinary home objects are placed on top of virtual layers and wireless sensors that are generally hidden from sight and unobtrusive [19]. The interaction features of objects and residents are used for data combination and approximation through AICO. Many Naive Bayes classifiers are exhausted to represent an action. This system is able to identify multiple activities that include listening to music while studying, such as studying or reviewing.

14.1.1.3.4 Wireless Identification and Sensing Project

The wireless identification and sensing project (WISP) enables sensor data communication by using passive RFID tags with sensors [20]. WISP, which is able to send data, are known as tags, and the single-bit message sending tag is known as the α-wisp. To accomplish this communication task between two distinct IDs in dissimilar inertial environments, ID modulation and mercury switch are used. The authors showcase a prototype in which they suggest the incorporation of sensing technology that's more power efficient with RFID technology.

14.1.1.3.5 LiveNet

LiveNet is focused on disease-specific research [21]. This mobile monitoring platform works in real time to report on the status of Parkinson's and epilepsy patients. This mechanism is capable of differentiating Parkinson's disease and epilepsy disease patients' varied symptoms of bradykinesia and hypokinesia.

14.1.1.3.6 Fall Detection System

A fall detection system was proposed by Wang et al. [22] that incorporates an accelerometer in the head to detect a fall and employs an algorithm to verify the fall. It can recognise eight different types of falling postures as well as seven different activities that people conduct on a daily basis: "standing," "walking," "jumping," "running," "lying," "sitting," and "stair-climbing." The algorithm utilises a formula that computes the variance between the percentage of time the body reaches close to the ground and the percentage of time the body is on rest in a specific time period.

14.1.1.3.7 HipGuard

HipGuard is a posture analysis application for use following hip replacement surgery to detect the posture to be used for recovery lasting 8 to 12 weeks [23]. This system is comprised of seven sensors that are strategically placed within close proximity to the surgical area. Data from sensors is transmitted to the computing part, which is then able to locate the hip's position and determine the amount of functional force on it. An alarm is elevated and physicians are contacted when unsafe movement or load is applied to the operated hip.

14.1.1.3.8 MobiHealth

The idea of MobiHealth is to collect data from all the wearables the average person carries every day [24]. Currently, one of the first attempts to collect medical data using sensors is ongoing. The device attempts to gather audio and video information in the event of an accident to aid response.

14.1.1.3.9 CodeBlue

CodeBlue is a podium that integrates medical sensors like "pulse oximeter," "two-lead ECG," and "motion sensor" using software architecture [25]. It is responsible for communication and coordination among medical devices. This system has the potential to greatly increase the efficiency of smart routing and network accumulation for a system that has been previously unadopted.

14.1.1.3.10 AlarmNet

A "biosensor network prototype" characterized by "heart rate," "pulse rate," "oxygen saturation," and "ECG" is a product of AlarmNet [26–38]. Temperature and humidity in the environment serve as spatial contextual data. A gateway is employed to connect the collected data with storage units that helps healthcare professionals to remotely monitor vital signs for patients using a graphical user interface for the process. Table 14.1 describes the applications of a CPS in the healthcare domain with different "architecture and sensing environments."

14.1.1.4 Some Popular Attacks on MCPSs

14.1.1.4.1 Stuxnet

To spread, this computer worm takes advantage of a number of previously undiscovered Windows zero-day vulnerabilities, including targeting and infecting not only computers but also PCs [39]. One of the primary goals of this Stuxnet was to inflict real-world consequences. By initially concentrating natural uranium gas, it is used to make enriched uranium that fuels nuclear devices, bombs, and reactors. When trying to infect a

TABLE 14.1

Application, Architecture, and Sensing-Based Mapping

Project	Application		Architecture		Sensing	
	Assisted	**Infrastructure**	**Data**	**Composition**	**Sensor Type**	**Parameter**
EMR [27]	Elderly living	Server	Heavy	Automatic	Heterogeneous	Multiple
CPeSC3 [28]	Elderly living	Cloud	Heavy	Automatic	Heterogeneous	Multiple
HipGuard [29]	Elderly living	Server	Light	Automatic	Heterogeneous	Multiple
iCabiNET [30]	In-home	Server	Light	User-defined	Homogeneous	Single
RFID CPS [31]	In-home	Server	Light	User-defined	Heterogeneous	Multiple
CPS-MAS [32]	In-home	Server	Light	Automatic	Homogeneous	Single
E-EPR [33]	In-home	Cloud	Heavy	Automatic	Heterogeneous	Multiple
ANGELAH [34]	Elderly living	Server	Light	User-defined	Homogeneous	Single
iPackage [35]	In-home	Server	Light	User-defined	Homogeneous	Multiple
iCabiNET [36]	In-home	Server	Light	User-defined	Homogeneous	Single
Mobile ECG [37]	In-home	Server	Light	Automatic	Homogeneous	Single
Kang [38]	In-home	Server	Light	Automatic	Homogeneous	Single

computer, it looks for Siemens "programmable logic controllers" (PLCs) that are connected to specific models of PLCs. In the above situation, a "programmable logic controller" (PLC) investigates how computers interact with and control industrial machinery such as centrifuges. Once the worm has completed a nefarious act of programming PLCs, it changes the programming and algorithm, which causes the centrifuges to spin too fast and for too long. In this case, delicate equipment is damaged or destroyed. Concealing and hiding what is running in the background is the reason for the PLCs' appearance to convey a fake message to the computer controller.

14.1.1.4.2 Distributed Denial of Services

Distributed denial of services (DDoS) attack is an attempt to damage a system or network by flooding it with bogus data or a flood of internet traffic. Mostly, the effectiveness of these attacks comes from using multiple computer systems as sources of attack traffic [40]. It is like a traffic jam that hinders regular traffic from reaching their destination, like a congested highway. Some recent DDoS attacks include GitHub (2018 – which used memcached rather than botnets to execute a massive DDOS attack, which lasted around 20 minutes), DYN (2016 – using a malware called "Mirai," they carried out the largest botnet DDoS attack to date), and others.

14.1.1.4.3 Man-in-the-Middle Attack

A man-in-the-middle attack is an intervention by the hacker that interferes with the communication between the server and the client, enabling the hacker to extract valuable and useful data from the communication channel [41]. This hack is carried out by re-placing the IP address of the hacker's computer with that of the customers and, as a result, the server falls for the con. Lenovo installed SSL Hijacking (also known as "man-in-the-middle" or MITM) adware called Super fish on their Windows PCs in 2014 as a modern approach to preventing MITM. This British couple (the Luptons) lost over $340,000 when their email account was compromised through a MITM attack.

14.1.1.4.4 Phishing Attack

The practice of sending emails from supposedly trustworthy sources with the intention of installing malware on the target system without the client's knowledge is referred to as phishing. Sandboxing is a good method for testing email content prior to deployment.

14.1.1.4.5 Insider Attack

An insider attack is considered an attack committed by a certified system user who has official permission to access the system and thus is referred to as a traitor. The team intends to launch an all-out attack on computer security and includes activities such as stealing sensitive data and the development of malicious viruses.

14.2 Review of Literature

M. Nandagaoli was the first to discuss perfect difference sets in 1938 that was unnoticed till incorporated into a perfect difference network (PDN) [42]. Because the construction was expressed in terms of points and lines in a finite projective plane, these were thought to have a high chance of being evolved into a network. PDN offer a diameter of 2 in an asymptotically optimal manner, according to the work of [43] et al. The work demonstrated PDNs allow O(d2) nodes that resulted in symmetry and connectivity result in balanced communication flow and high fault tolerance. Other work demonstrated that multidimensional PDNs provide a cost-performance compromise in the sense that a q-dimensional PDN has a diameter D = 2q and a node degree that grows as the (2q)th root of n for any fixed number q of dimensions [44].

PDN can be utilised in "network-on-chip (NoC)" applications. NoC is a system-on-chip (SoC)–based approach that aims to provide high-performance nanoscale structures [45,46]. Separating the communication infrastructure from the computational resources allows the network to be reused. PDN is a reliable, high-performing interconnection network for parallel and dispersed computing. PDNs may be desired for huge networks with cable connectivity, but they also make good wireless, nanophotonic, and optical linkages, as well as slighter constituent networks in hierarchical systems.

Integrated clinical environments (ICE) standardised by the ASTM foundation standards (ASTM F2761) introduce a patient-centric infrastructure that permits the exposed organization of assorted healthcare tools and techniques [47]. The ICE agenda is widely adopted by various agencies, the most popular implementation of which is OpenICE [48]. Almohri et al. [49] recently surveyed the leading-edge security techniques and evaluated their suit-ability for MCPS design. Another contribution details the development of a prototype that incorporates the ICE framework's security mechanisms and the OMG Data Distribution Service to help protect communications developed on that framework (DDS) [50].

A collaborative research approach on "social human-in-the-loop cyber-physical production systems (Social HITLCPPS)" is outlined [51]. According to the author, the ARTI model is suggested. This model combines directed control and simulation-based optimization, with control coming first and optimization following [52]. The results in [53] propose a classification of "human-in-the-loop cyber-physical systems (HiLCPS)." Although in [54], the author focuses on security by taking advantage of two complementary approaches, including approaches for acquiring multi-domain simulation to improve the overall attack resistance, as well as procedures and mechanisms that help in identifying attacked hardware, they manage to do so by dealing with security through a combined approach of these approaches. In [55], in the shape of a let-down and fault tolerance, a CPS is tailored in such a way that agents perform the usual functions, and processing is generalised as distinct transitions.

In the literature, only a few CPS architectures for healthcare applications [56,57] have been presented. However, Hu et al. [58] advocated the design of a medical CPS framework that incorporated service orientation. This proposal, however, lacks the architectural framework necessary to fully realise the concept. A new secure CPS architecture developed by Wang et al. [59] incorporated a WSN-cloud integrated framework. In a study published in 2003, the authers [60] familiarized demonstrating and examination of medical CPS. In the study conducted by Wang et al. [61], a secure architecture was proposed for CPS installations in health care. CPS-MAS was introduced by Banerjee et al. [62] to model and analyse MCPS. The research team led by Wu et al. [63] proposed a framework capability model (FCM) that incorporates "service-oriented architecture (SOA)" excluding the complete architectural setting.

Mohammad Mehedi Hassan and colleagues [64] demonstrated an efficient network system, which incorporates both WBAN and cloud to offer an efficient means of providing up-to-date healthcare data. The network system has four layers and provides continuous health data delivery. According to Gao et al. [65], bonds between a CPS and patients are growing stronger and sturdier with each passing year. As suggested by Abdol Hamid Pilevar [66], a new method is proposed where data recovery is performed based on the topic of the record. An IoT-dependent healthcare system is proposed by Kuo-hui Yeh [67] by way of using BSN architecture. This system aims to make the public Internet of Things a reality.

14.3 Methodology and Experimental Results

Connectivity is an important issue in the interconnection of networks for selecting the optimal path from source to destination. Interconnection of the network can be seen using a logical operator. The logical operator is very useful for selecting an alternative path such that our network becomes fault-tolerant and robust. In this paper, we are discussing logical operators who are clearly seen as very purposeful in the interconnection of networks below are the results of the logical operator (AND OR, EX-OR, and Conditional). In a multiprocessor organization, there are several "memory modules," "processing units," and "I/O modules." Each CPU has to contact memory modules and I/O units and exchange data between them. The linking of networks provides connectivity [68] between various components. Interconnection of networks is the heart of a parallel architecture [69]. In a multistage network, an interconnection network's goal is to transport data between two processors. The Von Newman design has a memory bottle-neck as a fundamental flaw. The processor performance suffers if the data exchange between processors is deferred. Each processor has a small local memory, while the multiprocessor system has one global shared memory.

Using an interconnection network, the processors can enter data deposited in a shared memory or memory related with another processor. As a result, interconnection networks play a crucial role in defining multiprocessor systems' inclusive presentation. The inter-connection networks are similar to traditional network systems with nodes and edges. The nodes are switches with a small number of input and output lines (say, n input and m output). Data is transported from input lines to output lines based on the switch connection. The interconnection network connects the multiprocessor network's numerous devices.

14.3.1 Interconnection Issues

Because a multi-core processor has multiple components on-chip, such as "cores," "ca-ches," "network controllers," and so on, the interaction between them might have an impact on the performance of interconnection issues that aren't resolved appropriately. The bus was used to communicate between the components in the first CPUs. The con-nectivity of components is done using crossbar and mesh topologies to reduce latency. Additionally, when thread parallelism rises, communication off-chip for memory access, I/O, and other functions increases. Packet-based connectivity is widely employed in si-tuations like this. Intel has employed this packet-based link (quick path interconnect) and AMD is using it as well.

14.3.2 Perfect Difference Network

For a clear understanding of the network, we can construct a direct interconnection network with $n = \delta^2 + \delta + 1$ nodes founded on the normal form perfect difference set $\{s_0, s_1,..., s_\delta\}$ with order δ, as depicted in Figure 14.4.

Definition 1: PDN is founded on the PDS $\{s_0, s_1,.., s_\delta\}$ accompying with $n = \delta^2 + \delta + 1$ nodes, ranging from 0 to n-1. Node i is linked via fixed associations to nodes i±1 and i±s_j(mod n), for $2 \le j \le \delta$. Because there is a reverse link from node j to node i for each link from node i to node j, the network can be depicted as an undirected graph. Chordal rings with a PDN grounded on normal form PDSs are unique. The links linking uninterrupted nodes i and i+1 are known as ring links, while those connecting non successive nodes i and i±s $_j$(mod n), for $2 \le j \le \delta$, are known as skip links or chords. The link concerning nodes i and i+s_j(mod n), for 2j $\le \delta$ is a "forward skip link" of node i and a "backward skip link" of node i+s_j(mod n).

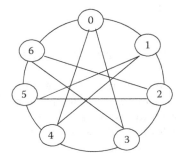

FIGURE 14.4
Graph Structure for PDN with Node 7.

TABLE 14.2

Incidence Matrix

0	1	2	3	4	5	6	
0	1	0	1	1	0	1	0
1	0	1	0	1	1	0	1
0	1	0	1	0	1	1	2
1	0	1	0	1	0	1	3
1	1	0	1	0	1	0	4
0	1	1	0	1	0	1	5
1	0	1	1	0	1	0	6

- Node 0 is linked with node (1,3,4,6)
- Node 1 is linked with node (0,2,4,5)
- Node 2 is linked with node (1,3,5,6)
- Node 3 is linked with node (2,4,0,6)
- Node 4 is linked with node (3,1,0,5)
- Node 5 is linked with node (1,2,4,6)
- Node 6 is linked with node (0,2,5,3)

While applying the AND operation to the incidence matrix (Table 14.2), we get a relation such that each processor at respective nodes can be connected through several links. Figure 14.4 provides alternative node diagonal connectivity when the AND operation is performed and, as such, the circuit matrix table following the relation like reflexive A relation R on a set A is called reflexive if and only if (a, a) for every element of a of A. For symmetric A relation is called symmetric if and only if for any a and b in A, whenever {R ∨ (a, b)€R we have (b, a) €R if aRbV ab€A} and for Transitive A relation R on "set A" is termed transitive if and only if for any "a," "b," and "c" in ("A"), whensoever relation satisfying the condition {R ∨ a, b, c €A if aRb bRc then aRc}. For example, the logical operation is performed between (row 0 and row 1) *row* 1: 01011010 Λ 10101100 resulting bit string is 00001000 in place of (4), i.e., node 4 is the alternate node for node 0.

Similarly, for

$$vec_0\Lambda \ vec_2: 01011010 \ \Lambda \ 01010110 = \{1, 3, 6\}$$
$$vec_0\Lambda \ vec_3: 01011010 \ \Lambda \ 10101010 = \{4, 6\}$$
$$vec_0\Lambda \ vec_4: 01011010 \ \Lambda \ 11010100 = \{1, 3\}$$
$$vec_0\Lambda \ vec_5: 01011010 \ \Lambda \ 01101010 = \{1, 4, 6\}$$
$$vec_0\Lambda \ vec_6: 01011010 \ \Lambda \ 10110100 = \{3\}$$

The substitute nodes for node 0, which are utilised to choose the best path from source to destination, are now discovered.

The AND operation is also supportive for showing transitive relation. Figure 14.5 shows the transitive property where we can communicate from source (0) to destination (2) via node 1 or node 3. Similarly, for destination node 5, communications are possible via node 6 or node 4. On the other hand, in the case of the logical OR operator, and conditional (implication) binary operator came up with the same results where 4 bit (1)

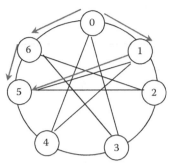

FIGURE 14.5
Transitive Relation.

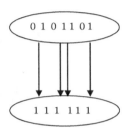

FIGURE 14.6
Connectivity of OR Operator, Four Bits Match (1st, 3rd, 4th, and 6th).

TABLE 14.3

Matrix for OR Operator (vec0 X vec0)

	0	1	0	1	1	0	1
0	0	1	0	1	1	0	1
1	1	1	1	1	1	1	1
0	0	1	0	1	1	0	1
1	1	1	1	1	1	1	1
1	1	1	1	1	1	1	1
0	0	1	0	1	1	0	1
1	1	1	1	1	1	1	1

match with the location at i.e., node 1, node 3, node 4, and node 6, showing that several processors can be connected. Hence, it can be concluded that the robust functionality is satisfied (Figure 14.6). However, both the OR logical operator and conditional statement have different functionality to operate as per truth table, but when applied to our matrix table given the same results (Tables 14.3 and 14.4).

When operation Ex-or is operated to the matrix, which is defined in Table 14.2 as b= {0 if a = b} or {1 otherwise} the condition a (a ⊕ b) = ⊕(a a) ⊕ b = b⊕ and (a a) ⊕ b = a⊕ (b b⊕) = a⊕ holds good for our matrix which shows we can limit the storage capacity of nodes (processors) and hence enables us to frame memory-saving processors with one or more nodes that can be connected to a single node. Suppose if L1 is the left and R1 is the

TABLE 14.4

Matrix for Implication Operator (Vec0 X vec0)

	0	1	0	1	1	0	1
0	1	1	1	1	1	1	1
1	0	1	0	1	1	0	1
0	1	1	1	1	1	1	1
1	0	1	0	1	1	0	1
1	0	1	0	1	1	0	1
0	1	1	1	1	1	1	1
1	0	1	0	1	1	0	1

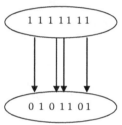

FIGURE 14.7

Connectivity on OR Operator, Four Bits Match (1st, 3rd, 4th, and 6th).

right node, then we have a link () = L1R1 for the rightmost node R1 = 0 and leftmost node L1 = 0. Therefore, it can be said that the nodes will run in polynomial time compute solutions at a given instance of an optimisation problem as demonstrated in Figure 14.7.

14.4 Conclusion

One of the fundamental problems that emerge in the interconnection of the network is how to improve connectivity and complexity. In this chapter, we deliberate and analyse the connectivity issue through the study of a perfect difference network for the interconnection of multi-core processors. The incidence matrix of PDN is produced in this research, and the accompanying graph data structure is examined, and node connection is established using the incidence matrix. Logical operations (AND, EX-OR, OR & ⇨) are applied on the incidence matrix of PDN, and the corresponding node connectivity relation is found. The AND operator has shown diagonal connectivity, and transitive relation and OR operator has shown that several processors can be connected to a particular processor, i.e., 1st, 3rd, 4th, and 6th, satisfying robust functionality, whereas when EXOR is implemented to enable memory-saving processors with two or more nodes connected to a single processor.

References

[1] Insup, L., Sokolsky, O., Chen, S., Hatcliff, J. and Jee, E. (2012). Challenges and Research Directions in Medical Cyber-Physical Systems, *Proceedings of the IEEE, 100*, 1, 75–90.

[2] Jonathan, G., Adepu, S., Tan, M. and Shan, L.Z. (2018). Anomaly detection in cyber-physical systems using recurrent neural networks. *International Journal of Pharma Research and Health Sciences, 6*, 1, 2075–2080.

[3] Fabio, P., Dörfler, F. and Bullo, F. (2013). Attack detection and identification in CPS, *IEEE transactions on automatic control, 58*, 11, 1–13.

[4] Amit, K.T. and Shamila, M. (2019). Spy in the crowd: How user's privacy is getting affected with the integration of internet of thing's devices. *Elsevier, 1(1)*, 12–21.

[5] Rasim, A., Imamverdiyev, Y. and Sukhostat, L. (2018). Cyber-physical systems and their security issues. *Computers in Industry, 100*, 212–223.

[6] Kyoung, D.K. and Kumar, P.R. (2013). An overview and some challenges in cyber-physical systems. *Journal of the Indian Institute of Science, 93*, 3, 1–8.

[7] Mourtzis D., Vlachou, E., Dimitrakopoulos, G. and Zogopoulos, V. (2018). Cyber-physical systems and education 4.0 – The teaching factory 4.0 concept. *8th conference on Learning Factories*, 129–134.

[8] Report of the President's Council of Advisors on Science and Technology (2007). [Online]. Available at: http://www.whitehouse.gov/sites/ default/files/microsites/ostp/pcast-07-nitrd-review.pdf. [Last accessed 05 May2021].

[9] Borja, D., Wael, M., Martínez, J., Villalonga, A., Beruvides, G., Castaño, F. and Haber, R. (2018). Towards the adoption of cyber-physical systems of systems paradigm in smart manufacturing environments, *IEEE*, 1–8.

[10] Meghna, M.N., Tyagi, A.K. and Goyal, R. (2019). Medical cyber-physical systems and its issues. *Procedia Computer Science, 165*, 647–655.

[11] Tawseef, A.S. and Rashid, A. (2019). Big data for better Indian healthcare. *International Journal of Information Technology, 11*, 4, 735–741.

[12] Almohri, H., Cheng, L., Yao, D. and Alemzadeh, H. (2017). On threat modeling and mitigation of medical cyber-physical systems. *2017 IEEE/ACM International Conference on Connected Health: Applications, Systems and Engineering Technologies (CHASE)*, 114–119, 10.11 09/CHASE.2017.69.

[13] Weizhi, M., Li, W., Wang, Y. and Au, M.H. (2020) Detecting insider attacks in medical cyber–physical networks based on behavioral profiling. *Future Generation Computer Systems, 108*, 1258–1266.

[14] Nilanjan, D., Ashour, S.A., Shi, F., Fong, S.J. and Tavares, J.M. (2018). Medical cyber-physical systems: A survey Share on. *Journal of Medical Systems, 42*, 4, 1–13.

[15] Ackerman, M.J., Burgess, L.P., Filart, R., Lee, I. and Poropatich, R.K. (2010). Developing next generation telehealth tools and technologies: Patients, systems, and data perspectives. *Telemedicine and e-Health, 16*, 1, 93–95.

[16] Markus S. and Marc H. (2016). Generative Manufacturing Technologies—The Future? M., Schönberger, M., Hoffstetter ed., Emerging Trends in Medical Plastic Engineering and Manufacturing. William Andrew Publishing, 107–174.

[17] Nithya, S., Sangeetha, M. and Prethi, K.N.A. (2018). Role of cyber-physical systems in health care and survey on security of medical data. *International Journal of Pharma Research and Health Sciences, 6*, 1, 2075–2080.

[18] Burton, J.H., Harrah, J.D., Germann, C.A. and Dillon, D.C. (2006). Does end-tidal carbon dioxide monitoring detect respiratory events prior to current sedation monitoring practices? *Academic Emergency Medicine, 13*, 500–504.

[19] Lu, C.H. and Fu, L.C. (2009). Robust location-aware activity recognition using wireless sensor network in an attentive home. *IEEE Transactions on Automation Science and Engineering, 6*, 4, 598–609.

[20] Philipose, M., Smith, J.R., Jiang, B., Mamishev, A., Roy, S. and Sundara-Rajan, K. (2005). Battery-free wireless identification and sensing. *IEEE Pervasive Computing*, 4, 1, 37–45.

[21] Sung, M., Marci, C. and Pentland, A. (2005). Wearable feedback systems for rehabilitation. *Journal of NeuroEngineering and Rehabilitation*, 2, 17, 1–12.

[22] Wang, C.C., Chiang, C.-Y. and Lin, P.-Y. (2008). Development of a fall detecting system for the elderly residents. *in Proceedings of the 2nd International Conference on Bioinformatics and Biomedical Engineering (iCBBE '08)*, 1359–1362.

[23] Iso-Ketola, P., Karinsalo, T. and Vanhala, J. (2008). HipGuard: A wearable measurement system for patients recovering from a hip operation. *in Proceedings of the 2nd International Conference on Pervasive Computing Technologies for Healthcare*, 196–199.

[24] Konstanta, D. and Herzog, R. (2003). Continuous monitoring of vital constants for mobile users: The MobiHealth approach, *in Proceedings of the 25th Annual International Conference of the IEEE Engineering in Medicine and Biology Society*, 3728–3731.

[25] Shnayder, V., Chen, B., Lorincz, K., Fulford-Jones, T.R.F. and Welsh, M. (2005). Sensor networks for medical care, *in Proceedings of the 3rd International Conference on Embedded Networked Sensor Systems*, 435–442.

[26] Wood, A.D., Stankovic, J.A. and Virone, G. (2008). Context-aware wireless sensor networks for assisted living and residential monitoring. *IEEE Network*, 22, 4, 26–33.

[27] Mendez, E.O. and Ren, S. (2012). Design of a cyber-physical interface for automated vital signs reading in electronic medical records systems. *in Proceedings of the IEEE International Conference on Electro/Information Technology (EIT '12)*, 553–562.

[28] Wang, J., Abid, H., Lee, S., Shu, L. and Xia, F. (2011). A secured health care application architecture for cyber-physical systems. *Control Engineering and Applied Informatics*, 13, 3, 101–108.

[29] Jin, Z., Oresko, J., Huang, S. and Cheng, A.C. (2009). Hearttogo: A personalized medicine technology for cardiovascular disease prevention and detection. In *Proceedings of the IEEE/ NIH LiSSA*, 80–83.

[30] Lopez-Nores, M., Pazos-Arias, J.J., Garc–Duque, J. and Blanco-Fernandez, Y. (2008). Monitoring medicine intake in the networked home: the iCabiNET solution. *in Proceedings of the 2nd International Conference on Pervasive Computing Technologies for Healthcare*, 116–117.

[31] Wu, N. and Li, X. (2011). RFID applications in the cyber-physical system. *RFID Applications in Cyber-Physical System*, 291–302.

[32] Banerjee, A., Gupta, S.K.S., Fainekos, G., and Varsamopoulos, G. (2011). Towards modelling and analysis of cyber-physical medical systems. *in Proceedings of the 4th International Symposium on Applied Sciences in Biomedical and Communication Technologies (ISABEL '11)*, 154–158.

[33] Poulymenopoulou, M., Malamateniou, F. and Vassilacopoulos, G. (2011). E-EPR: a cloud-based architecture of an electronic emergency patient record. *in Proceedings of the 4th ACM International Conference on PErvasive Technologies Related to Assistive Environments (PETRA '11)*, 387–394.

[34] Taleb, T., Bottazzi, D., Guizani, M. and Nait-Charif, H. (2009). Angelah: a framework for assisting elders at home. *IEEE Journal on Selected Areas in Communications*, 27, 4, 480–494.

[35] Pang Z., Chen Q. and Zheng L. (2009). A pervasive and preventive healthcare solution for medication noncompliance and daily monitoring. *in Proceedings of the 2nd International Symposium on Applied Sciences in Biomedical and Communication Technologies (ISABEL '09)*, 342–367.

[36] Sung, M., Marci, C. and Pentland, A. (2005). Wearable feedback systems for rehabilitation.*Journal of NeuroEngineering and Rehabilitation*, 2, 34–46.

[37] Kailanto, H., Hyvarinen, E. and Hyttinen, J. (2008). Mobile ECG measurement and analysis system using mobile phone as the base station, *in Proceedings of the 2nd International Conference on Pervasive Computing Technologies for Healthcare*, 12–14.

[38] Kang, W. (2009). Adaptive real-time data management for cyber-physical systems [Ph.D. thesis], University of Virginia.

[39] https://www.csoonline.com/in/ [Last accessed 20 April 2021].

[40] Jelena, M., Dietrich, S., Dittrich, D. and Reiher, P. (2004). Internet Denial of Services: attack and defense mechanisms. Prentice Hall.

[41] Alexander, K. and Clarkson, P. (2000). Good design practice for medical devices and equipment, Part II: Design for verification. *Journal of Medical Engineering & Technology*, 24, 2, 53–62.

[42] Nandagaoli, M.J. and Bakal, J.W. (2014). Study of perfect difference network. *International Journal of Computer Science*, 3, 6, 6465–6469.

[43] Behrooz, P. and Rakov, M. (2005). Application of perfect difference sets to the design of efficient and robust interconnection networks. *in proceedings of Proceedings of the 2005 International Conference on Communications in Computing, CIC 2005, Las Vegas, Nevada, USA*, 1–7.

[44] Tiwari, S. and Katare, R.K. (2015). A Study of fabric of architecture using structural pattern and relation. *International Journal of Latest Technology in Engineering and Management and Applied Science*, 4, 9, 1–5.

[45] Tiwari, S., Katare, R.K., Sharma, V. and Tiwari, C.M. (2016). Study of geometrical structure of perfect difference network. *International Journal of Advanced Research in Computer and Communication Engineering*, 5, 3, 1–11.

[46] Arney, D., Fischmeister, S., Goldman, J.M., Lee, I. and Trausmuth, R. (2009). Plug-and-play for medical devices: Experiences from a case study. *Biomedical Instrumentation and Technology*, 43, 4, 313–317.

[47] ASTM International (2013). Medical Devices and Medical Systems – Essential Safety Requirements for Equipment Comprising the Patient-Centric Inte600 grated Clinical Environment (ICE) Part 1: General Requirements and Conceptual Model, Active Standard ASTM F2761.

[48] Arney, D., Plourde, J. and Goldman, J. (2017). OpenICE medical device interoperability platform overview and requirement analysis. *Biomedical Engineering/Biomedizinische Technik*, 1–9.

[49] Almohri H., Cheng, L., Yao, D. and Alemzadeh, H. (2017). On threat modeling and mitigation of medical cyber-physical systems, *in Proceedings of the IEEE/ACM International Conference on Connected Health: Applications, Systems and Engineering Technologies*, 610, 114–119.

[50] Hamed, S., Arney, D. and Goldman, J. (2016). Toward a Safe and Secure Medical Internet of Things. *IIC Journal of Innovation*, 4–18.

[51] Cimini, C., Pirola, F., Pinto, R. and Cavalieri, S. (2020). A human-in-the-loop manufacturing control architecture for the next generation of production systems. *Journal of Manufacturing Systems*, 54, 258–271.

[52] Valckenaers, P. (2020). Perspective on holonic manufacturing systems: PROSA becomes ARTI. *Computers in Industry*, 120, 103226–103241.

[53] Nunes, D.S., Zhang, P. and Silva, J.S. (2015) A survey on human-in-the-loop applications towards an internet of all. *IEEE Communications Surveys & Tutorials*, 17, 2, 944–965.

[54] Eisenbarth, T., Kumar, S., Paar, C., Poschmann, A. and Uhsadel, L. (2007). A Survey of Lightweight-Cryptography Implementations. *IEEE Design & Test of Computers*, 24, 522–533.

[55] Johnson T. (2010). Fault-tolerant distributed cyber-physical systems: Two case studies, *Masters Thesis, University of Illinois, Department of Electrical and Computer Engineering, Urbana, USA*.

[56] High Confidence Software and Systems Coordinating Group. (February 2009). Highconfidence medical devices: Cyber-physical systems for 21st century health care. A Research and Development Needs Report, NCO/NITRD.

[57] Wu, F.J., Kao, Y.F. and Tseng, Y.C. (2011). From wireless sensor networks towards cyber-physical systems. *Pervasive and Mobile Computing*, 7, 4, 397–413.

[58] Hu, L., Xie, N., Kuang, Z. and Zhao, K. (2012). Review of cyber-physical system architecture, *in Proceedings of the 15th IEEE International Symposium on Object Component Service-Oriented RealTime Distributed Computing Workshops 78*, 91.

[59] Ahmadi, H., Abdelzaher, T., and Gupta, I. (2010). Congestion control for spatio-temporal data in cyber-physical systems. *International Conference on Cyber-physical Systems (ICCPS)*.

[60] Shah, A.H., Aziz, S.M. and Rahman, M. (2014). Review of cyber-physical system in healthcare. *International Journal of Distributed Sensor Networks, 10*, 4, 1–20.

[61] Wang, J., Abid, H., Lee, S., Shu, L. and Xia, F. (2011). A secured health care application architecture for cyber-physical systems. *arXiv preprint arXiv:1201.0213*.

[62] Jiang, Z., Pajic, M. and Mangharam, R. (2012). Cyber-physical modeling of implantable cardiac medical devices. *Proceedings of the EEE, 100*, 1, 122–137.

[63] Zhang, Z., Wang, H., Wang, C. and Fang, H. (2013). Interference mitigation for cyber-physical wireless body area Network System using social networks. *IEEE Transactions on Emerging Topics in Computing, 1*, 121–132.

[64] Mohammad, M.H., Lin, K., Yue, X. and Wand, J. (2017). A multimedia healthcare data sharing approach through cloud-based body area network. *Future Generations Computer Systems, 66*, 48–58.

[65] Jialin, G. (2017). A smart medical system for dynamic closed-loop blood glucose-insulin control. *Smart Health*, 18–33.

[66] Abdol, H.P. (2016). DISR: Dental image segmentation and retrieval. *Journal of Medical Signals & Sensors, 2*, 1, 42–49.

[67] Kuo, H.Y. (2016). A secure IoT – based healthcare system with BodySensor networks. *IEEE Access, 4*, 10288–10299.

[68] Wu C., Feng T. (1984). Tutorial, interconnection networks for parallel and distributed processing, Tutorial Texts Series. IEEE Computer Society Press.

[69] www.interconnection of networks, elements of parallel computing and architecture [Last accessed 22-May-2021].

Index